Wm. Cudworth

Rambles Round Horton: Historical, Topographical, and Descriptive

Wm. Cudworth

Rambles Round Horton: Historical, Topographical, and Descriptive

ISBN/EAN: 9783337190484

Printed in Europe, USA, Canada, Australia, Japan

Cover: Foto ©ninafisch / pixelio.de

More available books at **www.hansebooks.com**

HORTON OLD HALL.
THE RESIDENCE OF F S POWELL ESQ

Rambles Round Horton:

Historical, Topographical, and Descriptive.

By WM. CUDWORTH,

Author of "Round About Bradford," "Historical Notes on the Bradford Corporation," &c.

Published by Subscription.

1886.
BRADFORD: THOS. BREAR & CO., LIMITED.

Entered at Stationers' Hall. All Rights Reserved.

THIS VOLUME IS

DEDICATED BY THE AUTHOR

TO

FRANCIS SHARP POWELL, Esq., M.P.,

OF HORTON OLD HALL,

IN REMEMBRANCE OF HIS KINDNESS

ON MANY OCCASIONS DURING

ITS PREPARATION.

PREFACE.

The Author would fain hope that no apology is needed for the publication of "Rambles Round Horton," albeit the interest of the volume is of a comparatively limited character. Works of this nature form the basis of local history, treating as they do of "things great and small." It may be that many of the items included appear insignificant, but from the historian's standpoint they add completeness to the whole, and are therefore deserving of notice.

Under any circumstances the Author had no alternative but to issue the present work, such was the amount of interest evoked by the publication of the "Rambles" in the columns of the *Bradford Observer*. In bringing them before the public in the present form, he trusts that his patrons will not be dissatisfied with the result. No effort has been spared to secure accuracy, although it is obvious that accuracy cannot always be obtained even with the best intentions.

The Author has to acknowledge his indebtedness to many friends for the facilities they have afforded him for obtaining information; to his former coadjutor, Mr. W. G. HIRD, for his kind assistance in the tedious task of indicing; and to his numerous subscribers, without whose support the work could not have been undertaken.

The Author purposes to continue his rambles round the townships forming the Borough of Bradford, and to publish the account thereof uniform with the present volume, should this literary venture meet with favour.

January, 1886.

RAMBLES ROUND HORTON.

CHAPTER I.

Introductory — Boundaries — Streams — Roads — Conformation — Strata — Acreage — Origin of Names — Lords of the Manor — Manorial Customs — Ancient Tenants — Ancient Freeholders.

In olden times, when lords of manors enjoyed some degree of feudal importance, the ceremony of perambulating the boundaries of townships excited no small amount of interest in local circles. The ceremony would appear to have been of value, in so far as the feudal lord and his retainers took note of whatever changes might have taken place within the charmed circle they patrolled. In pursuing these "rambles," therefore, our immediate purpose will be to take note of the old landmarks still remaining, and refer as far as possible to some of their former inhabitants. In this way a foundation may be laid upon which a superstructure of township history may be raised, of which, so far as the townships of the borough of Bradford are concerned, no record exists. It will be acknowledged that ample material exists for such a record. Notwithstanding the common interest shared by all the townships of Bradford, an individuality pervades each locality which is sufficiently marked to justify individual reference without attempting the larger task of collating the whole into a history of the borough. Relieved from the necessity of recording the more important events which would be necessary in such a compilation, we can do greater justice to matters often only slightly touched upon or altogether left unnoticed.

Following in the track of ancient custom, therefore, we proceed to describe the boundaries of the township of the Hortons, Great and Little, as they are defined by natural lines of demarcation. The township is bounded on the west by the stream that divides it from Clayton, called Tanner Beck, which flows to Lower Lidget, and then through

Bulgreave Wood, when it becomes known as Bulgreave Beck. Flowing past Scholemoor Cemetery this beck joins the stream called Middle-broke, upon which Sams Mill is situate. From thence to the town of Bradford it is called the Bradford Beck, and forms the northern boundary of the township of Horton. On the east the township is bounded by Bowling Beck, and on the south by a portion of the township of North Bierley. Another portion of North Bierley obtrudes upon the south-east corner of Horton township, but if any modern lord of the manor essayed a perambulation of the boundaries he must needs wade through two Corporation reservoirs at Horton Bank-top. In addition to the above there are tributary streams rising in the township, although they are none of them of great volume. A stream, having several sources of supply near Cliffe Mill once fed the old corn mill at Beckside, and meandering down to Shearbridge was called Horton Beck. At Shearbridge the beck is joined by another, formerly called Broad Beck, having its rise in fields adjoining Horton Park.

The township boundaries formerly extended into Tyrrel Street by a triangular piece of ground called Broadcroft, which was appropriated by Henry de Lacy, Earl of Lincoln, and his mother of unsavoury memory. Horton being a mesne manor the lord thereof was not able to resist the encroachment, although he succeeded in establishing his claim to a rent of 3s. per annum. The triangular plot was described by a commission which sat in 1420 to determine as to the continuance of the rental, as "a plot of land in the township of Little Horton, lying within Bradford Brook, Bolling Brook, Horton Kyrkgate (*qy.* Chapel Lane), and the Field of Horton."

The principal roads in Horton township branch from what was formerly called the town-end of Bradford, and are now known as Horton Lane, Horton Road, Manchester Road (anciently Bowling Lane), and Legrams Lane. Manchester Road only passes through a portion of the easterly side of the township, and debouches into Bowling, whereas Horton Lane and Horton Road thread the township until they leave it, the former at Brownroyd Hill, Wibsey, and the latter at Clayton Heights on the old road to Halifax. Legrams is an old packhorse road, having been an outlet from Silsbridge Lane, joining the old road to Halifax by way of Green Lane, Toby Lane, Scarr Lane, Upper Green, Dog Lane, and what is still called the "old road" at Bank Top.

The hamlet of Lidget is also approached by Cemetery Road (formerly Thiefscore Lane). The oldest highway between Great and Little Horton is Southfield Lane, or Southgate. There are also other connecting links, such as Park Lane, Park Avenue, Laistridge Lane, Clayton Lane, Holme Lane, Thornton Lane, Aycliffe Lane, Jer Lane, Pickles Hill, Old Road, Hollingwood Lane, Cliffe Lane, and "bridle-stiles," too numerous for mention. Examples of the general character of these thoroughfares, useful during the period when the principal means of transit was by packhorses, existed in the road leading from Upper Green down Greenfield to Bracken Hill; in the one from Leventhorpe through Scholemoor by way of Foggs Lane to Horton; and in that leading from Thiefscore Bridge to Birks. The old road at Horton Bank, formerly the main coach road between Bradford and Halifax, is worth a visit if only to realise the contrast between the description of highway which served our forefathers and such thoroughfares as Park Avenue, for instance, a specimen of modern construction.

The conformation of the Horton township is agreeably diversified, the upper portion containing numerous eminences, from which extensive views are obtainable. The highest elevation is attained on the eminence known as Beacon Hill, 975 feet above the mean sea level. From this spot a commanding prospect may be had, embracing the companion beacons at Beamsley, Rawdon Billing, and Halifax, besides a fine sweep of country south and east. From Beldon Hill, Haycliffe Hill, Crag Hill, Pickles Hill, and Brow Hill good and varied views may also be obtained.

There is no moorland in Horton township, the only place bearing even the name being Scholemoor. From ancient documents, to which reference will subsequently be made, we learn that this hamlet was formerly waste land. Within a recent period, however, the only waste land was situate at

Horton Green and in Southfield Lane—the site of the Old Bell Chapel, for instance, and what are now called Upper and Lower Green. These "greens" are numerous, including Horton Green, Chapel Green, Low Green, Upper Green, Lidget Green, and Paradise Green. They, however, furnish no open spaces. Upon old maps what is called New England land is marked, being chiefly in the vicinity of Southfield Lane.

Although the surface land of the township is pleasantly undulated, it owes very little to the embellishment which a well-wooded locality receives from nature. In the sheltered valleys there are numerous trees, but not many of large growth, the most thriving plantations being those around Horton Grange, Bracken Hall, Springfield, and other residences, all of which have been planted within a comparatively recent period. As early as the year 1350 evidence exists that coal was found and used in the township. This fact we learn from an extract from the court rolls of the manor of Bradford, transcribed by Mr. T. T. Empsall and contributed to the journal of the Bradford Historical Society. In these rolls "Thomas del Halghes complains that one John the Milner, of Mickle Horton, had made divers wells in his land is search of *carbones marinos*, and that after taking away the coal he had left open the wells, whereby the cattle of Thomas del Halghes had fallen in and were drowned." Coal has also been extensively got on Beldon Hill and upon the slopes of Haycliffe and Crag Hills. Practically, however, the coal measures of Horton have now become exhausted; neither is stone obtained in large quantity.

The four principal landowners are Mr. J. A. Jowett, of Bolton; Mr. F. S. Powell, of Horton Old Hall; Mr. Wm. Ramsden, of Bracken Hall; and Mr. Geo. Turner, of Horton Grange. The manorial rights are held by Mr. James Cousen and Miss Rawson, the latter claiming the minerals and the former exercising a right over the remainder of the manorial property, which is very small. There are many small freeholders, which is accounted for by the fact that the holdings in the manor from very early times were granted in fee, subject only to military service and nominal rents. The township comprises 2170 acres of land, and is still nominally divided into the constabularies of Great and Little Horton, which until recently were defined by a boundary line, drawn from Fieldhead Dyeworks to Shearbridge, then following the course of the beck which runs through Horton Park it proceeds forward to the top of Haycliffe Hill, indicating the Horton wards of the borough. Since the recent extension of the borough, however, the old boundaries have been materially interfered with.

As to the origin of names found in the township we have no striking derivations to offer. Horton probably gave its name to the family which for generations held possessions there, although resident elsewhere. Originally we may assume that the "ton" or enclosure was situated upon the lower level, but the exact site is left to conjecture. Shearbridge probably obtained its name from the fact that there the streams, "sheared" or separated before, came together, the brooks from Beckside and Horton uniting in their onward course to Westbrook. As to Laistridge Lane, it may be that the immediate district forms the "least ridge" of the hills in the vicinity. Hollingwood Lane evidently derives its name from the holly bushes which once lined the neighbouring banks, and the name is perpetuated in the title given to Holly Bank, the residence of Mr. John Ramsden. Jer Lane is from Jeremiah Holdsworth, a yeoman in that neighbourhood. A former historian has jumped to the too ready conclusion that Beldon Hill owes it name to very remote times. It is not so. Beldon Hill is not the hill of Bael or Bel, but of one William Beldon, who owned land there so recently as 1800; while Pickles Hill has a similar origin. "Ewe Clews" is of less satisfactory explanation, as the place is variously styled Ewe, Yew, How, Hew, and High. It may have have been an inclosure for sheep, or a plantation of yew trees, or have taken its name from the clew or clough of the water-mill situate hard by. The name "Thiefscore" arouses unpleasant doubts as to the morality of the neighbourhood, but there is a Paradise in the township, which may be taken as a set-off. Many other possible derivations may be suggested as we patrol the township, but before doing this we must glance at the ancient history of the place.

From Domesday Book, that source of historic information to which the historian first turns, we learn that from the earliest times Horton formed a hamlet dependent on the manor of Bradford. The first man of consequence named in connection with the place was Robert de Stapleton, who is mentioned as living in the reign of Henry II. (1154-89). His son Hugh, who took the name of Horton, received from Robert de Lacy, the lord of the manor of Bradford, a grant of land extending to the very verge of the town, showing that he must have been in considerable favour with his superior lord. The land remained in the Horton family until the reign of Edward I., when Hugh dying without male issue it descended to his daughter, who had married Wm. Leventhorp. He was the head of the ancient family deriving their name from Leventhorp or Lenthrop, in Thornton township. In the reign of Henry VII. the manor of Horton passed into the hands of the Lacies of Cromwellbotham (a secondary branch of the greater Lacies), by the marriage of John Lacy with Alice Leventhorpe. The Hortons had by this time settled at Barkisland, in Halifax parish, and in 1639 William Horton, of Firth House, purchased the Howroyde estate, whose family have been in possession of to the present time, the present owner of Howroyde and the representative of the Horton family being Capt. Joshua Thomas Horton, J.P. In 1640, Joshua Horton, of Sowerby, a member of a junior branch of the Horton family, repurchased the manor of Horton formerly belonging to his ancestors, along with that of Thornton. His son Elkanah, a barrister, who died in 1728, lived at Thornton Hall. Thomas Horton, the grandson of Joshua of Sowerby, resided at Chadderton, near Manchester, which had been purchased by his father, and was Deputy-Governor of the Isle of Man. His eldest son, William, was made a baronet, and the present owner of Howroyde is the twice great grandson of Sir W. Horton's younger brother, Joshua Thomas. It is said that the Hortons, while lords of the manor, had in ancient days a manor house a little to the east of Great Horton, the site of which has been since known as Hall Yard, but there is no evidence in support of the tradition beyond the name.

The recent ownership of the manor of Horton may be recorded in few words. From Joshua Horton the manorial estate came to his descendant, Sir Watts Horton, of Chadderton, through his father, Sir William Horton. Sir Watts married Lady Henrietta Stanley, whose daughter, Henrietta Susanna, married Charles Rees, of Liverpool, who altered his name to Rhyss, and of the marriage came two sons and four daughters. Dame Henrietta died in 1827, leaving as her heir, Charles Horton Rhyss, who then came into possession of the manorial and other property of the Horton family. This gentleman led a somewhat erratic life, being a captain in the army, and for many years a comedian, acting under the *nom de plume* of "Morton Price." Upon several occasions he occupied Bradford theatres under that name, but was generally in the United States and Canada.

In October, 1858, he caused the manorial property to be sold by auction, when Mr. Wm. Cousen purchased the lordship of Horton, with hereditaments, &c., thereto belonging, comprising a messuage known as the Manor House, a cottage, the pinfold, &c., and also the fee farm rents, generally called "Lord's rents," which realised £12 7s. 8d. per annum. His son, Mr. James Cousen, is the present lord of the manor. Dracup's trustees purchased the old corn mill and water rights connected therewith, occupied by John Beanland, and comprising the dam field, West Croft, &c.

Much might be stated as to the manor of Horton which cannot be admitted here. But this may be observed, that whilst Bowling, for instance, was a mesne manor like Horton, yet none of the tenants of the former acknowledged as chief only the lord of Bolling, who himself, for all, did suit to the Lacies. The manor of Horton was practically independent while the tenants named held directly of the manor of Bradford. It is an anomaly which needs further explanation.

Before completing the story of the manorial succession, however, we may again make reference to the old Manor Court records as transcribed by Mr. Empsall, with the view of forming an estimate of the population of Horton during those early times. For this purpose the surveys made at the instance of the Lacy family afford some data, although to a large extent the township had been alienated from the Lacy fee, and was enjoyed by the Horton family. In the survey of 1342 only ten tenants of the Lacies are named, and they all belonged to the class of tenantry called "freemen," persons who had emancipated themselves from serfdom and had become possessed of land as customary tenants, *i.e.*, copyhold tenure. For their holdings they rendered certain services in the manor courts. Several of the tenants occupied an exceptional position, and of these was Roger de Manningham, who held a messuage and two bovates of land (about 16 acres) by the service of "going with his lord to Blackburnshire (of which they were lords) with a lance and a dog for forty days to hunt wild boars, receiving $1\frac{1}{2}$d. a day wages, also to be ready and willing to appear yearly at Bradford at the feast of St. Martin if required, to do suit of court at Bradford every three weeks, and give to the lord 3d. at the time of the Invention of the Holy Cross, in lieu of the work of one plough, and at seed time 1s. 4d. annually for his freedom." Thomas de Northrop, one of the Manningham tenants, had to render to the chief identical service with that of de Manningham in accompanying the lord in his journeys into Lancashire. But Northrop had six bovates of land, or about fifty acres, and three messuages, which were burdened on succession with heriots in the shape of the best beast in the herd to the lord. He had also to pay 8d. annually, in lieu of farm labour at seed time.

The Abbot of Kirkstall also held about forty acres of land in this township, by the gift of a pair of white spurs. The land in question was, after the dissolution of the monasteries, acquired by Richard Lyster, who, in addition to the spurs, rendered military service. But by an inquisition *post mortem*, 2nd Ed. VI., he held more than the abbots did, and it may be the extra land which imposed the latter burden. This land was held by the same tenure for several centuries, and was doubtless situate in Thornton Lane, extending to Burnet Field, in Bowling. William le Maisson held two bovates and a messuage, for which he tendered a ploughshare yearly to the lord on his coming to Bradford at the feast of St. Martin, and performed service of court every

Rambles Round Horton.

three weeks. Brian de Thornhill held a piece of land, for which he paid 2s. annually.

The remaining seven tenants of Horton held their allotments by foreign military service at the command of their lord. They also paid a rent varying from 1¼d. to 4d. per acre, and 1½d each per bovate instead of ploughing in spring. Hugh de Rochdale, one of them, for instance, held a messuage and two bovates of land, which was called the 16th part of a knight's fee, paying 2s. yearly for the land, and 3d. instead of labour, while William le Roy paid 6s. 6d. for a messuage and 1½ bovates, and 2¼d. instead of ploughing, and all other service similar to that rendered by Hugh.

Another source from which we may gather information as to the inhabitants of Horton during the fourteenth century is the lay subsidy or poll-tax of 2nd of Richard II. (1379). The list is as follows :—

Thos. filius Rogeri, mercator, & uxor	xijd.
Ricardus de Skircote & uxor...	iiijd.
Rogerus filius Rogeri & uxor	iiijd.
Thos. del Bryg & uxor	iiijd.
Willelmus Leman & uxor	iiijd.
Johannes de Wodehale & uxor	iiijd.
Thos. filius Gilberti & uxor	iiijd.
Johannes filius Ade & uxor	iiijd.
Thos. Machon & uxor	iiijd.
Wilhelmus filius Roberti & uxor	iiijd.
Wilhelmus Hawmerode & uxor	iiijd.
Thos. Gabriel & uxor	iiijd.
Thomas Hunsselet & uxor	iiijd.
Johannes de Holyns & uxor	iiijd.
Johannes de Newall & uxor	iiijd.
Wilhelmus de Hawmonrode & uxor	iiijd.
Thos. filius Wilhelmi & uxor...	iiijd.
Alicia filia Rogeri	iiijd.
Annabella Leman	iiijd.
Alicia filia Johannis	iiijd.
Agnes filia Johannis	iiijd.
Eva Machon	iiijd.
Johannis Sementhorn	iiijd.
Johannis de Bryg	iiijd.

Summa, viijs. viijd.

The list is copied *verbatim*, retaining the ancient form of spelling, and the amounts at which the inhabitants were assessed. Here, again, is a singular anomaly, not one of the military tenants of Horton named in the survey of 1342 occurring in the poll-tax list. Could it be that this class of tenants were exempt from this tax on account of their military service? It was the levying of this poll-tax which exasperated the populace to rise in rebellion under Wat Tyler. The total amount of the taxation raised, it will be seen, was 8s. 8d. Only one inhabitant at that period ranked as a merchant, and the amount extracted from him and his wife was 12d. The remainder were all of the humblest class of householders, and paid 4d. (a groat) each couple, a similar amount being apparently exacted from the single persons. Young persons under sixteen and persons in a state of mendicancy were exempted. While from these causes we are not able to number the population of Horton at that time, we can at least compare its standing with other places. Halifax, for instance, only raised 12s. 8d., and Bradford 23s., the tradesmen in the latter place being a fuller, a mason, two tailors, two shoemakers, and three innkeepers.

In only a few cases in the above list does there appear any semblance to existing Horton nomenclature. It would appear to have been generally deemed sufficient to distinguish a Hortonian by describing him as the son of his father, a like rule applying to the females. A similar custom still prevails in alluding to a person as Bob o' Doads o' Sams. In other instances it is evident that the Christian name was associated with that of the place whence the person came, as Richard of Skircoat, John of Newhall, and John of Woodhall. The Brygs and Hawmonrodes and Holyns are easy of identification with names still existing in the township, although in somewhat disguised forms, as in the case of the descendants of the Hawmonrodes, who are now known as Hammonds and Ormanroyds. The Christian names of William, Thomas, and John were evidently as common five hundred years ago as at the present day.

The following list of Horton freeholders, taken from the subsidy roll of 1608, which is preserved at Howroyd, confirms

Rambles Round Horton. 11

our impressions as to the principal families of the period. It is as follows :—

	Assessed.	Paid.
Robertus Boothe, in lands	xxxs.	iiijs.
Thos. Sharp, jun.	xxs.	ijs. viijd.
Thos. Sharp, sen.	xxs.	ijs. viijd.
John Lyster...	xxs.	ijs. viijd.
Georgius Holdsworth...	xxs.	ijs. viijd.
Will'ms Mortimer	xxs.	ijs. viijd.
John Feild	xxs.	ijs. viijd.
Johannes Nicholls	xxs.	ijs. viijd.
Gilbertus Brooksbank	xxs.	ijs. viijd.
Chrste'rus Swayne	xxs.	ijs. viijd.
John Sharp	xxs.	ijs. viijd.

Summa vill, xxxs. viijd.

Advancing a couple of centuries we are able from other sources to estimate with tolerable accuracy the material importance of the township of Horton, if not the number of its inhabitants. In Sir John Maynard's valuation of the tythes of Bradford parish, taken in 1638, the two Hortons are put down as valued at £603 0s. 6d. In this township the tythes were reckoned by oxgangs (or as much land as an ox could plough in a season), an oxgang containing, one with another, about ten acres, and the tythe of an oxgang was valued at £7. In Great Horton the principal contributor was Gilbert Brooksbank, who paid £35 on five oxgangs of land ; John Mortimer, of Scholemoor, £21 on three oxgangs ; Widow Holyns and Jonas Hammond, on two oxgangs ; Wm. Mortimer, three oxgangs ; John Booth, five and a-third. In Little Horton the principal contributors were John Sharp, jun., four oxgangs ; John Sharp, sen., two and three-quarter oxgangs ; John Lister, " who pretends his land is tythe free because of the Cistercian Order, yet pays tythe in kind to Sir Richard Tempest" (of whom or through whom he probably obtained it, Tempest and others having secured large quantities of abbey lands at the dissolution,, three and a-half oxgangs ; William Walker, two and a-third oxgangs ; Thomas Swaine, two oxgangs ; William Booth, two oxgangs ; Samuel Swaine, one and three-quarter oxgangs ; Thomas Balme, the eighteenth part of an oxgang, which was valued as one.

Rambles Round Horton.

What was called hearth-money or the hearth-tax was a levy upon all householders according to the number of their fires. It was originally established by William the Conqueror, and was continued under Parliamentary sanction by Charles II., but the impost was abolished under William and Mary. In the collection of this tax for the year 1666 we find the names of the following residents of Great and Little Horton, who were the most substantial people of the period, viz.:—Isaac Sharpe, five hearths; John Sharpe, seven; Thomas Swaine, three; Abm. Swaine, two; Robert Swaine, two; Joseph Lister, four; Andrew Hodgson, four; Thos. Pighles, four; Wm. Mortimer, four; Richard Thornton, three; Mary Mortimer, four; Gilbert Brooksbank, two; Will Hammond, three, The total number of hearths paid for in the township was 208, James Swaine being constable during the collection. The complete list of householders would have been interesting had space permitted of it being given. As compared with the township of Bradford, however, Horton appears to have stood well; Bradford East having had 206, and Bradford West 301 hearths taxed.

The land and property tax of 1704 contains a more complete list of owners of land and buildings at that period than can be obtained from any other source, and from it we cull the following particulars of the principal persons assessed in Horton. The tax was at the rate of 4s. in the pound, and was levied by order of Parliament in aid of the State. The list is as follows:—

	£	s.	d.		£	s.	d.
Gilbert Brooksbank—				Wm. Mortimer ...	3	15	0
For self and Booth's				Isaac Hollings... ...	1	6	0
land	4	17	7½	Thos. Hodgson ...	1	19	4½
Scholemoor land ...	1	2	6	Jas. Hall	1	0	0
Nichols' land ...	0	7	6	Thos. Pighills	1	10	0
Westcroft and				Wm. Blackburn ...	1	0	7½
Healds	0	6	3	John Ashton	1	11	10½
Sugden's land ...	0	5	7½	Robert Fox, for ye			
Hammond's land...	0	1	10½	milne	0	18	1½
Cockroyd's	0	1	3	Rich. Thornton ...	1	11	3
Jas. Swaine's land..	0	6	10½	Abm. Swaine, How			
Jewitt's land... ...	0	1	10½	Clews	0	11	3
Sarah Brooksbank	0	5	0	Henry Lancaster ...	1	2	6

Rambles Round Horton.

	£	s.	d.		£	s.	d.
Robt. Swaine, Hunt Yard	1	6	3	Chris. Swaine	1	15	6
Jonas Hopkinson	1	7	6	Jer. Roods	1	10	0
Wm. Mortimer	1	10	7½	Lionel Knowles	0	18	6
Thos. Swaine	1	10	7½	Abram Balme	0	15	0
Mr. Wm. Rawson, for cole mine	1	0	0	Mr. Wm Swaine	1	17	6
Mrs. Sharp	4	17	6	Thos. Ferrand	1	2	6
John Lister	4	0	0	John Bower	1	10	6
Joshua Stansfield	1	5	0	Mr. Rawson, for tythe	1	5	0
Isaac Sharp	3	11	3	Mr. Horton, for his Lord's Rent	1	0	0
Abm. Jewitt	1	2	6				
Mary Thornton	1	4	0	Total for the township	£100	10	5
Wm. Blaymires	0	6	0				

CHRISR. SWAINE,
THOS. SWAINE, } Assessors.

BARTHOLOMEW LANCASTER,
JAMES HALL, Jun., } Collectors.

CHAPTER II.

Surveys of 1802 and 1839—Parochial Matters—Horton Constables—Overseers—Old Workhouse—Highway Surveyors—Highway Board—Horton Councillors.

We have before us the plan of Great and Little Horton, the result of a survey made "by order of the inhabitants" in 1802, by William Basset, land surveyor. It contains references to the owners of every plot of land and field in the township at that period, and for the purposes we have in view is a most valuable record. We append a list of the principal landowners at the period in question, as follows:—Messrs. F. S. Bridges, Richard Hodgson, Charles S. B. Sharp, Joseph Stocks, Mrs. Lister, Mary Brooksbank, Mrs. Hodsden, Mr. Gorton, Miss Bower, Wm. Blamires, J. Blamires' trustees, John Booth, Gregory Fox, Susannah Swaine, James Swaine, Mr. Holden, Pollard & Co., Jarratt & Co., Jacob Hudson's trustees, Mrs. Hutton's trustees, John Balme, Jeremiah Thornton, John Tommis, William Beldon, and Jonas Jowett.

A survey was also made by Mr. Samuel Wormald, of Beeston, in 1839, including a valuation of the township, from which it appears that the total area was 1935 acres, and the ratable value £32,711. The principal land and property owners at that period were Francis Sharp Bridges, Miss Jowett, Ellis Cunliffe Lister, Mrs. Ann Giles, Colonel Fitzgerald, Messrs. Hird, Dawson & Hardy, Thos. B. Charnock, John Bower, Charles, Henry, and Alfred Harris, John and William Rand, Samuel and Wm. Blamires, Joseph Beanland's trustees, John Hustler, William Fox, Dracup's trustees, John Haley, Eli Suddards, Watson Cryer, Hudson's trustees, John Crook, Francis Ackroyd, Robert Stables Ackroyd, Nathan Bentley, John Blackburn, John and Squire Stowell, John Jennings, and Daniel Armitage.

The absence of any town's books or connected records of township business seriously interferes with the work of the historian, and, in respect to the township of Horton, practically results in our being obliged to leave the period prior to the present century almost a blank so far as parochial matters are concerned. After all, the omission may be imaginatively supplied by a knowledge of the routine of township government and township affairs in similar places. Horton would in the "olden time," we presume, be governed upon the most economical principles, its inhabitants expending as much upon the repair of roads and the salaries of its parochial officers as was consistent with a small highway rate, and no more—the burden of an additional penny in the pound upon a ratal valuation being as intolerable to Hortonian ratepayers as to those in any other part of the country.

The township officially managed its own affairs from a central point of inspiration, namely, the parish vestry, at which place all meetings affecting town's business were held, and where all appointments were officially made. Presumably, too, there would during each generation be a coterie of townsmen who, except they were more than ordinarily virtuous, worked for each other's benefit quite as much as for that of the township. Although these parochial patriots rendered service without recognised fee or reward so far as salary was concerned, tradition has it that the weekly dinners at Lidget Green were looked upon as some recompense, and were relinquished only after strong protests made by unprivileged ratepayers, whose notions of patriotic service failed to accord with such "guzzling" at the town's expense.

As already stated, the township of Horton is still nominally divided into the constabularies of Great and Little Horton, but practically into wards for municipal purposes. Prior to the advent of the Corporation, the jurisdiction of the old Lighting and Watching Commissioners of Bradford extended to "part of the hamlet of Little Horton," which, however, only included a very small portion of the hamlet, namely, that lying near to the junction of Manchester Road, Horton Lane, and Horton Road. The larger portion of the township, therefore, was managed as previously described, and left in darkness. It was left to the enterprise of the trustees of the Wesleyan Chapel to introduce gas into Great Horton, which they did for the purpose of lighting the chapel. It was soon afterwards made at Cousen's Mill, and at some other manufacturing establishments, until the Corporation ventured to assume that probably Great Horton might be a profitable customer, and carried gas mains to the place.

For highway purposes Great and Little Horton were divided, but in the administration of the Poor Law the township was united as at present. Once a year town's meetings were held at the vestry of the Bell Chapel, at which highway surveyors, churchwardens, overseers, and constables were appointed and a rate was laid, an occasion sufficiently exciting to arouse whatever local enthusiasm was existent. Bell Chapel, however, was only erected in 1808, and prior to that period parochial officers were elected at the parish vestry at Bradford. Among the earliest churchwardens whose names we have met with were Thomas Hodgson and Ezra Thornton, wardens for Great and Little Hortons in 1765; Samuel Swaine, Legrams, being overseer for the same year. Jos. Beanland, cornmiller, was the first churchwarden at the Bell Chapel, and held that office for many years, Messrs. Samuel and Richard Lumby also filling the office.

Horton constables of the manor of Bradford were also appointed at the "Court Leet," held for the purpose at Bradford, and of these a tolerable record is preserved, but we must be content with mentioning those holding office for the following years, viz.:—Gregory Fox, constable for 1795, Joshua Stanfield deputy; Samuel Lumby, constable for 1820, Francis Ackroyd, deputy; 1822, Joseph Barrans, Little Horton; Thomas Ramsden, Great Horton; 1827, Wm. Blamires, Great Horton; Wm. Cass, Little Horton; 1832, Dan Haley, Great Horton; John Stowell, Little Horton. As a rule, there were one chief constable and two deputies, and among the more recent chiefs were Wm. Swaine, Cowling Ackroyd, John Smith, Joseph Bakes, &c., and of the deputies Thomas Carter, John Haley, and John Liversedge. John Clough was bellman at Great Horton for several years, but was forcibly deprived by having the bell taken from him by Cowling Ackroyd and John Smith in 1839, for announcing a Chartist meeting. The inhabitants, indignant at such

Rambles Round Horton.

conduct, subscribed for another bell, and presented it to him to be used for all purposes. The town's bell was given to Samuel Fieldhouse, who held it for several years, and was succeeded by George Storey, who was for many years court-leet constable, bellman, and pinder for Great Horton. The office of court-leet constable is now inoperative, owing to the introduction of the borough police, but the appointment is still made at the Manor Court of the Honour of Pontefract, held yearly at the Market Tavern, Bradford, Mr. Wm. Greaves, solicitor, being steward and judge.

The administration of relief to the poor of Horton, happily never an arduous task, was effected during the early years of the century by a small, if not practically self-elected body, comprising amongst its number John Jennings, Wm. Blamires, Isaac Clough, Dan Booth, Richard and Sammy Lumby, and John Smith, with Abraham Balme, of Horton Green, as assistant-overseer and rate collector. This body met once a week to dispense the poor relief, the workhouse then being in the grounds now constituting Horton Park. Tom Carter, who was also a cow doctor and dentist, was the first workhouse master of whom we have any record. It is said that his practice of dentistry was attended with unpleasant effects upon some of the unfortunate inmates under his charge! Jeremy Haley succeeded Carter, and gathered the rates as well; and he was followed by Dan Booth and Wm. Marshall. At that period there were only nine or ten inmates of the "house."

The old workhouse was taken down about the year 182?, soon after the removal of the institution to a building now standing at Horton Green, which was erected for the purpose by the overseers of the township. The workhouse property at Great Horton having been purchased by Mr. Noble, a cloth merchant, of Leeds, for his son, Mr. Ed. Noble, the latter erected the residence now standing in Horton park, which he styled Wellclose House. He also planted the few old trees remaining in the park, and built a tower or bath-house over the cold spring of water, one of three springs known as the "tea well," the "bath well," and the "workhouse well," the latter having been used for bathing the paupers. Succeeding tenants of Wellclose House have been Mr. Richard Denton, who lived in it a long time, and Mr. Edwin Bentley.

The Bradford Union was constituted under the New Poor Law in Feb., 1837, and comprised among its twenty townships that of Horton, Mr. Abraham Balme being assistant-overseer. On Mr. Balme's retirement in 1839 Mr. Thos. Myers obtained the appointment to his office, and soon afterwards Mr. Jonas Jennings was made relieving officer, a position which he held for many years. In August, 1848, the Bradford Poor-law Union was divided, and the townships of the borough, viz., Bradford, Bowling, Horton, and Manningham, were formed into one union, and what is now known as the North Bierley Union into another. In the same year Mr. Myers, being wishful of being relieved from the duty of collecting the poor rates, gave up £70 of his salary towards the stipend of an assistant, and Mr. Benjamin Crabtree was appointed to the office. Mr. Richard Poole is the present assistant-overseer. The Bradford workhouse, which is in Horton township, is situated in an enclosure comprising about fourteen acres of land, and was erected in 1851-2, at a cost of £11,000. It has since been enlarged at a further cost of £16,000; thus, with the value of the site, the workhouse represents Union property worth £32,000. It has accommodation for 1000 inmates.

The records of the transactions of the highway surveyors are scarcely more ample than those relating to other parochial matters until we reach the period when the Board of Highway Surveyors was constituted. In the year 1840, at a meeting held at the old Bell Chapel, Messrs. Samuel Lumby, Scholemoor; John Jennings, Low Close House; Thomas Ramsden, High Street; Joseph Waterhouse, Bank Top; Samuel Dracup, Pickles Lane; Wm. Bakes, jun., Horton Road; and Robert Shepherd, Southgate, were appointed a board for the repair of the highways of Great Horton. At the same time Jeremiah Briggs was appointed acting surveyor. The first meeting was held at the Fleece Inn, kept by Wm. Bakes, the site of which is now occupied by the Congregational Schools, and the next meeting was held at the George and Dragon, the custom being to patronise the several "pubs" in the district in strict rotation. Almost the first item recorded in the proceedings for the year 1840 has reference to a matter which is still remembered as furnishing material for much angry disputation at the time it took place, namely, the question of the repair of Beldon Hill Road. In the minutes of the meeting of the Highway Board on June 1st we read :—

"That an appeal against the items expended on the Beldon Hill Road, and entered in the late Surveyor's accounts, be entered and prosecuted at the ensuing sessions to be held at Bradford, we the said Board not acknowledging the aforesaid road as belonging to the township, it having never been repaired at the expense of the township previously." Moved by Thomas Ramsden, and seconded by Samuel Lumby, and carried unanimously, "That Mr. Cowling Ackroyd and Mr. Nathan Bentley be appointed by this Board to enter and prosecute the aforesaid appeal at the ensuing sessions."

It appears that the road at Beldon Hill was, prior to 1840, in a very disreputable condition—almost impassable, or, as the old inhabitants describe it, "up tut knav i' muck." It so fell out, however, that Abraham Bairstow, of Hill End, was appointed surveyor, and, having some grounds for deeming the township liable to its repair, or else considering the existing state of things a reproach to the neighbourhood, he determined to exercise his authority as surveyor in the interest of the dwellers and frequenters of the uplands of Beldon Hill. Accordingly he put the road into a tolerable state of repair, rendering due account to the local authority. This course of the surveyor was stoutly resisted by the Board, representing for the most part those ratepayers who scarcely ever ascended to Beldon Hill, and led to the appeal referred to in the minute. Bairstow, however, resisted the appeal, and won the case; but even this did not appease the "Lords of Horton," who carried the case to the Court of Queen's Bench, compelling the patriotic surveyor to follow and maintain his cause. This he did principally at his own cost, and again came off triumphantly, but it is said that the drain upon his resources was such as to reduce him in worldly position—a circumstance not altogether to the credit of his neighbours, for whom he had waged and won a substantial point. At any rate, Beldon Hill Road, and Jer Lane as well, have been repaired at the public expense ever since Bairstow's victory, and are now in tolerable condition.

At a meeting of the Highway Board held in March, 1841, Thomas Myers was appointed clerk and treasurer of the Board without salary, Samuel Harrison being elected collector at a salary of £10 per annum, and Samuel Lumby overseer of the road-men. The highway rate for that period was 7d. in the pound. This arrangement continued until March, 1846, when Alfred Hind Denton was elected clerk at a salary of £2 per annum, and Wm. Keighley acting surveyor and treasurer, Samuel Harrison continuing his office of collector. The members of the Board had also undergone revision during the interval, Messrs. Richard Denton, Jos. Hirst, Wm. Keighley, David Mortimer, Chas. Bennett, John Parker, and Henry Sagar being the members for 1846, and Mr. Richard Denton chairman. We also meet with the several names of Nathan Bentley, Luke Blamires, William Keighley, William Fox, sen., David Mortimer, and William Moorhouse as having held the office. In April, 1847, " for certain considerations" understood between Mr. Horsfall, of the Mansion House, and the Board, that gentleman was allowed to enclose the plot of ground near his residence, then used as a dross-hill, and which was originally taken from the waste.

At the annual meeting held for the re-election of the Highway Board in March, 1849, something approaching to a "row" appears to have taken place, one section present being evidently determined to oust the members previously holding office and to substitute others. No less than four names were submitted for the office of chairman, but ultimately Mr. Wm. Buckle was elected; and a motion was proposed that the old members, viz., Messrs. John Wade, John Burrows, William Burrows, Jonathan Emsley, Samuel Wood, William Murgatroyd, Daniel Dracup, Dan Haley, John Bastow, Jeremiah Rudd, and William Moorhouse constitute the Board for the ensuing year. Whereupon a counter-list of names was submitted, containing those of Thomas Cockroft, Edwin Bentley, Luke Blamires, Job Robertshaw, Samuel Denton, William Buckle, John Jennings, and William Cousen. The old members, however, were carried by a large majority, and at the subsequent meeting of the Board the following officers were appointed :—Chairman, John Wade ; treasurer, William Moorhouse ; collector, George Laycock.

The books from which we derive this information give little more than the ordinary formal resolutions confirming what the surveyor might have done during the preceding month, such as the laying of a causeway or the removal of a rubbish heap. Neither do the account books offer much of interest, the following being the usual form of presenting the accounts. The period covered is for the year 1849 :—

		£	s	d.
Paid for day labour...		83	13	9
„	Contract work	85	1	1
„	Materials	78	4	11
„	Team work	49	18	9
„	Bills	68	12	5
„	Incidentals...	4	8	7
Total expenditure for the year		£368	19	7

This amount was raised in great part by the proceeds of a highway rate of 10d. in the pound, which realised £304 13s. 6½d., and by other small sums. At this period the Bradford Corporation had existed over two years, and Horton returned its councillors, but still the townships of the borough exercised control over their own highways, and, as it appears, levied rates for their maintenance. The anomaly, however, was removed by the passing of the Bradford Improvement Act of 1850, and by the enforcement of that Act the Board of Surveyors of Horton, as well as those of the other townships, was disestablished. The last meeting of the Board was held at the Four Ashes Inn, kept by Mr. Jeremiah Rudd, on the 3rd of March, 1851, there being present John Wade, chairman, Jeremiah Rudd, Saml. Wood, Wm. Moorhouse, Dan Haley, John Bairstow, Wm. Burrows, and William Murgatroyd. It may be stated parenthetically that a similar authority existed for Little Horton, of which Wm. Cass was surveyor, and Wm. Holdsworth collector. At a more recent date Isaac Rowntree officiated as highway surveyor of Little Horton, and was taken into the service of the Corporation.

Rambles Round Horton.

The Bradford Corporation was established in 1847, when the Horton townships was divided into two wards, three councillors being allotted to Great Horton and six to the Little Horton Ward, which had become very populous. The first burgess list of the borough comprised 5457 names, of which number Great Horton Ward had 536 and Little Horton 1206. The result of the first election of councillors invested the following Hortonians with municipal dignity, viz. :—Great Horton—Messrs. John Bartle, Wm. Buckle, and John Clough. Little Horton—Samuel Bottomley, James Bilton, John Clayton, John Hill, scale-beam maker, John Hill, maltster, and Samuel Smith. Hot contests ensued upon many subsequent occasions, especially in the Great Horton section of the township, but for years this ward has been practically given over to the Liberal party, so ardent in the Liberal cause being the majority of the inhabitants that active canvassers are in the habit of saying that Liberal voters may be counted by the house-row. In the Little Horton Ward the honours have been more equally divided.

CHAPTER III.

The "Good Old Times"—The Early Clothiers—A "Pot o' Four"—Primitive Habits—The Chartist Movement—The "Plug Riots"—The Cotton Manufacture—The Worsted Industry.

The antecedents of any community are not unfrequently reflected in the sayings and doings of the generations which follow, and so it has been in Horton. By this general term, however, we must be understood to mean suburban Horton, as distinguished from that portion of the township which is being rapidly absorbed in the great borough, and by the overgrowth of which its once pleasant fields are being covered with dwellings inhabited by people gathered from all quarters of the kingdom. The overwhelming process is not yet complete, however, and there still remains an element strongly Hortonian, in which may be found the characteristics distinguishing those who peopled the villages which were dotted here and there in the Bradford-dale of a past age.

In one important feature the villagers of Horton have maintained an honourable position, morally and socially. It is rare to see a drunken man in the Horton of which we speak. The people are thrifty and of a "saving" turn, without denying themselves the comforts of life; police regulations are almost superfluous; and in regard to material wealth, there are probably a larger number of small freeholders in Horton than in the majority of townships in the West Riding. In the various political struggles of the present century Hortonians have generally been to the fore, and many a veteran has suffered imprisonment for his zeal in political warfare.

We have, however, to deal with a period long anterior to this present age of school boards, commercial activity, and cheap bread—to a time when the two hamlets of Horton had undergone little change in their appearance for generations, with the exception of the erection now and again of an additional barn to receive the produce from a gradually extended cultivation of the surrounding uplands, or the rearing of a few one-storeyed dwellings for the young married men or labourers employed. At that time the processes of farming and of manufacturing, whether of cloth or other fabrics, went hand in hand—in one case the employers being styled "clothiers" and in the other "stuff makers." These manufacturers, as they may be termed, generally farmed their own small estates, and occupied themselves and their families alternately with the mixed labour of tilling their limited acres and in combing, spinning, carding, and weaving. In a large measure these old-time "manufacturers" spent a life of happiness and ended their days in honourable ease. Their indoor labours were at their own firesides; they had no factory bell to obey; if so disposed (which was not often the case) they could lie in bed an extra hour in the morning or take a stroll during the daytime, and while the father and his sons were engaged in sorting, combing, or weaving, the matronly dame and her daughters under her care and eye were busily engaged in spinning and reeling.

A pleasant picture this, but as time went on and the process of manufacture extended to a class who were not "master men" but were employed by others, the conditions of life were not of a character quite so pleasant as those described. Old Hortonians tell of a time when wool was brought about once a month from Leeds and other places to Horton, Clayton, Allerton, and other villages in Bradforddale to be carded, combed, and spun, the day of the arrival being held in festive celebrations, as on those occasions a "drop o' short" generally found its way into the villages. In summer-time the women took out their spinning wheels to the village green and upon the hillsides, which then were waste lands abounding with yellow furze and purple heather, interspersed with huge boulders. When the women had got a pound of wool from a neighbouring farmer it was spun into "cops," then reeled into hanks and carried back to "t'maister," who gave it out in the hank to the hand-loom weaver, who in turn had to spin it on to bobbins before weaving. A girl of fourteen or fifteen years would spin about ten hanks a-day, which would amount to less than sixpence. Nearly every farmer had a comb-pot and employed a comber or two; if he was the possessor of a "pot o' four" and a pair of looms he was in a large way of business. The class of goods made were called "calimancoes," and were from 16in. to 19in. broad, the weaver throwing the shuttle with one hand, catching it with the other, and throwing it back again. The warp and weft at that time were rougher than the roughest spun yarn of the present day. As a consequence, many long hairs protruded from the piece when completed, and these were removed by the process of singeing, performed by a man who went about with a piece of wood about the breadth of the warp, in which candles were placed at intervals.

As the processes of manufacture were of the most primitive kind, so were the habits of the people living in those times. Generally speaking their dwellings were of a mean description, consisting of one storey and one room, for which a rental of from 30s. to 40s. a year was paid. There were no weekly tenants in those days. The furniture of these cottages generally consisted of a pair of looms, a bobbin-wheel, a half-headed turn-up bedstead, the bed itself being made of chaff; a round table standing on three legs, a few turned, unpainted chairs, an old chest, and a cradle. Very few indeed were possessed of a clock of any kind, or even of a chest of drawers, and as the capacity of the cottage precluded the possibility of a second bedstead, it not unfrequently happened that the master of the house had two of his olive branches at his head and two at his feet while endeavouring to seek repose after the labours of the day! Where, it might be asked, were the comforts of the "good old times," as compared with those enjoyed at present? In process of time the cotton industry was introduced into Horton, and mills were erected specially for its manufacture, but the conditions of life of the operatives were little if at all the better for the introduction. It was nothing unusual for the cotton mills to commence at five o'clock in the morning and go on till eight at night, or any length of time that the masters chose to work them, as there was no limitation of hours. There was no setting off to Morecambe or the seaside then on Saturday afternoons, for the piece was to hook and "pike" before it could be paid for; then probably the wife had a jorum of clothes to wash or the baking to do for family use.

Nor were the "good old times" much to boast of in respect to food and living. The former was of the meanest description, consisting of oatmeal porridge and milk for breakfast; for dinner, potatoes and a bit of bacon fried together, with a piece of oat or "haver" cake dipped in the fat for a relish. An ounce of tea, which cost sixpence, served for a week, and if that failed, mint and herbs were called into requisition. Butter was only present on the table on Sundays. Flour and wheat bread were luxuries seen on particular occasions only in a working man's cottage. The former was seven shillings a stone, and if a large family could afford to exchange a gold piece for a stone of flour they did well. Almost every household had its "milk-stick," upon which notches were cut after each delivery—a most ingenious preventive of fraud, as there was no fear of the customer adding a notch, and he could not take one off! Tradition has it that at one time there was only one oven in Great Horton, and only one spoon for a neighbourhood, but tradition in this case is probably in excess of truth. It is certain, however, that porridge spoons did duty for both knives and forks, and so highly prized were they that within recent times a youth has been known to carry his spoon all day long stuck in one of the button-holes of his jacket! As to dress, a dyed cotton gown or lincey wolsey bedgown, and white calico "brats" for Sundays, sufficed for the women; while the men were proud indeed if they secured a piece of cloth for a coat twice in a score years.

The phraseology and mode of address of Hortonians of the past receive some illustration in the response once made to an exclamation of one of the "Horton Amateurs" (a noted body of Thespians years ago), who in the course of a stage speech was called upon to inquire, "Who am I?" "Whah," exclaimed one of the audience, "thar't one o' Robin o' Jack's lot for sewer!" The refinements of modern speech, however, are fast exerting an influence in Horton, making sad havoc with the mother tongue, but occasionally an unguarded native may be heard referring to a neighbour as "one o' Bill o' Sam's," or some equivalent form of expression.

Even in regard to Great Horton the ever-spreading borough is producing some change. The Horton of fifty years ago was a different place from the Horton of to-day. Half a century ago it formed a distinct place, divided from the town by a long stretch of green fields, the route by the highway having many long and lonely stretches, which on a dark winter's night were a source of dread to the timid pedestrian. The roads then were not so brilliantly lighted as now, and during the long, dark evenings the dim candles flickering here and there in the little shops were the only aid to the villager doubtful as to his whereabouts. Highway robberies and burglaries were then not unfrequent occurrences; so frequent in fact were they one winter, when flour was dear and work scarce, that the inhabitants of Horton were called up in batches to patrol the thoroughfares during the night.

This reminiscence takes us back to the time of the Chartist movement, as the patrol sometimes disturbed parties armed with pikes, &c., who were preparing for the great rising which was to take place if the Charter were still refused. During the palmy days of Feargus O'Connor's propaganda, Horton was a very hotbed of Chartism, and bristled with physical force men. The hand-loom weavers flourished the Radical colour almost to a man, and as for the woolcombers —and woolcombing was at that day an extensive industry in the village—they received O'Connor's gospel with special enthusiasm. Unlike the more taciturn hand-loom weavers, they worked in batches, and the discussion of the affairs of the nation, so far from hindering their work, deprived it of its monotony. And so through the long days and often far into the night—for these men had to work fourteen and even sixteen hours a day to earn a sorry pittance—the combing shops rang with wild denunciations of wrongdoers, or of fervid admiration of the champion of democracy.

These combing shops were centres for the dissemination of political information. The *Northern Star* was always subscribed for, and if a school lad could be got for a reader he was sure of a good audience, as all the neighbours who could find room congregated to hear him. The enthusiasm of some of these men was something remarkable, and though they may have been inferior to the working men of this day in some departments of knowledge, upon all questions appertaining to politics they were infinitely superior. The difficulty was not then to find speakers at the many public meetings which were held, but rather to find places for all who were anxious to unburden their souls. Old Chartists will remember the tremendous enthusiasm evoked in the village by the visit of Feargus O'Connor. No royal personage could have been received with greater honour than was the then leader of democracy in England on that day. All the village was astir almost before the morn broke, and when O'Connor appeared the horses were taken from his carriage and he was drawn through the streets amidst the wildest enthusiasm.

The movement known as the Plug Riots—a sort of mixture of Chartism and trades unionism—was somehow regarded with very little sympathy in Horton, and very few compromised themselves by joining it. The sight of that huge crowd of people as they marched from Halifax to Bradford was not such indeed as to induce many to throw in their lot with them. It was a spectacle which once seen it is impossible to forget. The crowd came pouring through Horton, taking the whole breadth of the wide road—a gaunt, famished-looking, desperate multitude, armed with huge bludgeons, flails, pitchforks, and pikes, many without coats and hats, and hundreds with their clothes in rags and tatters. Many of the older men looked footsore and weary, but the great bulk were men in the prime of life, full of wild excitement. As they marched, they thundered out to a grand old tune the Union hymn :—

> Oh, worthy is the glorious cause,
>   Ye patriots of the Union ;
> Our fathers' rights, our fathers' laws,
>   Demand a faithful union.
> A crouching dastard sure is he
>   Who would not strive for liberty,
> And die to make old England free
>   From all her load of tyranny ;
>   Up, brave men of the Union !

As the wild mob swept onward, terrified women brought out all their eatables, and in the hope apparently of purchasing their forbearance handed them to the rough-looking men who crowded to the doors and windows. That some of them had need of food was evident from the fact that one poor famished wretch, after struggling feebly for a share of the provisions, fell down on the roadside, and died just about where the Liberal Club now stands.

Before referring to the growth of the worsted industry, to which the township of Horton with other portions of the worsted district owes its material prosperity, we may supplement what has been already stated with regard to the cotton manufacture, which at one time bade fair to find employment for a goodly number of the inhabitants of Horton and adjoining places. This industry had obtained a footing during the closing years of last century, providing employment principally for weavers of cotton pieces at their own homes. The central market was of course Manchester, to which place all the finished goods were conveyed by waggons, and from whence warps were brought to the Horton manufacturers.

Old people speak of Johnny Ward, of Bank Bottom, and Robert King, of Town End, as among the earliest carriers engaged in this business; they being succeeded by Isaac Knight (or "Neet," as he was generally called), father of John and Benjamin Knight, who afterwards played a conspicuous part in this manufacture. Isaac Knight was succeeded in the carrying business by John and then by Tommy Knight, who was the last of the family who were carriers. Their large covered waggons with big wheels went to Manchester and other places. John Nichol (properly Nicholson) succeeded the Knights, having been brought up by them. Some of the larger makers employed their own waggons, keeping them constantly upon the road between Horton and Manchester, the time occupied in going and returning being three days. Considering the bad condition of the roads at that period, which were at some portions of the year almost impassable, it may well be imagined that the difficulties of transit operated materially against the prosperity of this particular branch of industry.

From an old directory we learn that the following calico manufacturers from Horton attended Manchester market at the beginning of the present century, namely, Richard Bolton, Abraham Haley, John Knight & Co., George Norton, James Tetley, Edward Peel, and Thomas Wardman. All these persons apparently resided in the upper portion of the township: Richard Bolton in Low Green, where he kept scores of persons weaving for him; Abm. Haley in Paternoster Fold; Jas. Tetley (another large manufacturer) in Southfield Lane; Edward Peel, also of Southfield Lane, where he owned a large number of cottages tenanted by calico weavers; and Thos. Wardman, in Cross Lane. The firm of Knight & Co. we shall have to refer to subsequently. The Trafalgar coach passed through Great Horton daily on its way to Manchester and Liverpool, but it was either not considered trustworthy enough for some of the Horton manufacturers, or for some other reason not explained, they commenced a conveyance of their own, which ran to Manchester, and was known as the "Calico coach."

The above-named, however, were not the only persons engaged in the cotton manufacture in Horton, there being in addition others resident at Little Horton, some of whom were in an extensive way of business, such as Benjamin Kaye, of Horton Green, who, after his removal to Allerton Hall, was succeeded by his nephew, Abraham Balme; and in the same locality were James Swaine, John Riley, and others.

The Knights, to whom reference has been made, were of especial prominence in the commercial world of Horton. John Knight was for years regarded as one of the "kings of Horton," his will being generally considered law. About the year 1806 John Knight, in company with his brother Benjamin, erected a cotton factory, the site of which is occupied by the present worsted spinning mill of Messrs. J. J. Broadbent & Co. It was only a small erection, however, as compared with that which at present exists upon the site, but it served to find employment for a considerable number of "hands," who toiled during the long hours previously stated at very low wages. John Knight erected a good house adjoining the mill, his brother Benjamin purchasing in the year 1821 the old mansion now standing opposite Broadbent's mill, from Gorton's trustees, for the sum of £2500, the purchase including West Croft adjoining. Of this amount, however, he would appear to have mortaged the property for £2000.

Up to this period the firm of John Knight & Co. were in a prosperous condition in public estimation, and so continued until the year 1826, when, consequent upon the failure of Messrs. Wentworth, Chaloner & Co., the Wakefield banking firm, and the commercial disasters which shook the credit of scores of firms in this neighbourhood, Messrs. John and Benjamin Knight succumbed, and with their downfall the calico trade of Horton sustained a serious blow. Their estate was taken possession of by the Commissioners in Bankruptcy, and in great measure passed into the hands of Messrs. Harris & Co., bankers, of Bradford, the principal creditors, who rebuilt the mill and adapted it for a worsted factory.

The cotton trade, however, was destined to sustain an even greater shock than this, by the failure of the firm of Messrs. Butterworth & Brooke, of Manchester, about the year 1845. The consternation which followed upon this event, when the news reached Horton by coach, was very great, as many cotton piece makers in the township were pecuniarily involved in the affairs of the firm, the extent of whose collapse may be judged from the fact that a dividend of only 8⅝d. in the pound was subsequently realised. Even at this low rate a combined dividend amounting to £6000 was paid over to Horton manufacturers as their share of the wreck. The effect, however, was disastrous, scores of little masters who were doing business with the bankrupt firm being more or less crippled in their resources, some of whom were only able to tide over their difficulties by the help received from Mr. Bridges, of Horton Old Hall. The cotton trade, however, finally collapsed in Horton in the presence of its more vigorous rival, the worsted industry, to which reference may now be made.

With regard to this feature of the subject our remarks may be prefaced by the following list of worsted manufacturers

of Great and Little Horton who attended the Bradford Piece
Hall in the year 1821, viz. :—

Bakes, William	Hardaker, John	Parker, Andrew
Bakes, William	Hindle, Joseph	Peel, Thomas
Barstow, Abraham	Holder, John, sen.	Robertshaw, Jeremiah
Bentley, Joseph	Holder, John, jun.	Shackleton, Robert
Bentley, Joseph	Holdsworth, Jeremiah	Sharp, Daniel
Bentley, Nathan	Holdsworth, John	Smith, W. and E.
Binns, John	Holdsworth, John	Swain, Joseph
Birtwistle, William	Holdsworth, Jonas	Tordoff, Squire
Blakeborough, Richard	Hudson, John	Whitaker, John
Blaymires, Joseph	Jennings, John	Whitaker, Timothy
Booth, Joseph	Keighley, Abraham	Wilkinson, David
Clough, Isaac	Keighley, James	Wood, Joseph
Denton, Samuel	Mitchell, Thomas	Wooller, Samuel
Emsley, John	Murgatroyd, William	Wright, Jonas
Emsley, Thomas	Parker, Abraham	Wright, George
Fox, Samuel	Parker, John	Wright, William
Greenhough, Benjamin	Parker, Samuel	

Several of the above persons had been previously engaged in the cotton trade, but had turned their energies in the direction of worsted. The list is not complete, however, as it omits mention of other and larger manufacturers whose places of business were in Horton, such as the firm of Messrs. John Rand & Sons. Rand's mill was one of the earliest worsted manufacturing works in the township, but the interest attaching to it and the families connected with it call for a more extended notice than can be given in the present article.

In order of seniority the mill at Bank Top, now the property of Mr. T. Priestley; and Mitchell's Mill, Manchester Road, come next, both having been erected in the year 1817. Bank Top, or Mirypond Mill, as it was formerly named, was erected by Mr. Ellis Cunliffe Lister, whose family owned considerable property in Horton at that period. The first occupant was Mr. Thomas Ackroyd, son of old Francis Ackroyd, who brought up a numerous and influential family of sons, most of whom were manufacturers, namely :—Joseph, Thomas, William, Francis, Cowling, and Robert Stables. Thomas Ackroyd left Bank Top Mill nearly half a century ago, and removed to Birkenshaw, where he established the business afterwards carried on by his sons, as spinners and manufacturers, colliery proprietors, and timber merchants. William went to Otley, where he founded the extensive business firm of Messrs. Wm. Ackroyd & Co.; Cowling succeeded John Knight & Co., at Great Horton; and Robert-Stables Ackroyd built Fieldhead Mills, afterwards occupied by Messrs. A. Tremel & Co., and since owned and occupied by Messrs. John Smith & Sons, the firm now represented by the Mayor of Bradford, Alderman Isaac Smith.

The original portion of the extensive pile now owned and occupied by Messrs. Mitchell Bros. was erected by Mr. Richard Smith, and was formerly well known as "Dick Smith Mill." It was occupied by the owner as a worsted-spinning mill until it was taken for the same business by Messrs. Turner & Mitchell. The parties to this firm were George Turner and Thomas Mitchell, father of Messrs. Abraham and Joseph Mitchell, who have subsequently so largely extended the premises. Messrs. George, John, and Robert Turner afterwards went into business at Holme Top Mill and Beckside Mill, John and George subsequently settling at the latter place. John Turner died in 1860, leaving George in business, and he was joined by Mr. S. Ackroyd, in the firm of George Turner & Co.

What is still known as "Marshall's Mill," in Manchester Road, was erected in the year 1818, having been built by Mr. James Marshall for his two sons, Joseph and John. Mr. Marshall was an ironmonger opposite the Old Manor Hall in Kirkgate, and was a man of some enterprise, he having, in company with Mr. Henry Leah, some time previously purchased the Bierley Ironworks. Marshall's Mill was unfortunately burnt down in 1822, and the worsted business carried on in it collapsed some time after its re-erection from the effects of the commercial disaster which told upon the owners and occupiers. Messrs. Joshua Wood & Co. were subsequently tenants of the premises, and Messrs. B. Berry and Co. Some years ago the property was sold to Messrs. Geo. Brown and John Sowden.

In the year 1819 Mr. E. C. Lister erected for Messrs. Francis & John Mitchell Old Bowling Lane Mill, in Horton township.

c

Two worsted mills were built in Horton township during the year 1820, namely, Cliffe Mill, Great Horton, and a mill in Nelson Street. The latter was erected by Mr. James Duckitt, and was first occupied by Messrs. Aked & Co. and Messrs. Chapman & Co. It has latterly been owned and used for woolcombing by Messrs. M. Todd & Sons. The premises have, however, been recently acquired by the Corporation for the purposes of street improvement. Cliffe Mill, on the other hand, has been wonderfully extended, and is at present one of the chief sources of employment for the factory workers of Great Horton. Cliffe Mill was built by Joseph Beanland, corn miller and colliery proprietor, of Shuttleworth Hall, and was run by his sons-in-law, Samuel Helliwell, Joseph Wilkinson, and Edward Knight. It was afterwards occupied conjointly by Mr. Cowling Ackroyd and his brother, Robert S. Ackroyd, also by John Bartle and Samuel Field; and Messrs. Henry and George Mason commenced business there, being succeeded by Messrs. John Priestman & Sons. The premises are now owned and occupied by Messrs. Wm. Ramsden & Co., of whose extensive works the old Cliffe Mill forms a very inconsiderable portion. Joseph Beanland also built the original portion of Beckside Mill for the purposes of corn-milling, the premises, however, being subsequently purchased by Samuel Dracup, and adapted for a worsted factory. The premises were occupied until recently by the firm of Messrs. George Turner & Co., and now by Messrs. Benn & Sons, spinners and manufacturers. Samuel Dracup's trustees are still the owners of the property. Mr. Dracup also built a mill in Cliffe Lane, the first tenant of which was Mr. John Bartle. Messrs. W. Bunting & Co. were subsequently tenants, and on the retirement of Mr. Bunting his partner, the late Mr. Henry Snowden, took the business.

Cross Lane Mill comes before the two last-named in order of erection, the original structure having been commenced in 1821 by Mr. Eli Suddards. Mr. Suddards came from Todmorden as a corn dealer, and carried on that business in an old house at Low Green. He, however, did not complete the erection of the mill in Cross Lane, which was completed by Mr. James Cousen, who commenced running it as a spinning mill under the name of James Cousen & Son. Mr. Wm. Cousen, the son, afterwards succeeded to the business. The adjoining shed was erected by Mr. Moses Topham and run by him in 1867. The entire premises are now owned by Messrs. John Rand & Sons, and occupied by the firm.

In 1826 Cannan Mill was built by Mr. Samuel Cannan, who farmed Tommy Barraclough's land at Primrose Hill, and sent out "travelling Scotchmen." The old mill, known as Sammy Cannan Mill, was occupied by several tenants, among others by Mr. George Oxley, afterwards Willett & Oxley, merchants; Mr. Wm. Foster, of Queensbury; Mr. John Buckle; Mr. John Smith, afterwards of Fieldhead Mills; Mr. Thos. Myers, and others. An alarming accident happened in connection with Cannan Mill on the 6th of January, 1839, when the chimney suddenly fell, cutting the mill into halves. The new mill was built by Mr. Charles Tetley, and called by the owner Cannon Mill. It had been completed some time when Mr. John Ashley, spinner, &c., became the first tenant in the year 1854. He had been bookkeeper and cashier with the firm of Messrs. John Smith & Sons. Some time after Messrs. Whitaker & Booker, spinners and manufacturers, became tenants also. In the year 1874 Mr. Ashley from various causes was obliged to suspend payment, an arrangement being made to pay the creditors 17s. 6d. in the pound, with guarantee. Twelve months after, each creditor received a sum equal to 20s. in the £ with interest, thus furnishing another instance of commercial integrity which it is a pleasure to record. In admiration of his upright conduct a handsome service of plate was shortly afterwards presented to Mr. Ashley by Mr. Richard Fawcett, on behalf of a few friends, and on the same occasion a gold snuff box was presented to Mr. Samuel Ackroyd, of Great Horton, in recognition of his judicious management of Mr. Ashley's affairs during his temporary embarrassment. Mr. Ashley now lives in retirement in Summerseat Place.

Mr. Chas. Tetley, the builder of the new portion of Cannon Mill, was of the firm of Rennie, Tetley & Co., and was sometimes called by his friends Pump Tetley, from the fact that he was the inventor of the centrifugal pump. Mr.

Tetley was a very clever man, but short of some of the qualities which go to make a successful man of business. He was for many years manager of the Laxey Mine in the Isle of Man, where he died a few years ago. The premises are now owned by Mr. George Rennie Tetley, of Bingley, son of the late Mr. G. G. Tetley.

In the year 1827 the mill at Great Horton erected by John Knight for a cotton mill was converted into a worsted mill by Messrs. Harris & Co. for Mr. Cowling Ackroyd, who commenced life in partnership with his brother Robert Stables Ackroyd at "Cowling Mill," as it was termed. When Mr. R. S. Ackroyd went to Fieldhead, his brother Cowling remained at Horton, and for a long period was intimately identified with its interests. He retired from business, however, and the mill stood empty for a time. Messrs. Harris pulled down the old mill and built the present one, when Messrs. J. J. Broadbent & Co., who had been at Atlas Mills, Bradford, came to it in 1861, and purchased the property, since which period the works have been much extended.

Brief reference can only be made to subsequent erections, among which may be named Northside Mill, Legrams, built by Mr. Nathan Bentley, and occupied by him and his sons, Edwin, William, Bakes, Nathan, and Henry, afterwards purchased by Mr. Simeon Townend, and now owned by Mr. Alfred Illingworth, M.P. Bentley's Mill suffered from a disastrous fire on November 25, 1852, when it was almost burned to the ground.

Stowell's Mill at Holme Top was erected in the year 1835 by Messrs. John and Squire Stowell. It was occupied at one time by Messrs. George, John and Robert Turner, and afterwards purchased and extended by Messrs. Michael and Samuel Smith, who occupied a portion of the premises.

Britannia Mills, Manchester Road, erected by Messrs. Christopher and Edward Waud in 1836, were at the time of their erection the largest spinning mills in the Bradford district, and so persuaded were some persons that the worsted trade did not justify so large an outlay that the erection of these mills was looked upon as an extravagant piece of folly!

Albion Mill, Manchester Road, was erected by the late Mr. Thomas Dewhirst, previously with Messrs. Pearson and Whitehead, of Laisterdyke, upon the ground first purchased after the opening up of the Skinhouse estate in 1850.

Shearbridge Mills, erected by Mr. Thomas Firth in 1850, are now the property of the late Mr. Wm. Dewhirst's executors. This property also suffered seriously from fire, the premises having been burned to the ground on July 10, 1866. They were, however, rebuilt quickly, five feet wider than originally planned.

Among those who deserve especial mention in connection with the manufacturing interests of Horton and the neighbourhood are the Dracup family. Sammy Dracup, whose family was originally from Idle, was a most ingenious and persevering man. His family acquired a considerable reputation as shuttlemakers and makers of harness, also in rendering the jacquard engine applicable to the worsted business. Mr. Dracup commenced making these engines in 1838. When first introduced into Horton they could only be worked by hand. It is stated that Mr. Thomas Ackroyd, of Horton Bank Top, set the first jacquard engine to work by power in the neighbourhood of Bradford. In connection with this subject it is worthy of note that Mr. S. Dracup also made the first card-cutting machine in the year 1833, and in the succeeding year he produced his repeater, a kind of stereotype for designs. The family acquired considerable property in Horton, which they still hold.

CHAPTER IV.

Pioneers of the Worsted Industry—The Rands—The Ramsbothams—The Swaines.

Referring in a previous article to the commercial interests of Horton we reserved what it might be desirable to place on record with regard to several important families which were largely identified with the township of Horton and the interests of the worsted trade generally. Among the number the Rands, the Ramsbothams, and the Swaines call for especial notice, as being pioneers in that important industry. Although many beside them had long been engaged in the making of worsted stuffs, it was reserved to members of the above families to concentrate the industry within the walls of a worsted factory.

The first erection of this character is attributed to Mr. Henry Ramsbotham, with whom were associated Mr. Swaine and Mr. Nathaniel Murgatroyd. The mill was situate in the Holme, and was adjacent to the beck-course dividing the townships of Horton and Bradford. This was in the year 1798. A second mill was erected in 1801 by Mr. Benj. Peile for his nephews, Benjamin and Matthew Thompson, and in 1803 one was built in Horton Lane by Mr. John Rand. It would appear, however, that the force of circumstances impelled some of the persons named to a course of action which they had resolutely opposed in others. In James's History of Bradford there is given a curious document, showing that an enterprising gentleman named Buckley, residing in Bradford, formed in 1793 the design of erecting a factory to be worked by a steam engine, a site for which had been purchased in a field near the bottom of Manchester Road, known as the Brick Kiln Field. So opposed were the residents of the locality to the erection of a smoking factory chimney, however, that a number of inhabitants signed a document threatening Mr. Buckley with an action at law if he persevered in his design, and that gentleman, seeing the array of influential names against him, quietly gave up the project, and withdrew to the Todmorden valley. The signatures attached to this threatening missive were as follows:—Toms. Atkinson, Nathl. Aked, John Smith, Isaac Willson, Thos. Holdgate, Jonas Bower, John Rand, Wm. Whitaker, Jno. Hardy, Henry W. Oates, Mary Laidman, Betty Swaine, Frs. Town, J. Lupton, and John Aked.

It is somewhat significant that several of the signatories took a leading part in later years in promoting the erection of objectionable mill chimneys, among them being Mr. John Rand. Betty Swaine was Mr. Rand's mother-in-law, and Mary Laidman was Mrs. Swaine's sister. The Rev. Dr. Laidman, husband of Mary Laidman, was vicar of Calverley, and it is worth notice in passing that that position was in later times held successively by the Rev. Saml. Redhead, who married Mary, eldest daughter of John Rand (grandniece of Mrs. Laidman), and the Rev. Alfred Brown, who married Jane, third daughter of Samuel and Mary Redhead. Thomas Atkinson was a woolstapler in Tyrrel Street, and was the employer of John Rand. John and Nathaniel Aked were members of a family which resided in a low old-fashioned house where the New Inn now stands—a family long identified with the wool trade. John Hardy, the grandfather of the present Lord Cranbrook, lived in the good house opposite Mr. Rand's ; Wm. Whitaker was the principal partner in the Old Brewery near at hand ; and Henry W. Oates was also a member of the firm. Isaac Willson, the clerk of the Court of Requests, resided at the house at the corner of "Bowling Lane," afterwards occupied by Mrs. Bacon. Jonas Bower belonged to the respectable family of that name in Chapel Lane ; and Thos. Holdgate was the minister at Horton Lane Chapel.

It will be seen therefore that the "protest" was extensively signed by the gentry of the Town End, as that portion of Bradford was called, and remembering the salubrious character of the locality at that time, it is scarcely to be wondered at that they should have taken alarm at the threatened pollution by smoke of the neighbourhood. However, as history proves, some of the protestors soon changed their views, and not only entered heartily into the initiatory stages of development through which the worsted industry necessarily passed, but left representatives who in an eminent degree deserve the gratitude of the present generation for the enterprising spirit in which they promoted that industry in subsequent but not less critical stages.

In this category rank the Rand family. The Rands sprang from Norwich, the father of John Rand, the elder, being named Hewett Rand, who was a merchant of that city. Through his mother's line John Rand was descended from the Columbines, a Huguenot family, who, after the revocation of the Edict of Nantes, settled in Norwich. That city was towards the close of last century and during the earlier portion of the present one, celebrated for the manufacture of a class of worsted goods akin to those produced in Bradford, and probably arising out of this circumstance Hewett Rand apprenticed his son John with Mr. Thomas Atkinson, of Tyrrel Street (one of the signatories of the famous Buckley "protest"), and with whom John learned his business so far as a knowledge of the wool trade was concerned.

In March, 1785, John Rand married Mary, the only child of Samuel and Betty Swaine, Mr. Swaine afterwards entering into partnership with Mr. John Rand in the worsted trade. Samuel Swaine formerly lived in a homestead in Legrams, nearly opposite to Horton Grange, but afterwards built and resided in the house in Horton Lane adjacent to which Rand's Mill was built, and he owned the land required for that erection. On Mr. Rand's marriage with their daughter, Mr. and Mrs. Swaine gave up this house to Mr. Rand, who resided there until his death in 1835, at the age of seventy-six years.

The picture of this veteran stuffmaker, with his powdered queue, knee breeches, black silk stockings, and buckled shoes, is yet in the remembrance of "old inhabitants," and it may be recorded that he was the last man in Bradford who held to the above costume. His wife died in 1837, aged seventy-seven years. Their family comprised three sons, viz., Samuel, who died in 1808, aged twenty-two years; John, and William; also four daughters:—Mary, who married the Rev. Samuel Redhead, vicar of Calverley; Sarah, who married the Rev.

Henry Ives Bailey, incumbent of Drighlington ; Elizabeth, who died young, unmarried ; and Annie, who married George Dodsworth, Esq., of Wheldrake, near York.

To the memory of John and William Rand, the surviving sons of John Rand the elder, ample justice can scarcely be done in sketches of the character we propose. Of both of the first-named gentlemen it may be said that they assisted in the development of the worsted industry from its most primitive stage until it reached a position of assured stability—they were, in fact, connecting links between the generation which inhabited Bradford when it was a mere village and that which has made it one of the most influential towns in the kingdom. There are but few in Bradford who remember the "Bishop Blaize" celebrations of sixty years ago, but those who do can tell with what a lusty voice John Rand pronounced the famous "speech" beginning "Hail to the day," &c., which, doggerel though it be, was deemed by our ancestors the laureate-poem of Yorkshire. But Mr. John Rand was more than a tradesman, and his name will long be associated with the various religious, social, and philanthropic movements of his time. Mr. Rand married a sister of the late Dr. Macturk, but left no issue. His death occurred in June, 1873, in the eightieth year of his age. A tablet has been erected in Bradford Parish Church by his widow, who died during the year 1884.

William Rand was born in 1796, and, in conjunction with his brother, devoted much time to the development of the worsted business. In public matters his name stands connected with the Waterworks Company, of which he was chairman until it was bought up by the Corporation. Over the latter body he was elected to preside as Mayor in the year 1850-1, having been an alderman of the borough since its incorporation in 1847. For many years Mr. Rand lived at the family house in Horton Lane, but subsequently removed to Baildon, where he died in December, 1868, aged seventy-two years. He was never married.

It may be stated that the original mill erected by John Rand was adapted for the spinning of cotton as well as of worsted, and is still standing parallel with Horton Lane.

That portion of the premises adjoining the burial ground of Horton Lane Chapel was erected many years afterwards upon the site of the mill-dam, and subsequently the premises have been much extended in the direction of Great Horton Road.

The history of Swaine and Ramsbotham's Mill in the Holme is interesting on account of its being the first erection of the kind in Bradford. Although it is just outside the Horton boundary, it may be noticed in these papers by reason of its associations, and its initiation by men who were intimately connected with Horton. From the fields in which it was situate being from "time immemorial" called the Holmes, it may be inferred that they formed a dry spot in a swampy place, or possibly at one period an island may have been formed by the divergence of the streams from Horton and Thornton. It was in these meadows that the famous Bishop Blaize demonstrations were marshalled before proceeding round the town. The road to the Holme, and subsequently to Holme Mill, was by way of Brewery Lane, and across the beck at the bottom. There was also a nice plantation of wood at that time upon the slopes of the hill upon which Westbrook House (now the Alexandra Hotel) stands.

After the erection of Holme Mill by Mr. Henry Ramsbotham, he was joined in partnership by one of the Swaines. Mr. Nathaniel Murgatroyd, a cotton manufacturer and father of the late Mr. Wm. Murgatroyd, having some interest in it. The leading spirit, however, was Mr. Ramsbotham, who, it is said, had prior to 1798 turned a quantity of spinning machinery in his premises near the site of the Bradford Banking Company's bank by means of a horse-gin, a course adopted by several other manufacturers. It would appear, too, that Mr. Ramsbotham was an authority in trade matters generally, as we are told that he and the late Edward Pease, of Darlington, met every three months at the Golden Lion in Leeds, or at the Star and Garter at Kirkstall, to arrange the list of prices to be charged for worsted yarns during the ensuing quarter! How delighted would any two or three spinners of the present day be to possess such a privilege!

Rambles Round Horton.

After the Holme Mill had been erected about four years a serious fire occurred, and almost destroyed the edifice. On that occasion the corps of the Bradford Volunteers, captained by Mr. Samuel Hailstone, had an opportunity of distinguishing themselves by putting out the flames. With this view we are told they " saged " or severed the leaden pipe which supplied the town's reservoir in Westgate, and thus obtained the necessary fluid. That was in March, 1804. It is not at all unlikely that the fire was the work of some malicious person or combination of persons, inasmuch as it is upon record that Mr. Ramsbotham had to encounter considerable opposition during the erection of the mill. While the stones were being conveyed for its erection a large number of inhabitants of the town assembled to prevent their being deposited on the site, and Mr. Ramsbotham had to strip and show fight before the horse and cart was allowed to proceed ! The engine supplying the propelling force was of 15-horse power. After the disastrous fire the premises were rebuilt and enlarged by the original partners, but were shortly afterwards purchased by Mr. Richard Fawcett, who at the time was also erecting a mill in Union Street, and in both places he carried on a successful business for some years. Holme Mill again suffered from conflagration in 1868, and since that period the premises have been occupied as machine works by Messrs. Sowden & Stephenson.

The Ramsbothams originally came from Lancashire. A member of this family settled in Halifax some time about the year 1730, as an oil merchant, and his son Robert Ramsbotham very early in life came to Bradford, and married Eliza, a daughter of William Swaine, of Legrams, brother to Samuel Swaine, the father of Mrs. John Rand, who also lived in Legrams. Robert Ramsbotham died in 1796, leaving three children, viz., Henry (of whom mention has been made in connection with Holme Mill) ; William, who died without issue ; and Elizabeth, who married Dr. Mossman, of Bradford, and had children : George Robert, solicitor, father of Mr. G. R. Mossman, of Crow Trees, and clerk to the West Riding and borough justices ; and Margaret, who married Wm. Taylor, Esq., of Hunsworth. It will be seen, therefore, that the connection between the Rands and the Ramsbothams came through the Swaines.

Henry Ramsbotham married Ann Elizabeth, daughter of Thomas Shepley, Esq., of Tadcaster. He died in 1810, and his widow afterwards married Dr. Mossman. Henry Ramsbotham had two sons, Henry Robert and John Hodgson. Robert, after being in partnership with the Rands for many years, founded the firm of Messrs. H. R. Ramsbotham & Co., and lived at Allerton Hall, afterwards removing to Finchley, where he died, unmarried, in 1880. John, the second son, was apprenticed with Mr. Blakey, surgeon, of Bradford, and practiced as a medical man for a time in London and afterwards in his native town. Being compelled by ill-health to retire from the active pursuit of his profession, he accepted in 1838 the stewardship of the Thornhill estates at Fixby and Calverley. In 1845, having had his attention drawn to the method of treatment put forth by Hahnemann, then a novelty in this country, he gradually resumed practice, and by his enthusiasm as one of the pioneers of homœopathy in the north of England, made many converts to the new doctrine among his professional friends. He was well known as a successful practitioner, first in Huddersfield and then in Leeds, where he died in 1868. He married Mary, eldest daughter of the Rev. Samuel Redhead. Of his sons, two have become connected with the Bradford trade, viz., Robert Redhead, who was in partnership with Mr. Wm. Firth as a worsted spinner, and died in 1873, and John Rand, who is associated with his cousin Frederick Mossman in carrying on the business of H. R. Ramsbotham & Co. His eldest son, Samuel Henry, succeeded him in practice at Leeds, and his youngest son, Francis Shepley, is an assistant master at Charterhouse School, Godalming. His daughter, Mary Elizabeth, married the Rev. Edward Kemble, formerly vicar of Yeadon, now vicar of Coniston Cold, in Craven.

The Swaines are a very ancient family. By the will of Miles Swayne, of Horton, dated 1515, he gave his body to be buried in the church of St. Peter and St. Paul at Bradford, and left 3s. 4d. for church work. He also mentioned Alice, his wife, and made James and Christopher Swaine, his sons, his executors. In 1596 a Robert Swayne married Elizabeth Sharp, of Horton, and numerous entries might be given from documents before us showing a continuous succession of Horton and Bradford Swaines to the close of last century. That members of the family were considerable landowners may be gathered from a perusal of the land tax for Horton in 1704, of which Chris. Swaine and Thos. Swaine were assessors, and in which occur the following names :— Abm. Swaine, of Hew Clews ; Robert Swaine, Hunt Yard ; Thos. Swaine, Chris. Swaine, and " Mr." Wm. Swaine.

The Swaine family had numerous branches, the various lines of which it would be undesirable to trace except for strictly antiquarian reasons. Following the more important branches so far as their connection with Horton is concerned, we append notes culled from family documents and the silent testimony of the burial ground of Chapel Lane Chapel, where many members of the family lie interred.

As we have seen, the Swaines were located in Horton early in the sixteenth century, and probably before. The family, however, have a clear descent from 1596, when Robert Swayne married Elizabeth Sharp, one of the members of the Horton family of that name. Their son, Thomas, married in 1633 Grace Pearson, and the eldest son of this marriage, Samuel, married Susannah Feild, also of Horton. In 1701 Robert Swaine, a son of the above, married Sarah Balme, of Bowling. From this marriage sprang the several branches of the family, who in various ways were largely identified with the interests of the neighbourhood. Robert Swaine lived at Newall Hall, and had three sons and two daughters, several of whom were baptised in the Presbyterian Chapel, Wibsey Bankfoot, called Hill Top Chapel, where their grandfather, Samuel, was interred. This reference gives rise to the interesting question where this place of religious worship, the predecessor of the old Presbyterian Chapel in Chapel Lane, was situate. This moot point, however, will receive attention in a subsequent paper.

Robert Swaine subsequently resided in the house at the entrance to Legrams Lane, afterwards occupied by Mr. Henry Oates, and Mr. Robt. S. Ackroyd. He was in partnership with his sons, Samuel and William, as worsted stuff makers in Legrams. Robert Swaine died in September, 1775, at the age of eighty-four years, and he and his wife Sarah, who also reached her eighty-fourth year, are interred in the Presbyterian burial ground, Chapel Lane. Besides Samuel and William he had an elder son, Joseph Swaine, born at Newall Hall in 1703, and married to Bathshua Hesketh, daughter of the Rev. Robert Hesketh, of Tingley, who traced her descent from the Lords Eure, of Witton Castle, Durham, and Stokesley Manor, Cleveland. Joseph Swaine for some time resided at Lower Burnet Field, one of the residences purchased by him, and he had also lands at Esholt and Hawksworth.

Joseph Swaine appears to have been a man of some business energy, and to have acquired considerable property. In a cancelled will, dated 1770, he is described as of Horton, woolcomber, and after devising to Bathshua, his wife, and Edward Hesketh, his brother-in-law, certain property, he bequeathed his Hawksworth estate to his second son John, of Burnet Field, stuff maker. In 1780 Joseph Swaine was resident in the mansion at Great Horton now occupied by Mr. John Denton, and was a merchant. He afterwards farmed lands in Manningham, but again removed to a house in Little Horton Lane, where he lived with his unmarried daughter and son, John, then a widower. He died in 1787, in the eighty-fifth year of his age, and with his wife, lies in the burial ground in Chapel Lane.

Joseph Swaine's eldest son Robert married the daughter of Mr. Nathaniel Priestley of Northowram, and lived for some time at Cross Hill, Halifax, afterwards joining in business with his brother John, and his nephews, Joseph and Edward, at Gomersal Mills. He died in 1812, without issue. John, the second son of Joseph Swaine, was twice married, first to Mary, daughter of Mr. Robert Fieldsend, of Waddington, and secondly, to Ann, daughter of Mr. John Greenwood, of Bridge House, Haworth. By his first marriage he had a son, Joseph Swaine, born in the house in Horton Lane, in 1781. He afterwards resided at Copley Gate near Halifax, and then removed to Brier Hall,

Gomersal, where he, in partnership with his half-brother Edward Swaine, who died at York, in January, 1885, in the ninety-fifth year of his age, took a sixty years' lease of what was then called the Gomersal Cloth Hall, from Sir Henry Ibbetson. Joseph Swaine died at Brier Hall, in the year 1870, at the advanced age of eighty-nine years. His daughter, Miss Caroline Frances Swaine, born in 1806, now lives at Field Head, Gomersal. Her brother William Edward, of Leeds, born in 1809, died while staying at Ilkley in 1880, leaving as the head of the Swaine family in England Mr. Henry Paget Swaine, of Brabœuf Manor, Guildford, Surrey. The family bear arms—A maiden figure couped, proper, crined or, between wings of gold.

Edward Swaine, the third son of Joseph Swaine, sen., was the progenitor of the German branch of the family. He lived in London for a time, but for many years resided in Leipsic and Weimar, Germany, where he died in 1837, over eighty years of age. Of this stock several branches exist— viz., that represented by Col. Leopold Victor Swaine, military attaché at Berlin and Lord Wolseley's military secretary in the Egyptian campaign ; and Capt. Ernest Edward Swaine, son of Dr. W. E. Swaine, formerly physician extraordinary to H.R.H. the Duchess of Kent. Another branch is represented by Freiherr Richard von Swaine, who married the Princess Lowenstein Wertheim.

We have still to notice the brothers of Joseph Swaine, sen., who died in 1787. They were, as stated, William and Samuel Swaine, the former having a daughter Elizabeth married to Mr. Robert Ramsbotham ; the latter, Samuel, being the father of Mary Swaine, married to Mr. John Rand, sen. Samuel died in 1787, aged seventy-four years ; and his wife Betty (who signed the " Buckley protest ") in 1793. William died in 1789, aged eighty-two years. He had also a son, Samuel, who married his cousin, a daughter of Joseph Swaine, sen., who died in 1841, having reached the ninety-first year of her age. All the above were engaged in the Bradford worsted trade, and one of them was associated with Mr. Ramsbotham in the erection of the Holme Mill. Samuel, the father-in-law of John Rand, erected the good house near Rand's Mill, which his daughter and Mr. Rand occupied until their deaths.

The record of the Swaine family is remarkable for the long ages attained by many of its members. Of the nine persons above referred to, eight lived to over four-score years, three of the number being over ninety years of age. The Swaines were undoubtedly the oldest Presbyterian family in Bradford, several of its members having been upon the trust since the foundation of the chapel in 1717, when Abraham Swaine's name appears. Joseph Swaine, of Brier Hall, his half-brother, Mr. Edward Swaine, of York, Mr. W. E. Swaine, of Leeds, and his brother John, were all trustees, but now Mr. Henry Paget Swaine, of Guildford, is the only representative. When the foundation-stone of the new chapel was laid in 1868, the ceremony was performed by Mr. Edward Swaine.

Other members of this family were resident in Great Horton, to whom subsequent reference may be made, and there was also an influential branch more immediately connected with Bradford. Dr. Swaine, who was connected with this branch, and resided in Hall Ings, was an eminent apothecary in Bradford in the first half of last century, and was a great friend of Abraham Sharp, the Horton mathematician. He was one of the few persons who were admitted to the workshop of the recluse by the process of rubbing a stone upon a certain place in the wall, but even he had often to return disappointed, Sharp being either too much absorbed to notice the signal or indisposed to see company. Mr. Charles Swaine Booth Sharp, of Horton Hall, succeeded to the property of this gentleman. In what way the Horton Swaines were connected with Dr. Swaine we have not ascertained, but it is said that next to Mr. C. S. B. Sharp, Joseph Swaine, of Brier Hall, was heir-at-law to the property of the Bradford Swaines.

CHAPTER V.

Chapel Lane—The Bower Family—Presbyterianism in Horton—Horton Meeting-house—Chapel Lane Unitarian Chapel—Former Ministers—Spring House, Mrs. Bacon—Ebenezer Chapel—John Hardy—Samuel Hailstone—Edward Hailstone, F.S.A.

Having alluded to various features connected with the township of Horton without reference to locality, we may now take a ramble round the township, commencing with that portion of it adjacent to Bradford "town-end."

A perusal of the map of Bradford will show nearly the whole of Chapel Lane to be just within the township boundary of Horton. Although now essentially in the heart of Bradford, the residences which formerly lined Chapel Lane were pleasantly situated, away from the centre of the town and the bustle of the market place, which was situate in Westgate. In the reference book to the township map of 1801 we find mention of "Chapel Lane Gardens," and within more recent times we have pleasing recollections of a grass-covered lawn opposite the old Unitarian Chapel.

At the commencement of the present century the principal residents of Chapel Lane were Miss Swaine, Joshua Jennings, Geo. Dodgson, Wm. Goodchild, James Pullan, Benjamin Key, and Miss Bower. The last-named lady was also a large landowner in the neighbourhood.

The Bower family had been resident in Chapel Lane for a long period, and ranked among the leading gentry of the town. Jeremy Bower and Thomas Bower were important tradesmen of Bradford in Queen Elizabeth's time, being put down as "mercers." Thomas Bower also kept "Ye Swanne," and carried on an extensive tanning business, besides that of "hair-beard," or barber. It was probably this Bower who was appointed to make out the return for Bradford in Barnard's Survey of 1577. Simeon Bower was a "lawyear," a profession followed by more recent members of the family. Jeremiah Bower was postmaster of Bradford in the latter half of the seventeenth century, and a Jeremy Bower kept the Talbot Inn in Kirkgate in the year 1691. The Paper Hall in Barkerend, and considerable property in Horton, once belonged to the Bower family. For many years, however, the leading representatives of the family have been removed from the town. Mr. John Bower, who resided here in the early part of the century, died at Middlethorpe, York, in 1843, at the age of seventy years. His son, also named John, a barrister, and the last of the family who lived in Bradford, died a few years ago. Mr. Abraham Bower, another son, lived at an estate purchased by him many years ago at Ripon, and died there, at the age of eighty-one, during the year 1884.

In the early part of the century the gardens and orchard attached to Townend House extended up Manchester Road (or Bowling Lane) for some distance. There was also a toll-bar at the bottom of the lane which effectually commanded all the traffic entering the town from that direction. The toll-house was on the Chapel Lane side, and was kept by John Lee. It was afterwards occupied as a flour shop by one Craven. The toll-bar, however, which had long been a nuisance, was removed in 1826.

The principal object of historic interest in Chapel Lane is undoubtedly the Unitarian Chapel. The date of its erection was about the year 1718-19, it being at the time the only dissenting place of worship in Bradford. The founders were the old Nonconformists or Presbyterians. The history of this section of Christians would take our thoughts back to troublous times in the annals of the Christian Church, and if space permitted, lead us to notice the two diverging tendencies of the Puritan party in the seventeenth century, which at last settled down into what were known a century later as Old Dissent and New Dissent, Rational Dissenters and Orthodox Dissenters, synonymous with the English Presbyterians or Unitarians, and Independents or Congregationalists, of the present day. Immediately after the Revolution of 1688 Presbyterianism first took root in Bradforddale, and a chapel was built at Little Horton for the use of the Dissenters of the neighbourhood, who were not only numerous but comprised several influential adherents; among these may be included some members of the Sharp family, also of the Swaines, the Hodgsons, the Hollings, and others. In the list of meeting-houses registered at Wakefield Sessions after the passing of the Toleration Act in 1688 we find the following entries :—

Under date January, 1689.—"That Thomas Sharp, of Little Horton, nigh Bradford, clerk, doth make choice of his own house to assemble in for religious worship."
January, 1691.—"The dwelling-house of John Smithies, of Little Horton, recorded a place of religious meeting. Signed—Samuel Swayne, John Smithies, John Butterfield, Robert Parkinson."
January, 1695.—"The house of Thomas Ferrand, of Bradford, for religious worship."
January, 1696.—"The house of Thomas Hodgson, of Bradford, recorded."

The erection of a chapel for the use of those who from conscientious motives dissented from the forms adopted in the Church as by law established would doubtless be the means of gathering together the various sections of devout persons attending these meeting-houses, but it is not clear where that chapel was situate. The site of it was either given by or purchased from Thomas Sharp, of Horton Hall, a man eminent for his theological attainments, and who, as we have seen, had licensed his own house for religious worship, whither, it is recorded, "numbers flocked to hear him." In his will, dated 1693, Thomas Sharp bequeathed to his daughter Elizabeth a close of land at Little Horton, called Higher End, which is described as being "near the new meeting-house." In Fawcett's "Life of Oliver Heywood," it is said that "the people had previously (to the erection of the Presbyterian Chapel at Bradford) worshipped at Little Horton, and at a place not far from Wibsey."

The house usually pointed out as the site of the "new meeting-house" is situate in Thornton Lane, and is still known as Chapel House, while Chapel Fold and Chapel Green are well-recognised names in the immediate vicinity. Over the door are the initials $_I T_M$ the letters I and T standing for Jeremiah Thornton, and M for the name of his wife. The date, 1739, does not correspond with the period when the "new meeting-house" was erected, but might refer to a time of rebuilding, as there are indications of portions of the house being older than the period referred to.

The late John James discredited the claim of the Thornton Lane residence, and stated that he had seen references to Chapel Fold at Bradford long before, assuming the site of the earlier edifice to be in Chapel Lane. To still further complicate the subject, we have evidence that members of the Swaine family, who were amongst the earliest Presbyterians, were both baptised and buried at the "Presbyterian Chapel, Wibsey Bankfoot, and called Hill Top Chapel." Wherever this place of worship was situate, it was undoubtedly the birthplace of Nonconformity in Bradford.

The Rev. Samuel Hulme was a resident of Little Horton about the year 1700, and was minister of the Presbyterian congregation. His son, Joseph Hulme, M.D., was born in the village, and was educated for the ministry under Dr. Philip Doddridge, but, changing his profession, he became a skilful physician. He died in the ninety-second year of his age. The Rev. Samuel Crowther, who died in 1706, and the Rev. Eli Dawson succeeded Samuel Hulme at Little Horton. In 1716 the congregation was called Presbyterian, having 500 hearers, forty of them having county votes.

In the year 1719, however, the congregation removed to the new chapel in Chapel Lane. The site of it is described in the trust deed as "the north corner of Murgatroyd's Croft, in Horton," and was given by Robert Stansfield, a drysalter, who married a daughter of Thos. Sharp, and whose son Robert afterwards purchased Esholt Hall. The dimensions of the site were about thirty yards in length and thirty yards in breadth, and it was bounded on the north by Back Lane, then probably called Toad Lane, and now rejoicing in the better-sounding name of Chapel Lane. On the west it was bounded by land belonging to the daughters of Mr. John Hollings, while to the east and south lay the rest of the croft.

The trustees were Abraham Sharp, of Little Horton; Samuel Stansfield, of Bradford, salter; Thomas Ferrand, Bradford, grocer and mercer; Abraham Rhodes, Bradford, yeoman; Jeremy Dixon, Heaton Royds, yeoman; Abm.

Rambles Round Horton. 53

Swaine, Bradford, yeoman ; John Lister, Bolton, yeoman ; Isaac Wilkinson, Little Horton, yeoman ; John Atkinson, Bradford, butcher (?) ; Wm. Hodgson, Bowling, yeoman ; and James Aked, Bradford, yeoman, who are described as being " Protestant Dissenters from the Church of England ; " and the date of the conveyance is December 2nd, 1719.

From a document printed in the *Bradford Antiquary* we learn that many of the materials came from Howley Hall, near Batley, built in 1590 by Sir John Savile, and dismantled through the caprice of its subsequent owner, the Earl of Cardigan, during the early part of the eighteenth century. Among these items are the following :—

	£	s.	d.
May 24, 1719.			
Pd. for Hooley windows...	3	0	0
Pd. for 14 loads of ye same leading to Bradford, at 5s. per load	3	10	0
Charges at Hooley when best ceiling was taken down	0	0	10
Paid for 6 pilasters at Hooley	0	9	0
Paid John Crocker for Hooley gates leading	2	5	0

The woodwork and fittings were therefore old at the time they were brought to Bradford. The total cost of the erection was £340 3s. 5d. The old gateway, since its removal from Chapel Lane, has been re-erected in the grounds of Mr. Arthur Briggs, Cragg Royd, Rawdon.

The Rev. Eli Dawson continued his pastorate at the new chapel in Chapel Lane until 1728. He was followed in 1731 by the Rev. Joshua Hardcastle, who continued until his death in 1753, and was succeeded by the Rev. John Smith, of Mixenden, a graduate of the Glasgow University, and a relative of the Sharps. For a long time Mr. Smith concluded his sermons with the Trinitarian Doxology, and to the last attended the week-day services of the Church. He died in 1768, and lies in Mixenden Chapel yard.

He was succeeded by the Rev. John Dean, who was his son-in-law, and who ministered there from 1768 to 1813. Mr. Dean was treasurer to the Bradford Library when it was formed in 1774, and was father-in-law to the late Mr. C. H. Dawson, of Royds Hall. During Mr. Dean's ministry the congregation became Unitarian.

Rambles Round Horton.

From 1813 to 1817 the chapel had for its minister the Rev. Henry Turner, whose name is yet fresh and honoured. He left to occupy the important pulpit of the High Pavement, Nottingham, where he succeeded Dr. Hutton, but died there in 1822, in the thirtieth year of his age.

To him succeeded the Rev. Nicholas Heinekin, the son of a Bremen merchant, and a Lutheran, who had come to London and joined the ranks of the Old Dissent. He was

Old Gateway, Chapel Lane.

born in London, March 8th, 1763, and is still remembered with respect and affection. He died suddenly in 1840.

The Rev. George Vance Smith, B.A., was the minister from 1841 to 1843, when he removed to Macclesfield, and afterwards to Birmingham. The Rev. G. V. Smith subsequently acquired the degree of doctor of divinity, and had the honour of forming one of the body entrusted with the Revised Version of the Scriptures.

From 1844 to 1864, the Rev. John Howard Ryland ministered. Mr. Ryland was a gentleman of very active habits, and took a prominent part in the work of the Mechanics' Institute, of which he was president in 1858. He was very generally respected in Bradford.

In 1845 the Dissenters' Chapels Bill encouraged the congregation to make improvements in the old chapel. A new vestry was built and new schools projected, which were opened the following year. In 1846 also a fresh batch of trustees was appointed, comprising C. H. Dawson, of Royds Hall, his sons, C. H. Dawson, jun., Joseph Dawson, and John Dawson; Joseph Swaine, of Gomersal, cloth maker; Edward Swaine, Gomersal, cloth maker; John Swaine, Gomersal, cloth maker; Wm. Ed. Swaine, Leeds, merchant; Thomas Hollings, Manningham, gentleman; Stephen Humble, Idle, gentleman; Alfred Bankart, Bradford, worsted spinner; and Charles Bankart, Bradford, woolstapler. Of this number only Mr. John Dawson, living at Exmouth, remains upon the trust.

Mr. Ryland retired in 1864, and was succeeded in that year by the Rev. T. W. Freckelton. On the removal of Mr. Freckelton in 1866 to Plymouth, the Rev. Richard Pilcher, B.A., London, was chosen minister. Subsequent ministers have been the Rev. W. J. Knapton, who afterwards joined the Church of England; the Rev. Robert Laird Collier, D.D., and the Rev. J. Cuckson.

The chapel was endowed by Jeremy Dixon, one of the old trustees, who, by his will, dated 22nd February, 1724, gave a farm at Denholme, called Birchin Lee, to the trustees of the chapel. The income from this source now realises about £100 per annum. New schools were erected in 1867, and in February, 1868, the corner-stone of the present handsome chapel was laid by Mr. Edward Swaine, of York, whose family had been connected with the chapel from its foundation. The style of the erection is Gothic, the accommodation is for 500 worshippers, and the cost was about £5400.

At the corner of Manchester Road there was formerly a garden gate admitting to the grounds of Spring House, at one time the property of Isaac Willson, clerk of the Court of Requests. This house was in danger of being sacked by an exasperated mob in 1793, in consequence of the unpopularity of Mr. Willson or of his office. More recently it was the residence of Mr. Wm. Bacon, and subsequently of his widow, a lady well known for her piety and benevolence. Her father was Mr. John Balme, a worsted manufacturer. He built the house subsequently occupied as a Baptist College at Horton. Mr. Balme was a zealous Independent, and was one of the parties to the original trust of Horton Lane Chapel, erected in 1782.

Mr. Bacon, of Spring House, died in 1818; and Mary, his widow, in 1853, aged eighty-three. By her will Mrs. Bacon left £1000 each to the following institutions:—the Bible Society, the London Missionary Society, and the Home Missionary Society, and a sum of £12,000, the proceeds of which were to be devoted to the relief of aged and infirm ministers, their widows and daughters. Her sister, Miss Sarah Balme, was equally benevolent in disposition, and in accordance with her request, valuable property at Undercliffe and Fagley was conveyed to the trustees of Airedale College (then at Idle), and upon a portion of which a college was afterwards built.

Another daughter of John Balme was married to Samuel Broadley, who lived in the house in Kirkgate upon the site of which the Bradford Banking Company's premises were erected. She died in 1825, bequeathing large sums for charitable purposes, including £5000 to Horton Baptist College.

Directly opposite to Mrs. Bacon's house was situate the Bowling Alley, to which in times past the well-to-do people of the "town-end" resorted for a bout at bowls. A portion of this ground was acquired about the year 1836 for the erection of the Ebenezer Chapel, which stood upon the boundary line dividing Horton from Bradford. The movement for the erection of this place of worship originated with Mr. Wm. Grandage, of Brownroyd, who, having been connected with the New Connexion denomination in his native town of Halifax, gathered together a few persons in sympathy with himself upon coming to Bowling Dyeworks. Being but "feeble folk," however, they were unable to afford the high price of £2 per yard asked for a corner plot at the end of Thornton Road, but accepted the offer of the Rev. Godfrey Wright of the site at the bottom of Horton Road, at the price of £1 per yard for 700 yards. The parties to the deed of purchase were Wm. Grandage; John Carter, banker's clerk; John Fearnside, Green Row; Wm. Ackroyd, grocer, Manchester Road; and two others. Mr. Grandage was also the first class-leader. The new building cost about £1700, exclusive of the £700 paid for the ground.

The first minister was the Rev. Wm. Trotter, who officiated with such acceptance that soon the membership was raised to over 150 persons. After a few years, however, serious discord was created among the congregation by the conduct of the Rev. Joseph Barker, a minister of the denomination settled at Leeds, who, being on terms of great intimacy with Mr. Trotter, induced him to join in the editorship of a magazine giving publicity to doctrines which by the orthodox New Connexionists were considered unsound. Both individuals were ultimately expelled the Connexion, although, so far as Mr. Trotter was concerned, that course was regarded with great regret by the congregation worshipping at Ebenezer. In consequence of this unpleasantness, a portion of the congregation seceded and erected a small chapel in Croft Street, Mr. Trotter taking charge of it. After a lingering existence the separationists collapsed.

The Ebenezer Chapel being pronounced unsafe, from some defect in its construction, it was rebuilt in 1861 upon an improved model, but that edifice has also disappeared, owing to the property having been scheduled in the Bradford Improvement Act of 1873, the Corporation at that time contemplating the construction of a thoroughfare in continuation of Manchester Road to Thornton Road. That project, however, has never been carried out, but the scheduling of the property led the congregation to secure another site, resulting in the erection of the present handsome edifice at Mannville, Horton Road. That chapel was opened on March 26th, 1879, and with the adjoining school buildings cost nearly £20,000.

There were formerly two good houses adjoining the site of Ebenezer Chapel, and now forming part of the Old Brewery premises, about which were many interesting associations. In one of them, nearest to Brewery Lane, lived John Hardy, the grandfather of Lord Cranbrook, and here was born his son John, returned in 1832 as one of the first members of Parliament for Bradford. Mr. Hardy previously resided at Horsforth. He used to attend Bradford in his professional duties, and eventually removed here, having succeeded to the business of Mr. John Eagle, a solicitor who piloted the first Leeds and Liverpool Canal Act, and eventually Mr. Hardy was its solicitor and law clerk. He was also one of the first partners of the Low Moor Iron Works. There was a basement room to the back of the house at the bottom of Great Horton Road, which was his office. In this office Mr. Samuel Hailstone served his articles with Mr. Hardy, afterwards joining him in partnership. The office, however, was afterwards removed to the corner house at Brewery Lane, and there the business was carried on for some years, and when Mr. Hardy ceased practice it became Mr. Hailstone's property. Previous to that occurring Mr. Hardy had removed to the Manor Hall in Kirkgate.

Mr. Samuel Hailstone came to Bradford from York in the year 1783, and lived in a house in the Old Market, in Westgate, just above the Central Coffee Tavern. After succeeding to Mr. Hardy's practice, Mr. Hailstone took into partnership Mr. Mason, who became a partner in the Bowling Ironworks, and gave up his profession, marrying a Miss Barber, the daughter of a Bradford attorney. Mr. Paley married another daughter, and the fortunes they received were put into the Bowling Ironworks, along with that invested by the Sturges family. At one time Mr. Hailstone had the late Greenwood Bentley for a partner, and afterwards he took in Mr. John Thompson (the elder brother of the present Mr. Jo. Thompson). Mr. Thompson married a Miss Skelton, the sister of Colonel Skelton, and lived in the house where Mr. Hardy did. He and his wife were passengers in the ill-fated *Rothsay Castle*, wrecked in Menai Straits in 1831, and both perished.

Mr. Hailstone removed to a small house in Great Horton Road, where he erected the first greenhouse perhaps seen in Bradford, and after he left it the house was enlarged and occupied as a school by the Rev. S. Redhead, who married Miss Rand, and was the first clergyman of the old Bell Chapel. About the commencement of the present century, Mr. Hailstone bought Croft House from the Faber family and largely increased it, and resided there with his family till 1834 or 1835, when he removed to Horton Hall, previously occupied by Mr. John Wood. In 1837 Mr. Hailstone offered for sale the whole of the land lying between Croft House and Bridge Street, which had formed the orchard and grounds to Croft House, and it was bought up for building ground. The demolition of Croft House followed some time after the formation of Croft Street.

Mr. Hailstone died in December, 1851, in the eighty-third year of his age. His connection as law clerk with the Leeds and Liverpool Canal was of long standing, and to the close of his professional career he sustained a prominent part in its affairs. When he joined as a shareholder, the shares were at a discount of £50, but his sagacity led him to look for a very different state of things, and, as is well known, the navigation became a most lucrative concern. His legal practice also was large, and of a high-class character. Mr. Hailstone was a gentleman of high scientific culture, a good botanist and geologist, and possessed a considerable love for the pursuits of natural philosophy. For his attainments he was elected a fellow of the Linnean Society.

Mr. Hailstone had several sons. One son, Samuel, died at Horton Hall. Another son, the Rev. John Hailstone, was vicar of Bottisham, Cambridgeshire, afterwards of Anglesea Abbey, in the same county, and died in 1872.

His youngest son, the present Mr. Edward Hailstone, F.S.A., was born at Croft House. In one way or other this gentleman has been connected with the legal profession for half a century, and for the last thirty-three years has been the law clerk of the Leeds and Liverpool Canal Company. Since the year 1870 Mr. Hailstone has resided at Walton

Hall, near Wakefield, formerly the abode of the eccentric naturalist, Squire Waterton, and has long enjoyed the reputation of possessing one of the largest and most valuable private collections of books, manuscripts, and antiquarian treasures in the north of England. In local literature and MS. the Walton collection is specially rich, and its resources have been largely drawn upon in the compilation of works relating to the history of Bradford. Indeed, to Mr. Hailstone we are much indebted for material required in the preparation of these papers on Horton—a place in which, from long association, he maintains more than ordinary interest.

The Rev. Lamplugh Wickham, who took the name of Hird, and was the father of Mr. H. W. Wickham, M.P., resided in the old house nearest to Ebenezer Chapel, and Mr. George Anderton and Mr. Titus Salt were subsequent occupants.

CHAPTER VI.

The Old Brewery—Richard Fawcett—Early Methodism—Old Octagon Chapel—Randal Well—The Mann Family—Early Independency—Horton Lane Chapel—Former Ministers.

Excepting the Old Brewery, we have already noticed all the objects of interest at the "town end" of Bradford calling for special reference. Unlike some of the landmarks in the immediate vicinity which have given place to new creations, that institution still survives, having long ago entered upon the second century of its existence. It is therefore justly entitled to its appellation as the Old Brewery. The date of its origin is the year 1757, when Joseph Storey and Thomas Aked, of Bradford, were in partnership as common brewers with John Whitaker, of Halifax. In 1763 Aked and Storey conveyed their shares to Whitaker, who was succeeded by his son William. Benjamin Thompson, uncle of Mr. M. W. Thompson, married a daughter of Wm. Whitaker, and upon Mr. M. W. Thompson marrying his uncle's surviving daughter, he became the sole owner of the Old Brewery. Considerable interest attaches to the Thompson family through several of its members, but as they have had more immediate connection with the township of Manningham than with that of Horton, we may defer further reference until we touch upon Manningham. Mr. Henry Oates, of Fieldhead, Mr. James Marshall, ironmonger, Kirkgate, Mr. Thos. Pullan, and Mr. Henry Leah were formerly partners in the brewery along with Mr. Whitaker.

Having disposed of the "town end," we are prepared to ascend to the upper portions of Horton township, and, in making a start, occupy a similar position to that in which Mr. Gladstone was once placed, in having "three courses" open to us. We may ascend either by way of Manchester Road, Horton Lane, or Horton Road. A more convenient arrangement, however, remains, namely, to notice what objects of interest attract our attention in that portion of Little Horton lying nearest to our present standpoint, leaving the higher portions for future reference.

An examination of the township survey of 1801 is suggestive of several names of residents in the lower part of Horton Road, in addition to those already mentioned, and among them are those of Thomas Hodgson, Richard Fawcett, and John Wood, sen. These were all substantial men of the period. The gentleman last named, who resided in the good house at the bottom of Mann Lane, called Southbrook Lodge, commenced the erection of what afterwards became Messrs. Wood & Walker's worsted factory. The purpose for which that building was erected, however, was not that of worsted spinning, but the manufacture of horn, ivory, and tortoise-shell combs, lanterns, leather ink-bottles, &c., for which the town of Bradford had a reputation before it became famous for worsteds. It was Mr. John Wood, jun., who, with townsmen like Richard Fawcett and others, established the worsted industry.

Mr. Fawcett was an eminent Hortonian, having been born at Hunt Yard, Great Horton, where his father, a nephew of Dr. Fawcett, the celebrated divine, resided. As we have seen, Mr. Fawcett erected a factory in Union Street, besides owning the mill in the Holme, in the earliest stage of development through which the worsted industry was passing. So identified was he with the district in which we are immediately concerned, that to this day "old inhabitants" speak of Fawcett Holme and Fawcett Hill. Upon the little knoll bearing the latter name Mr. Fawcett erected Westbrook House, the position being regarded as one of the most favoured in Bradford. From the windows of his residence there was not only a good view across the Holme valley, down which meandered a clear running stream, but there was an uninterrupted view of green fields on the other side in the direction of the Bowling valley.

While comparatively young Mr. Fawcett entered with energy into business, and in conjunction with his father, also named Richard, he purchased the interest of Messrs. Swaine and Ramsbotham in the Holme Mill. He was also a gentleman of great public enterprise, and took part in all movements in which the welfare of his native town or fellow-townsmen was concerned. He was one of the old Highway Commissioners created by the Act of 1803, and fulfilled the duties for forty-two years. Mr. Fawcett was in fact the leading man of his time, and to such an extent was he so regarded by his fellow-townsmen that he was often familiarly styled "King Richard." Unfortunately, his various schemes of enterprise suffered from commercial depression and other causes, and he died in 1845, if not a wealthy at least an honoured citizen. Mr. Fawcett was one of the old type of Wesleyans, with a strong attachment to the Church of England, and one of his sons, the late Canon Fawcett, M.A.,

Octagon Chapel.

who married a sister of Mr. H. W. Wickham, M.P., was for over thirty years incumbent of Holy Trinity Church, Low Moor. Another son was the late Mr. Richard Fawcett, woolstapler.

In immediate contiguity to Westbrook House there stood, until the year 1810, the old Octagon Chapel, the first place of worship erected by the Wesleyans of Bradford. In addition to the undoubted interest attaching to it from this circumstance, the building, from the peculiarity of its construction—having eight sides to it—elicited the remark of John Wesley that it was "the largest octagon we have in

England, and the first of the kind where the roof is built with common sense, rising only a third of its breadth." The dimensions of the chapel were fifty-four feet square. It was opened during the summer of 1766.

Ten years before, however, the disciples of Wesley in Bradford had been gathered into a congregation, according to the Rev. W. W. Stamp, the historian of Methodism in Bradford, when the second floor of a large building near the Cock-pit in Aldermanbury, having been vacated by the Baptists, was rented by the society. To this, doubtless, Mr. Wesley refers when in 1757 he observes in his journal:—

Thursday, May 12th.—The latter end of the week I spent in Bradford. Sunday, 15th.—At five the house contained the congregation, but at eight they covered the plain adjoining it

From the east end of the building, where Mr. Wesley stood when addressing the multitude, "the plain" to the Sun Inn, was then an open space, interrupted only by the beck and the old prison which stood on the site of what are now denominated the Sun Bridge Buildings, whilst to the right, with the exception of three houses forming the west side of Tyrrel Street and one or two small cottages intervening, was a yet further extension of "the plain." Such, with fields extending where Thornton Road now runs, together with the deserted cockpit and dog kennel in juxtaposition, was the neighbourhood in which this early preaching-house was situate.

During the interval of Mr. Wesley's visits in 1759 and 1761 the room near the cockpit, being deemed no longer safe, was given up; and Mr. James Garnett, piecemaker, then residing at the Paper Hall, kindly offered the use of his barn in Barkerend until better accommodation could be secured. The offer was at once and thankfully accepted, and there for a season the services of Methodism were regularly held. Mr. Stamp also states that Mr. Garnett, to whom Methodism was thus indebted for its second sanctuary in Bradford, was for several years a member of the society. Eventually, however, in conjunction with Messrs. Smith, Balme, Hodgson, and others he assisted in founding an Independent church, meeting for awhile in an upper room in the Brewery yard,

Rambles Round Horton.

and then removing to a newly-erected chapel in Little Horton Lane.

In the autumn of the year 1765 land was purchased for the erection of a Wesleyan chapel in Horton Road. The deed, which bears date December 21st, 1765, describes the purchase as an assignment on lease of 999 years, subject to an annual rent of £3 12s., of "all that close or parcel of arable, meadow, or pasture ground called or commonly known by the name of the Hilly Close, formerly in the possession or occupancy of Edward Jobson, and late of Thomas Aked, deceased, and containing two days' work, be the same more or less, situate in Horton, in the parish of Bradford."

The property was conveyed to the following persons as trustees:—Richard Stocks, grocer and draper, Bradford; John Hodgson, stuff maker, Horton; Henry Atkinson, stuff maker, Manningham; Nathaniel Dracup, shuttle maker, Horton; Ebenezer Pyrah, stuff maker, Wibsey; John Butler, stuff maker, Bradford (afterwards of Kirkstall Forge); and John Murgatroyd, stuff maker, Horton. What subscriptions were obtained towards the erection of the Octagon in Bradford, or what the collections at its opening, does not appear, but it is upon record that when John Murgatroyd and Richard Fawcett (father of the Richard Fawcett who in after years played so prominent a part in Bradford) sallied forth on a collecting expedition, the first contribution received was the magnificent sum of twopence towards the outlay of £997 8s. 9d.!

In order that the services might not interfere with those of the Parish Church, the times of worship at the Octagon were nine in the morning, two in the afternoon, and five in the evening; nor was it till the removal to Kirkgate, forty years afterwards, that the Sacrament was administered in the Methodist chapels of Bradford. In the year 1767, a preacher's house was erected adjoining the chapel, the whole expense of both house and furniture being under £200. In 1810 the property, including the chapel and adjoining houses, was sold to Mr. Richard Fawcett, jun., for £1575, and that gentleman subsequently purchased the adjacent plot and built upon it Westbrook House, where he resided, the chapel

E

site being disposed of to Thomas Horsfall. Kirkgate Chapel was opened in May, 1811. It has received enlargement several times since. While not recording further the history of the Kirkgate sanctuary, we may note as a curiosity that the bottom step of the flight in front of the chapel is said to be the longest stone ever delved in these parts. It is 22 ft. long, and came from Copy Delf.

Randal Well Close, adjoining the old Octagon Chapel, originally formed part of Sagar's Charity land, left by James Sagar in 1665, out of the proceeds of which 20s. yearly was to be paid to the minister of Thornton Chapel, and the residue to the most needful poor of Thornton. The close obtained its name from the existence of a spring of water arising in a small plantation near the side of the beck. Formerly there was a draw-well there, but when Mr. Fawcett purchased the Holme Mill he put in a pipe from which the residents of the neighbourhood, after crossing the beck by means of a plank, obtained a never-failing supply. The Randal Well was a common gossiping place up to the year 1820. The well is now enclosed in Messrs. Thwaites Bros.' engineering works.

Within a short distance of the Randal Well Close was reared a mansion of some pretensions called Mannville, associated with the family of Mann. This family is of some interest, from the fact that they were the first stuff merchants in Bradford. The family sprang from Spen Hall, Cleckheaton. Thomas Mann seems to have been the first to come to Bradford, where he commenced business in the woollen drapery trade in a shop at the corner turning into the yard still known as Mann's Court, in Kirkgate. He also embarked in the artificial cork-leg trade, by which he obtained much popularity and money. These cork-legs were covered with leather by John Brunton, a leather breeches maker, and great Southcottian, whom Rushton celebrates in one of his effusions against Southcottianism as "the cripple mender." It is said they were really the invention of one David Haigh, whom Mann employed. This cork-leg business was afterwards sold to Mr. Swithenbank, who carried it on until a late period in premises in Toad Lane. Thomas Mann, however, seems to have had both this business and the shop in Kirkgate on his hands when he, with his brother John, started the business of stuff merchants, which yielded the family considerable wealth. This business was carried on in a warehouse behind the shop. John Mann, the brother, built Springfield House, now occupied by Sir Jacob Behrens, in Manningham Lane.

Thomas Mann erected Mannville, in Great Horton Road, which is said to be built both inside and out with dressed stone. He had three sons, Joshua, John, of Boldshay Hall, and Thomas, who were united, as they came of age, with their father and uncle in the stuff trade. Joshua succeeded his father at Mannville, where he died, and Mr. John Rawson, the solicitor, lived there afterwards for some years.

John Mann, of Manningham Lane, the uncle, was married but had no children. He brought up a daughter of his brother Robert, of Spen Hall, and left her most of his property. She married Mr. W. M. Harris. Joshua, of Mannville, died a bachelor, and left his property to Miss Wells, his niece, the daughter of Mr. Wells, who married his sister. Thomas died a bachelor. John resided at Boldshay Hall, and had a family.

Another place of worship, the congregation of which during the year 1882 celebrated its centenary—was erected not far from the Octagon, namely, Horton Lane Chapel. The history of the congregation of Independents worshipping at Horton Lane is in great measure bound up with that of Chapel Lane already noticed. Among the congregation worshipping at the latter place were many who were unable to accept the Unitarian creed which, under the influence of Mr. Dean's teaching, was substituted for the old Presbyterian doctrine of the Trinity, and being joined by a few Episcopalians, and others whose doctrines were in harmony with those of Whitfield, but whose church principles were Congregational, united in forming an Independent Church. This was in the year 1780. For twelve or eighteen months they met in the malt chamber of the Old Brewery, meanwhile making arrangements to build a more suitable place in which to assemble for worship. Hence the erection of Horton Lane Chapel.

From the original conveyance of the site of this chapel, dated 20th December, 1781, we learn that the ground was purchased from Charles Swain Booth Sharp, Esq., of Horton Hall, by James Garnett, worsted stuff maker, of Bradford; John Smith, of Bradford, stationer; Thomas Naylor, Bradford, tobacconist; William Wilkinson, Bradford, worsted stuff maker; Thomas Hodgson, of Scholemoor, worsted stuff maker; John Balme, Bradford, worsted stuff maker; Joseph Wright, Bradford, worsted stuff maker; Robert Benson, Frizinghall, maltster; Joseph Robinson, Idle, butcher; Jonas Smith, Bolton, carpenter; William Smith, Wibsey, worsted stuff maker; and John Hutton, Eccleshill, cloth maker.

The land is described as "all that piece or parcel of land situate, lying, and being in Horton aforesaid, containing thirty-seven yards in length, as the same is railed off from the bottom or north-east end of a close of land called the Croft, the property and in the possession of the said Charles Swain Booth Sharp; up the said close, the breadth of the same close; which said piece of land abuts on the lane called Little Horton Lane, on the south-east end thereof; on a piece of ground the property of Samuel Swaine on the north-east side thereof; on a close of land the property of Mr. Bower on the north-west end thereof; and on the remainder of the said close of land from which the piece of land is taken on the south-west side thereof." The amount of the purchase money was £122 10s.

The trust deed contains a full enumeration of the articles of faith of the purchasers, and also declares that if any of the original trustees shall cease to be of the sect of Dissenters above mentioned, or change their religious views, or that any of them shall not attend at the intended place of worship for the space of thirteen weeks, except prevented by sickness or other evident call in Divine providence, that it shall be lawful for the remaining trustees and the majority of the church members to nominate and elect other persons in their place. The deed is witnessed by John Brogden and Richard Milnes. At a meeting, held in the vestry of the chapel, December 28, 1808, the following persons were chosen to act as trustees in place of several who had died, viz.:—John Balme,

Richard Hargreaves, William Pearson, Benjamin Kaye, James Wilkinson, Thomas Waddington, James Cousen, and Joseph Smith.

In June, 1815, consequent on the "great increase of population and of Dissenters in Bradford and the neighbourhood," it was decided to extend the chapel by seven yards, upon ground in the rear purchased from Mr. John Bower, being portion of a close of land called Wilson Well Croft. The amount of the purchase money was £39 10s. The parties to the deed of purchase were Wm. Wilkinson, Joseph Wright, Jonas Smith, Wm. Smith, and James Hutton (original trustees), and James Cousen, woollen draper; Thos. Waddington, calico maker; Jas. Wilkinson, cabinetmaker; Wm. Pearson, worsted spinner; Benj. Kaye, Allerton, merchant; James Garnett, woolstapler; Lister Naylor, tobacco manufacturer; Wm. Hargreaves, Idle, scribbler; Abm. Balme, worsted manufacturer; William Smith, worsted manufacturer; Robert Milligan, linen draper; John Bottomley, accountant; John Hutton, jun., Eccleshill, clothmaker; Francis Ackroyd, worsted manufacturer; John Bonnell, saddler; and James Hargreaves, Eccleshill, clothmaker.

An enlargement of the burial ground also took place in 1837 by the additional purchase from the Rev. Godfrey Wright (who had succeeded to Mr. C. S. B. Sharp's estate) of a piece of ground adjoining the minister's house, comprising about three roods, for the sum of £998, being at the rate of 5s. 6d. per yard. In addition to the surviving trustees the parties to the deed of purchase were—Richard Garnett, Joseph Smith, William Hardcastle, John Russell, James Garnett, Robert Monies, Edward Ripley, Henry William Ripley, John McCroben, William Milnes, James Rennie, Alexander Robertson, and Jonathan Holdsworth.

By successive enlargements Horton Lane Chapel and Schools grew to the dimensions familiar to many of our readers prior to their being supplanted by the present handsome chapel and school premises. The first step towards the erection of this imposing pile was the building of the schools, which were opened on the 7th September, 1861, and on the 9th September the foundation stone of the new chapel was laid by the late Sir H. W. Ripley, who was a large contributor to the building fund. The completed edifice was opened on September 30th, 1863, having cost about £12,000. Of this large sum all but about £40 had been received up to the close of the inaugural services, and this small amount was subscribed the next morning.

During the hundred years' existence of Horton Lane Chapel five pastors in succession have filled the pulpit. Of this number the first only preached one Sunday, and died during the following week. The second held the pastoral office twenty-five years; the third twenty-seven years; the fourth nineteen years; and the fifth twenty-eight years. Practically, therefore, the century's pastorate was discharged by four ministers, giving an average of twenty-five years to each.

The first pastor, the Rev. Jas. Crossley, was a native of Saltonstall, in Warley; he was a disciple of the Rev. W. Grimshaw, incumbent of Haworth, and the first minister of Booth Chapel. After twenty years' service at Booth, he was induced to leave a people to whom he was much attached and come to Bradford, but his ministry here was prematurely cut short, for after preaching one Sunday he died.

The next minister was the Rev. Thos. Holdgate, who laboured from the year 1783 until 1807, the year of his death. The only unpleasant episode of Mr. Holdgate's ministry so far as any record exists, was brought about by the attempt to introduce a bass viol into the singing-pew, and so bitter were many of the congregation against it that it was but rarely used.

The next pastor of the church was the Rev. Thomas Taylor, who came from Ossett to Bradford in 1808, and under whose ministrations Horton Lane Church and congregation attained a position of considerable influence in Bradford, comprising within its roll of membership the names of Garnett, Milligan, Forbes, Salt, Ripley, and many others, who were literally the makers of Bradford. Mr. Taylor was a man of remarkable shrewdness and strength of character, and left the imprint of his mind and labours not only upon his congregation, but upon the town of his adoption. He was greatly beloved and respected, and was familiarly known and spoken of in the town as "good old Mr. Taylor." It was during Mr. Taylor's ministry that Sunday schools were established in Bradford, and two new congregations were sent out from the parent chapel. After retiring from the pastorate he lived to a serene old age, enjoying the profound respect of all, and died in October, 1853.

Mr. Taylor having retired, the Rev. Jonathan Glyde became his successor in the autumn of 1835. Mr. Glyde, who was a native of Exeter, differed in many respects from his predecessor. A man of original talent, of the purest type of piety, high culture, and one of the gentlest of mankind, he was greatly beloved by his congregation and fellow-townsmen. After nineteen years of devoted pastoral work he died in the forty-eighth year of his age, in December, 1854. The Rev. James Robertson Campbell, D.D., entered upon the pastorate at Horton Lane in 1855, having previously ministered at Edinburgh. Dr. Campbell was a worthy successor of the good men who had preceded him. Possessing many Christian virtues, a gentleman of scholarly attainments, and imbued with a lofty regard for the responsible office of a Christian minister, he ably filled the pulpit of Horton Lane Chapel during a period of twenty-eight years, retiring only in the autumn of 1883. Dr. Campbell's sudden death, in December, 1884, a little more than a year after he had resigned his pastorate, is still a sorrow in the hearts of his former charge.

After an interval of two years from Dr. Campbell's retirement, the pastorate was accepted by the Rev. Dr. Anderson, of Troy, U.S.A., a gentleman of great ability as a preacher and a devoted pastor.

As the parent Independent Church in Bradford Horton Lane has a numerous progeny. Of these may be named the congregations at Wibsey, Little Horton, Lidget Green, Eccleshill, Salem, Lister Hills, Saltaire, Bowling, Ryan Street, and Laisterdyke, all directly springing from it. In addition to this list may be named Borough West School, which, as an elementary school, has long enjoyed a reputation of a high order.

CHAPTER VII.

St. John's Church — St. James's Church — Parson Bull — Bowling Lane — The Old Skinhouse — Jacob Hudson — His Curious Will — The Blackburns — The Cordingleys — Clayton Lane — Baptist College — Dr. Steadman.

St. John's Church, Manchester Road, was erected during the years 1838-9, at the expense of Mr. J. Berthon, a gentleman residing in the Isle of Wight, and under licence of the Bishop of Ripon service was for some time performed in it, but without any assigned reason it was then closed. For several years afterwards the building remained unconsecrated, the unfortunate loss of a sum of money set aside for the endowment being stated to be the reason. In the year 1844 the church was offered for sale, but was afterwards consecrated for public worship. It has subsequently been pulled down, and upon the site a music-hall and theatre have been erected. The new church of St. John the Evangelist in Horton Lane was opened in its stead in 1871.

St. James's Church, Manchester Road, was erected at the sole expense of Mr. John Wood, junior, of the firm of Messrs. Wood & Walker, upon land purchased from the Fitzgeralds. It is a handsome structure in the lancet style of Gothic architecture, with accommodation for about 1200 worshippers. The first stone was laid by the generous founder on October 31st, 1836, and he also endowed it, and erected the school and parsonage house adjoining. The cost of the whole was stated to be about £10,500. Mr. Walker Rawsthorne, an architect of some repute in Bradford at that period, prepared the design.

The first incumbent of St. James's was the Rev. G. S. Bull, or "Parson Bull," as he was frequently termed, who was intimately associated with Mr. John Wood, the philanthropic manufacturer, Richard Oastler, the Earl of Shaftesbury, and others, in furthering the progress of the Factory Act or Ten Hours Bill. It was during the agitation of that measure that Mr. Wood proposed to erect and endow a church and schools for the use of his workpeople, and he gave the appointment to Mr. Bull, who was then officiating at Bierley Chapel. He was fortunate in securing in Mr. Bull a gentleman who was equally at home in superintending building operations, in expounding a sermon, or in delivering philippics from a platform. The schools adjoining the church he built first, and there prepared, as he used to say, the living stones by the time the material church was ready to receive them. Mr. Bull personally superintended the whole of the building works, both as regards the parsonage, church, and schools. The rev. gentleman had been in the navy, and on the erection of the church spire "swarmed" up the scaffolding, and placed the capstone on the top with his own hands.

It must not, however, be supposed that Parson Bull was wholly absorbed in bricks and mortar. During the period referred to he was faithfully preaching the Gospel, and making speeches everywhere on behalf of the Church Missionary and Pastoral Aid Societies, besides advocating the abridgment of factory labour for children with fearless courage, vigorous eloquence, and untiring perseverance. No wonder that the name of Parson Bull became a household word throughout a great part of the West Riding of Yorkshire. It was never known why Mr. Bull left Bradford, but in all probability the unflinching position he took up on the factory question often brought him into unpleasant collision with many whom he otherwise might have counted among his friends. He, however, removed to Birmingham, and began afresh at the Church of St. Matthew's before it was consecrated. The names of two of his successors, the Rev. William Sherwood and Canon Burfield, will also long be had in remembrance in connection with St. James's Church.

As we have drifted into Manchester Road, or Bowling Lane as it used to be called when St. James's Church was erected, we may as well note the appearance of that thoroughfare in the early part of the century. Long after the abolition of the toll-bar at the "town end," there was one placed at the top of the street leading down to St. James's Church. Excepting a few houses clustered near the toll-bar, almost the entire length of Bowling Lane towards Bradford was destitute of buildings of any description. A little above Mrs. Bacon's grounds there stood and still stands the maltkiln owned by John Tordoff, and afterwards occupied by Thomas Hill. At John Tordoff's house there lodged the first German merchant who came to settle in business in Bradford. All the land at the rear, extending to Horton Lane, was open, and belonged to Mr. C. S. B. Sharp; and the same remark applies to Miss Bower's land, extending up Manchester Road from the maltkiln to Isaac Rountree's flour shop, near the toll-bar.

Providence Primitive Methodist Chapel was erected in 1824, and about the same period Hope Street, King Street, and Clarence Street were laid out and filled with working-class dwellings upon the "back-to-back" system, principally by Messrs. J. & R. Turner and Mr. John Wood. Owing to the effects of a calamitous fire the chapel was totally destroyed in 1861, and rebuilt shortly afterwards.

A similar fate befell the Borough Corn Mill opposite on the 1st of January, 1874, after it had been much enlarged by Messrs. James Ellis & Co., who purchased the property in 1870 from Messrs. W. & J. Pilling. Messrs. Pilling, who had previously occupied Sams Mill, near Thiefscore Bridge, completed the erection of their new mill in Manchester Road in 1843. Messrs. Thomas Burnley & Co. were the builders, and the engines and boilers were supplied by the Low Moor Iron Company.

Upon the opposite side of the road there resided about this period Mr. Wm. Murgatroyd, afterwards of Bankfield, Bingley, his partner, Mr. Miles Illingworth, and Mr. John Russell, the head of the firm of Russell, Douglas & Co. Closely adjoining was the lawyer's office occupied and owned by Mr. Samuel Hailstone—to whom reference has already been made; then came an open plot of ground belonging to Miss Hartley, afterwards occupied by Mr. Robert Crosland's engineering works; and next to this plot came Croft House, purchased by Mr. Hailstone from Mr. Faber, of the firm of Faber & Duffield, merchants, and bought by that gentleman from a Mr. Edward Taylor.

The erection of Marshall's Mill in 1818 led to the building of a few houses in the neighbourhood of Portland Street, a step followed shortly afterwards by Mr. Wm. Rand, who added many working-class dwellings to this street. Subsequently Adelaide Street, Queen Street, Caledonia Street, and Marygate sprang into existence, through the building enterprise of Messrs. Jere. Parker, John Crook, Ed. Ripley, John Wood, and others, the opposite side of the road occupied by Grafton Street, Fitzgerald Street, &c., still remaining vacant. It will thus be seen how comparatively new are the densely-packed dwellings and shop property in Manchester Road. The new road to Halifax was opened in 1826, and from that period the name Bowling Lane gave place to that of Manchester Road.

Beyond the toll-bar there is no object calling for special reference except the old Skinhouse, situate near to Albion Mill, one of the few homesteads of the seventeenth century remaining in this part of Horton. Above the entrance are the initials $_A{}^A{}_H$ and the date 1660. The old Skinhouse is typical of the period when the early stuffmakers of Bradford farmed their own small estates, occupying themselves and their families alternately with the mixed labour of weaving and combing, and tilling the land. Of this class in the middle of last century was Jacob Hudson, woolcomber. He was a man of industry and frugal habits, and in those virtues his sober-minded wife Grace joined. She "jigged" and he "straightened" until in the course of a few years, by investing his savings in small parcels of wool, and working them into tops, he was enabled to accomplish the grand object of his heart—the purchase of an estate of land, and accordingly bought and afterwards resided at the Skinhouse estate, consisting of a farmhouse and twenty-two acres of land.

Jacob Hudson was a singular character in many respects. He was a regular attendant at the old Presbyterian Chapel, Chapel Lane, and a very worthy man, but he apparently lacked a forgiving disposition, for we are told that on one occasion a member of the congregation gave him some cause of offence, and he declared that henceforth he would not sit in the same building with him. Jacob went regularly to chapel, but he never sat down in it. His remains, with those of his wife, lie in the chapel yard.

Old Jacob, in making his will in 1772, did not forget that his wife had greatly contributed to the getting of the estate, and determined (as they had no children) that her relations should join with his in the benefit of it. He accordingly determined that what had been gathered so hardly and come into the family so slowly should never depart from it. Calling in an old lawyer named Brogden (father of the last Mr. Brogden, of Bradford), they concocted what they conceived would bind it in the family to all eternity. Jacob gave to each of nineteen persons (his relatives) and their heirs sums varying from £1 to £6 a year out of the rents and profits of the estate for ever, an arrangement which was never to be altered.

But the law abhors what old Jacob loved — namely, perpetuities, or keeping an estate in the same family for ever — and the will was therefore soon pronounced to be in that particular defective. As, however, he had so bound it that it could not be sold, the estate still remained in the same families, although the parties entitled to the rents had, through very numerous descents, increased to a great number. Some of them only received out of the estate a few shillings a year. The estate was well adapted for building sites. It was therefore resolved by the parties entitled to it, as the only course for loosing old Jacob's bonds, that application should be made to Parliament for an Act to enable them to sell it. The application was made in 1848, and an Act obtained at great expense enabling them to sell the property and divide the proceeds — this being probably the first private estate bill ever solicited from Bradford.

The Act above referred to enumerates the various relatives who were made devisees under Jacob Hudson's will, among them being Jacob Lister the elder, John Lister, Joseph Lister, Mary and Grace Lister, John Lister of Tingley, Mark Brook, John Booth, Grace Harrison, Mary Atkinson, Joseph Gaunt, Jonathan Gaunt, Ann Birk, and Martin Gaunt, being the names of persons mostly residing in Bradford and its immediate neighbourhood. The estate out of which the small annuities were to be paid was vested in John Bower, Isaac Hollings, James Garnett, and John Balme, as

Rambles Round Horton.

The Old Skinhouse, Manchester Road.

trustees. The trustees acting at the period of the passing of the Act were Messrs. Richard Garnett, James Garnett, Wm. Hardcastle, and Joseph Smith, and upon the three trustees first named devolved the disposal of the estate. In addition to the homestead, there were several closes of land, called the Five Day Work, the Croft, the Low Field, the Great Ing, the Round Hill, and the Andrew, occupied by Benj. Blaymires, and other closes in the occupation of John Cordingley and Samuel Cordingley, besides two closes of land in Horton called the Upper and Lower Westcroft.

The Cordingleys had, long prior to 1848, the date of the Hudson Estate Act, occupied a portion of Jacob Hudson's estate, and being fellmongers gave the appellation of the Skinhouse to the building. In 1801 James Cordingley and Abraham Blackburn occupied the estate betwixt them. The latter was the father of Mr. Bailey Blackburn, of Bradford, and was a maltster and corn merchant. In 1812 he removed to Cropper Lane, and had a lease of the Soke Mills, at Bradford. The Blackburn family originally came from Knaresbro' Forest.

A singular and fatal incident befell James Cordingley during his occupancy in October, 1827. Either from pleasure or in order to guard his premises he kept several ferocious dogs, which at night were allowed to roam at large. This circumstance proved fatal to their master, for, returning home one night somewhat inebriated, the dogs did not recognise his voice, and worried him upon his own doorstones to such an extent that he died. A mysterious fatality also attached to that portion of the homestead inhabited by the Blamires family, who succeeded Abraham Blackburn in a portion of the Skinhouse; John Blamires was found dead in the garden in front of the house, with his head overhanging a well which still exists.

The Skinhouse was purchased along with an adjoining close of land by Mr. Thomas Dewhirst, of Laisterdyke, in 1850, this being the first purchase under the Act obtained by Hudson's trustees, and upon the vacant land adjoining Mr. Dewhirst erected Albion Mill. The remaining building ground still perpetuates the name of its former eccentric proprietor, one of the streets being named Jacob Street and another Skinhouse Street.

Following the lead of Manchester Road from the Skinhouse we should soon cross the boundary dividing Horton from Bowling, so must retrace our steps, noticing by the way that the Lister's Arms Inn, in the immediate locality, dates from the opening of the new road to Halifax in 1826, having been erected by Mr. Ellis Cunliffe Lister, who owned considerable property in the neighbourhood. Prior to its erection there had been a "public" at Four Lane Ends, just behind the Skinhouse, kept by William Blackburn, brother of Abraham Blackburn, who removed to the Lister's Arms in the new road when the licence was transferred there. In November, 1828, he was succeeded by John Blackburn, who was landlord until 1841. For some time after its erection there was no public-house between the Lister's Arms and the New Inn in Tyrrel Street upon one side, and the Craven Heifer in Smiddles Lane on the other. The house was made use of by passing coaches, a large copper kettle being kept on the hob in winter time filled with good home-brewed, and spiced with sugar and ginger for the comfort of passengers. The back parlour of the house was generally patronised on a Sunday morning by a few celebrities, who, after the beadle with his staff, and John Andrew his constable, had paid their morning visit, discussed the events of the week while enjoying their home-brewed — for there were little spirits consumed in those days.

Clayton Lane took its name from John Clayton, who erected a substantial house, dated 1776, in that remote thoroughfare. In the same lane there once existed a Jerusalemite Church, where in former times assembled a goodly number of the disciples of Johanna Southcott. An interesting chapter might be written of the vagaries of this body of misguided fanatics, led by Prophet Wroe, but their peculiar doctrines were not confined to the township of Horton. A little higher up Clayton Lane was erected in 1839 a Wesleyan Chapel to commemorate the centenary of Methodism. It has since been superseded by the more graceful erection called Annesley Chapel. The top of

Clayton Lane once rejoiced in the name of Sodom, the immediate locality being the abode of hand-combers and others engaged at " Dick Smith Mill."

The Baptist College, situate near the top of what is now known as Park Road, was founded under the auspices of the Northern Baptist Education Society in the year 1805. The premises occupied for the academic studies and residence of the young men intended for the ministry, comprising a warehouse and dwellinghouse, were purchased from Mr. John Balme in 1817, and were rebuilt in 1825. Towards the foundation of this institution (removed to its present site at Rawdon in 1859) Samuel Broadley, of Bradford, gave £5000, and other Baptists very liberal sums.

The Rev. Wm. Steadman, D.D., was the sole tutor until 1818, when he became minister at Westgate Chapel. He died in 1837, and was succeeded as president and theological tutor by the Rev. James Acworth, LL.D., the Rev. Francis Clowes being classical tutor. Dr. Steadman was a native of Herefordshire, and a man whose learning was of solid foundation, being blessed with a memory so retentive that what he once learnt he always retained. Of his character as a Christian teacher much has been already published. His sympathies were of the broadest, with a special leaning towards those less endowed in intellectual gifts than himself. Personally he was somewhat ungainly in appearance. His corpulent personage, awkward manners, negligent dress, well-known cough, bad eyesight, and singular physiognomy, although yet dimly remembered by few, are gilded over by the image of the old doctor as he sallied forth, staff in hand, upon some errand of mercy, with his pockets full of apples for children, and with more valuable gifts for those of larger growth. During the long period of forty-six years he preached about 11,000 times, baptized 700 professed disciples, educated for the ministry about 100 young men, attended more than 100 ordinations, and officiated at the opening of forty places of worship !

During the period when Dr. Steadman was in his prime, and even up to the time of his death in 1837, Little Horton Lane was a solitary part of the town. Between Horton Lane

Chapel and Rand's Mill there was a stretch of open fields extending to Melbourne Place, where the first break in the monotony was made by Mr. Jonathan Cordingley in 1838, by the erection of a house fronting to Horton Lane. The late Mr. Wm. Andrews followed suit a little higher up on the other side of the lane, a retired Scotch gentleman named Corson erecting an adjoining residence, and shortly afterwards Mr. Joseph Smith, land agent, built the house long occupied by him. The opening out of the estates of Colonel Fitzgerald, of Boldshay Hall, brought into existence Fitzgerald Street and other outlets to Manchester Road. For some time after this, however, a toll-bar stood at the top of George Street, now Grafton Street.

CHAPTER VIII.

Horton House—Joseph Hinchliffe, Schoolmaster—The Lister Family, of Horton and Shibden—Joseph Lister, Historian—The Fitzgeralds—Lawrence Sterne, Author of "Tristram Shandy."

From the point at which we have arrived in these "rambles" a good view is obtainable of Horton House, which is only divided by a lawn from Horton Lane. In former days the greensward in front of the house generally presented a lively aspect, the adjoining residence being at that time an academy for young gentlemen, kept by Joseph Hinchliffe. A generation ago this scholastic establishment was held in high repute for the excellence of the teaching given there. Not a few gentlemen of Bradford and the neighbourhood who subsequently attained exalted positions owed their educational training to Joseph Hinchliffe, and for many years his former pupils formed a " Hinchliffe Club," and dined together once a year. One of his assistants was Mr. Joseph Riley, a gentleman who afterwards gained a reputation as a schoolmaster at Rawdon and Steeton, subsequently removing to Pannal, near Harrogate. His brother Edmund Riley, another Bradford schoolmaster, also received his training as assistant at Horton House Academy. We believe that Mr. Hinchliffe took up the teaching connection of Mr. Nesbitt, a celebrated schoolmaster in Westgate, whose works on "Mensuration" and " Arithmetic" had a far more than local reputation.

Mr. Hinchliffe was a Moravian, and chiefly through his influence the Moravian Chapel at Holme Top was erected. He was also most zealous in teaching the young collier lads at Wibsey, gathering them on Sundays for that purpose at the place of worship long maintained by the Moravians at Chapel Fold, Brownroyd Hill. Mr. Hinchliffe was the author of several works on the art of speaking ; and one of them, entitled the " Academic Speaker," illustrated with plates, attained some reputation, and he also published several books of poems. Mr. Hinchliffe was a man of a very active and energetic mind, and fully alive to the all-important duties of his position. His bodily activity was so great that he might be literally said to be always occupied. The latter years of his life were, however, unfortunately embittered by the loss of the greater portion of his hard-earned savings, which, although invested with care and apparent prudence, were lost by others over whom he had no control. As soon, however, as his difficulties became known, his former pupils formed a committee and immediately raised amongst themselves a very substantial pecuniary testimonial, amounting to upwards of £700 ; thus alleviating, as far as possible, the pain which loss of property almost invariably occasions to those who have no longer the physical power to retrieve their position. Mr. Hinchliffe was interred at the Moravian settlement at Fulneck in April, 1853, aged seventy-two years.

Horton House at the period of which we write was the property but not the residence of Colonel Fitzgerald, who lived at Boldshay Hall, Barkerend. The property came to him, however, by his marriage with the daughter of Dr. Crowther, who had married a niece of Samuel Lister, of Horton. The Lister family, therefore, were the ancient possessors of Horton House, and bore the same arms (ermine on a fess sable, three mullets or, a canton gules), and were, like the Listers of Ovenden and Shibden, descended from the Listers of the township of Halifax.

The Listers of Horton may be traced to a remote period in local history. From abundant documentary evidence before us it appears that the family held land in Northowram by copy of court roll in succession from father to son from the year 1422. The descent of the family might even be traced to the year 1272, when Bate le Lister, or, according to the Latin rendering, "tinctor," of Halifax, purchased half an acre of land in Northowram, in Hipperholme greaveship, of William of Halifax, the miller (molendinarius). From him descended John Bate-son, living in 1329, and Richard, son of Bate. In 1382 Robert Lister, probably the son of Richard, had a licence for dyeing granted to him for life by the Monastery of Lewes, the priors whereof were lords of the manor of Halifax, and he served as constable of Halifax in 1372.

From the above enumeration we derive some interesting information as to the origin of names. A dyer in remote times was known as a *lister, iyster, lyttester, dyer, dyster,* or *dister,* while in legal documents the Latinised form of *tinctor* was employed. Thus Bate the "tinctor," or dyer, became Bate the "lister," and ultimately the latter became the surname of the family. Another name seems to have sprung from the same root. Bate the "lister" had sons, one of whom in 1329 is called Bate-son, and thus we have the now common name of Bateson. In a similar manner have become localised such names as Walker, one who thickened cloth by treading it before the invention of fulling machinery; Webster, a weaver; Barker, a tanner, and others.

Resuming our notes of the Lister family, we find that the Robert Lister who in 1382 held the exclusive privilege of dyeing in the manor of Halifax was succeeded by Richard, who in 1412 was constable of Halifax and an important man. He held a lease of the tolls of the town of Halifax, and in addition to the inheritance from the above-named Robert of a messuage and land in Halifax, he was the owner by purchase of several estates in Halifax and Northowram, and paid in 1409 the highest rent of all their Halifax tenants to the lords of that manor—the Prior and Convent of Lewes. In 1421 he purchased from John Naylor two acres lying under "Haylay Bank." In 1429 he also purchased a close of land in Northowram, called the "Yvepighill," of John Symson. In 1435 Richard Lister took of the lords of the manor a certain parcel of waste land in Halifax adjoining the "North Brige," near which was a mill pond belonging to him, and doubtless used by him in his business, and in 1439 he released to Richard Moore his rights in a close of land called Horlawgreene Close, in Northowram, which formerly belonged to Richard Illingworth, and whose daughter, Cecilia, Moore had married.

The names given above will be readily identified by those acquainted with the locality. The Ovenden and Northowram estates continued in the Lister family until sold in 1756 by Samuel Lister, J.P., of Horton, to Mr. John Watkinson. The farm at Ovenden was called "Parklands" or "Parkroyd."

In 1452 the Northowram estates of Richard Lister were surrendered by him to the use of his son William, who had evidently begun to assume a position in the locality. In Glover's Visitation, 1612, the pedigree of the Listers of Hull is traced to this Richard, as is also that of the Shibden family, as recorded in the Heralds College.

The Listers, although owning lands at Horton, appear to have lived at Ovenden until John Lister, grandson of the above-named William Lister, about 1524 came to reside here; and paid to the subsidy levied in that year "for £3 lands, 3s.," in Horton township. In the muster roll for the "liberties of Bradford," temp. Henry VIII., under the head of Horton, we find that this John Lister was one of the five township-men who furnished a "horse and harness" apiece, and he is described as one of thirty who carried "bills." His son was Richard, who succeeded to the Horton and Ovenden lands in 1543, and died in 1546, seised in fee by military service (the sixteenth part of one knight's fee) of "one messuage, 20 acres of land, 12 acres of meadow, and 100 acres of pasture in Horton." Richard Lister's successor was his son Thomas, three years old at his father's death. He appears to have lived chiefly at Parklands, Ovenden, and to have died there, as his children were all baptised at Halifax. An ancient deed, dated 1591, however, affords presumptive evidence that prior to his decease there were members of the Lister family resident at Horton, as Thomas Lister and John Lister are both parties to a conveyance by William Collinson to Robert Collinson of "two closes in Horton, abutting on lands belonging to John Armitage, of Kirklees, on the south side, and on the north by the moor or common of Horton." The deed was drawn by Abm. Lister, attorney, of Bowling.

Thomas Lister died in 1606, seised, according to a *post mortem* inquisition of the Court of Wards, in fee by military service, of "one messuage and 3½ bovates of land, meadow and pasture, containing 40 acres, to the same messuage belonging in Horton, and also of 14 acres of land in Horton, and one other messuage and 10 acres of land, meadow and pasture, in Ovenden."

Thomas Lister married Sibella Northend at Halifax, and left two sons, John, his heir and forty years old at his father's death, and Samuel. The latter married, in 1598, Susanna, daughter of William Drake, of Northowram, and was the founder of the Shibden Hall branch of the Lister family. Shibden Hall is situate in the lower portion of Shibden Dale, and is a fine example of the timber-built residences of the earlier part of the fifteenth century. The earliest possessors were a family named Otes, who appear to have been well settled there by the year 1410. Owing to careful treatment at the hands of subsequent owners, the hall retains much of its original character, and it is not likely to suffer while under the guardianship of its present owner, Mr. John Lister, M.A., a lineal descendant of Samuel Lister, named above.

John, the elder brother of Samuel Lister, succeeded to the Horton and Ovenden estates, and resided at Little Horton. In 1612 it was found by an inquisition that "John Lister, of Little Horton, payeth yearly *one pair of white spurs* to the King." The curious nature of this tenure had its origin in the feudal disposition of lands generally. In the great survey taken in 1311 of all the territorial possessions of the Lacies, the Abbot of Kirkstall, for four oxgangs (or 48 acres) of land in Horton, was only required to present yearly a pair of white spurs. Such tenures were not unfrequent at the period referred to, especially in respect to lands held by religious houses. It has been assumed by Mr. John James that the land in question was the gift of the Lacies, and that it lay near to Burnet Field. A sister of John Lister, of Little Horton, was married in 1602 to Caleb Kempe, B.D., vicar of Bradford.

A succession of Johns, three in number, followed. By the terms of a revoked will made in 1678, John Lister, gentleman, described as late of Ovenden, but now of Horton, devised "all that messuage called Parkroyd, in Wheatley, with lands, &c., to his son Joseph, also his interest in the lease of Mixenden Mills, which he had of my lords Halifax." Two messuages, lands, and farms in Horton, in his own occupation and that of Thomas Fox, together with his Halifax and Lancashire estates, he left to his son John the younger, for the term of "fourscore years if he should live so long," and after his death to his son Samuel Lister, his heirs, &c., and in default of such issue then to John Lister, a younger son of John his son. To Samuel Lister, as eldest son of his father John, the family property descended, and as heir to his younger brother, also named John, whose will was dated 1705, he succeeded to "all those two messuages or tenements situate in Ovenden, late in the several occupations of John Allinson and Jonathan ——; and also that tenement called Park House, now in the tenure of James Smith, and also those two messuages situate in Horton, in the occupations of the said testator, and also his other tenements wheresoever situate."

Samuel Lister married Martha, a daughter of William Midgley, of Scholemoor, one of the influential families of the period. He died in 1752, leaving issue an only son Samuel and a daughter Elizabeth. Samuel Lister, the younger, born in 1714, married Mary Midgley, another member of the Scholemoor family of that name, for his first wife. She died in 1764 without issue, and he married secondly Dorothy, daughter of Wm. Lister, of Shipley. There was no issue of the second marriage.

Samuel Lister lived at Little Horton, and probably rebuilt the present substantial residence called Horton House. He was for some years a justice of the peace, and an influential member of the community. He disposed of the Ovenden estates inherited by him to John Watkinson, jun., in 1756, but must have added considerably to the extent of his Horton property, as his name frequently occurs in deeds of conveyance as mortgagee or purchaser of land and messuages in the neighbourhood. Under the deed of settlement made in 1766 on the marriage of Samuel Lister with his second wife Dorothy, the Horton estates are described as "all that capital messuage in Little Horton wherein he dwelt, together with closes known as Hargreave Land, Hollingreave, Hutchen Yard, and Great Flatt, occupied by Benjamin Stables; Narr Langside, purchased by Samuel Lister of Benjamin Kennet, clerk, and inherited by him from his grandfather, Mr. Stockdale; also the messuage wherein Abraham Balme did dwell, and the Great Laistridge, Little Laistridge or Mary Hind Fields, occupied by Abraham Balme; also Boggard Close, occupied by John Balme; Three Nook, occupied by Henry Blagburn; also Bowling Ing, Pudding Ing, Tumbling Hill, and other closes in Horton occupied by John Whitaker; also the Norcroft Brow, purchased by Samuel Lister of Thomas Aked, and previously owned by Faith Sawrey, widow; also the Far Silbridge, occupied by Richard Hargreaves; and three messuages in Kirkgate occupied by John Fearnley, John Tottie, and Samuel Wilkinson; and another house in Kirkgate, occupied by Mr. Sedgwick, together with two closes of meadow land at Piper Grave and Manningham Stoop, in the occupation of Mr. Sedgwick; also a road 14 ft. wide, called the Cockholme, leading to the School Holme, Mr. Bartlett's Holme, the Norcroft, and the Langsides above mentioned," &c.

Samuel Lister died in 1769. In his will, made before the death of his first wife, Mary, and after provision made for her, he bequeathed his estate in trust to his friend Benjamin Bartlett, of Bradford, with a provision that a sum of £200 should be paid to him for his trouble in realising outstanding mortgages, and in seeing to the discharge of all his debts. The residue of his estate he devised to "Samuel Lister, of Horton, gentleman," during the term of his natural life, and in default of heirs male to his the testator's niece, Mary Hemingway, with the proviso that in case of her marriage she and her husband should take the surname of Lister, and reside at Horton House. In the event of these conditions not being complied with, the estates were to pass to Japhet Lister, of Northgate House, Halifax (brother to Jeremy Lister, of Shibden Hall), and his heirs male. Japhet Lister, however, died leaving only one daughter.

The "Samuel Lister, of Horton," to whom the Horton estates were thus bequeathed, subsequently resided at Manningham, and was an attorney-at-law and clerk to the trustees of the turnpike road between Bradford and Keighley, by way of Toller Lane and Cottingley; also of the turnpike between Dudley Hill and Killinghall. He married Mary, the daughter of Dorothy Stapleton (who was a Sharp,, and died

Horton House.

Rambles Round Horton.

without issue in 1792. He is described as a cousin of the Listers of Shibden. At any rate, he never came into the property, nor did Mary Hemingway.

In explanation, it should be stated that Elizabeth, sister of Samuel Lister, married in 1740 Henry Hemingway, a noted attorney, then residing at Boldshay Hall. She died in 1772, leaving an only daughter, Mary, the "niece" referred to in Samuel Lister's will, and who was married to Dr. Crowther, of Leeds, and subsequently of York. Samuel Lister, however, married again, as stated above, Dorothy Lister, and she became tenant for life of her husband's estates. At his decease Dorothy married for her second husband Richard Hodsden, and it was only after her death in 1814 that Miss Elizabeth Crowther, the only surviving daughter of Dr. Crowther and Mary Hemingway, entered into possession of the Lister estates as heir-at-law of Samuel Lister, besides succeeding to the Boldshay property.

In 1819 Elizabeth Crowther married Colonel Thos. Geo. Fitzgerald, of Turlough Castle, Ireland. Of this marriage were Henry Thomas George Fitzgerald, born at Boldshay in 1820, and two daughters. Colonel Fitzgerald married for his first wife Delia, daughter of Joshua Field, of Heaton Hall, and sister of Mr. John Wilmer Field, and had one son, who took the Irish estates. Colonel Fitzgerald resided at Boldshay Hall, and took a position among the gentry of the period. His son, Major Fitzgerald, who is still living in the south of England, married Elizabeth Harriet Yates, eldest daughter of the Rev. S. W. Yates, of Reading, and has three sons and two daughters.

In collating the above from voluminous manuscripts we have confined our remarks pretty generally to the line of the Horton Listers. There were evidently, however, various branches in and around Bradford, and probably of the same parent stock—the Listers of Halifax. Confirmation of this is furnished by the lists of guests invited to funerals of members of the Lister family of Shibden Hall, in which the Listers of Wibsey, Horton, Manningham, and Bolton are mentioned, and in some cases are referred to as "cosins."

The Listers were zealous friends of the Parliamentarians during the Civil Wars, and in "James's History of Bradford" we find the following reference to that period :—

John Lister, the father, and Joseph Lister, the son, resided in a house on the site of Horton Low Hall, and were clothmakers, and suffered terribly from the pillage of the town by the Royalist troops after the seige of Bradford in 1643.

The original document setting forth the claim for compensation put in by the family is in the possession of Mr. Hailstone, of Walton Hall, who has kindly furnished us with the following extract from it :—

Certificate of money paid by John Lister, the father, and Joseph Lister, the son, inhabitants in Horton, in the parish of Bradford Dale, being constant in their affections and actions for the Parliament and loss at the taking of the said town by the Earl of Newcastle's army upon the 2d and 3d July, A.D. 1643, as followeth :—

Items			
Lent upon the public faith...	£10	0	0
Item one meare put into Colonell Bright's Troop with her garniture ...	5	13	4
Item in free quarter ...	72	4	2
Total of the Account	£228	4	6

Put in Dec. 17, 1649.

Many other items are contained in the original document referring to articles taken away or destroyed by the Royalist troops, while other entries show that necessaries had been provided by the Listers for the Parliamentary forces. It will be noticed that the account was not sent in with a view to obtain payment until six years after the siege of Bradford.

It was to another member of the Lister family that subsequent generations have been indebted in a great measure for an account of the memorable siege of Bradford, namely, Joseph Lister, who was an eye-witness, and whose description Mr. James spoke of as "artless and simple, and bearing internal evidence of its truthfulness."

Joseph Lister, in his Autobiography, describes himself as having been "born at Bradford, of godly and religious parents, in June, 1627." He would, therefore, be sixteen years old at the period when he was witness of the events which he narrates. At fourteen years he was apprenticed to learn the trade of a clothier with John Sharp, Little Horton, the father of Abraham Sharp, the famous mathematician, residing at Horton Hall. In 1657 he married Sarah Denton, and had two sons, one of whom, Accepted Lister, was born at Bailey Fold, Allerton, and was minister of Kipping Chapel, Thornton. Both father and son died in 1709, within a few days of each other.

Some doubt exists as to the parentage of Joseph Lister, the historian of the siege. From the information given in Holroyd's valuable tracts on Bradford history, and notes supplied by Mr. Empsall, we gather that his father was named Edward Lister, who in 1618 married Sarah Hill, sister of Edward Hill, M.A. The latter gentleman was some time vicar of Huddersfield, and afterwards of Crofton, from whence he was ejected by the Act of Uniformity in 1662. Under the Five-mile Act he afterwards removed to Shibden, near Halifax, preaching, like Oliver Heywood, where he could, and according to Wright, died in 1669, at Shibden Hall. He was the first subscriber to the *Vindiciæ Veritatis* in 1648. A "cousin," Edward Hill, is referred to in private memoranda of the Lister family of Overbrea and Shibden Hall, who resided in London, and was son of the Rev. Edward Hill. He was a partner with Samuel Lister, of Shibden, as cloth merchants. Joshua Hill, minister of the chapel at Bramley, was another brother of Sarah Hill.

It is worthy of note, however, that there was a family of Listers residing at Bolton, who were in intimate relationship with the Listers of Shibden and Horton, and were often referred to in Oliver Heywood's diaries. Is it probable that Joseph Lister, the historian, was of this family? In Vol. II. there is the following entry:—"—— Lister, of Bolton, near Bradford, buried there July 23, 1683, grandfather to Mr. Jo. Lister, preacher, aged eighty." The dates correspond with the statement of Joseph Lister that he was born in 1627. He, however, states that he was born at Bradford, but Bolton is very near to Bradford, or his father might have removed there.

Another name is also suggested by a perusal of the Lister pedigree of more than local reputation, namely, that of Sterne. At two periods in the family history relationship was established between the Listers and the Sternes; from the latter, it may be stated, were descended Richard Sterne, Archbishop of York in 1683, and the Rev. Lawrence Sterne, author of "Tristram Shandy" and "The Sentimental Journey." It may not be generally known that the vivacious author was for some time a pupil at Hipperholme Grammar School, Halifax (see note). In his Autobiography he says:—"In the autumn of that year, 1722 (or the spring afterwards, I forget which), my father got leave of his colonel to fix me at school, which he did near Halifax, with an able master."

An elaborate record of this family would exhaust more space than can now be afforded. Suffice it at present to state that Simon Sterne, of Woodhouse, near Halifax, left a numerous family, the eldest son being Richard Sterne, who married in 1703 for his first wife Dorothy, relict of Samuel Lister, of Shibden Hall, where, until the death of the said Dorothy, he resided; and, secondly, Hester, daughter of Timothy Booth, of Halifax; also a son Roger, the father of the celebrated Lawrence Sterne. Of Richard Sterne's second marriage was, with other issue, Dorothy, married to William Lister, of Shipley, whose daughter, also named Dorothy (evidently a favourite name), married, first, Samuel Lister, of Horton, and secondly, Richard Hodsden, a London gentleman. Their only daughter, Frances, was married to George Carroll, son of George Carroll, gentleman, of county Wicklow. Mr. Carroll, who lived for some time at Horton

---

NOTE ON LAURENCE STERNE.—The accuracy of this statement is questioned by an old pupil of Heath Grammar School, who contends that the latter well-known school, situate on the other side of Halifax, was that to which Sterne was sent. A similar contention is held by another local antiquary. On the other hand we have the testimony of a gentleman near Hipperholme, in whose family is preserved the tradition that Sterne habitually called at the family residence while walking to and from school, and who points out that at the period referred to there certainly was not the "able master" at Heath alluded to by Sterne in his Autobiography, while there was at Hipperholme in the person of Nathan Sharp. Then we have the evidence rendered in the history of Heath Grammar School, compiled by Mr. Cox, a late master, who is of opinion that it was at Hipperholme School that Sterne received his education, and not at Heath, although he might have first been sent there.

House, subsequently removed to Boston Spa, and died in 1861. His sons were Coote Alexander, a West Riding magistrate, and high sheriff of county Wicklow in 1862; Richard Sterne, a West Riding magistrate, lately deceased; George Frederick, now living at Boston Spa; and Francis Rawdon, deceased.

In concluding this notice of Horton House it may be stated that the property remained in the hands of the Fitzgeralds until a short time ago, when it was disposed of by public auction.

CHAPTER IX.

Horton Hall—The Sharp Family—John Sharp, the Parliamentarian—The Rev. Thos. Sharp, M.A.—John Sharp, M.D.—Abraham Sharp, the Mathematician; his Workshop at Horton Hall—Charles Swain Booth Sharp—Madam Sharp—Mrs. Giles.

No district in the township of Horton has retained its primitive character more than the neighbourhood of Horton Green; and probably from this reason there is no more desirable place of residence in the borough of Bradford. Situated at a medium altitude, and lying well open to the western breezes, the line of dwellings fringing the "Green" enjoy an immunity from the evils attendant upon an overcrowded neighbourhood which is possessed by few residential districts, having open fields both to front and rear. It is not to Horton Green and its former residents, however, that this chapter is intended to be devoted, but to the leading family which for hundreds of years has been associated with the locality. In subsequent papers we shall not overlook those of humbler rank and station.

In a lecture delivered by the late Canon Fawcett, of Low Moor, relating to old Bradford families, the following remark occurs:—" There is scarcely any name associated with the early history of Bradford parish of more real interest than that of the Sharps of Horton." The worthy Canon might have added that none of the several respectable families associated with the township could boast of so continuous a connection with it as the Sharps can. So early as the year 1365, as appears from a deed executed at that period, Wm. de Leventhorpe, the then lord of the manor, conveyed to Thos. Sharp two bovates or oxgangs, being as much land as an ox could plough in a year, and a messuage in Little Horton, adjoining to lands belonging to the Abbot of Kirkstall.

In previous papers reference has been made to the easy payment required of the monastic head of the Abbey of Kirkstall for his holding, namely, the annual presentation to the lord of the manor of a pair of white gilt spurs. Whether the "messuage" referred to occupied the site of Horton Hall, so long associated with the Sharp family, we have no information. From documents dated 1390 evidence exists that two members of the Sharp family had acquired a position entitling them to grants from the surrounding wastes; for at that period William, the son of Jordan de Bradford, conveyed to John, the son of Thomas Sharp, of Little Horton (probably the Thomas named in the 1365 deed), half an acre of land situate in Horton. The second document, dated " Friday, in third week of Lent," 1390, is a

Grant by feoffment from William de Leventhorp, of the parish of Bradford, to John, son of William, son of Robert de Horton, and Thomas, son of —— [qy. John] Scharpe, of Little Horton, of the Manor of Leventhorpe, in Bradforddale. Rent, 5 marks per annum. Witnesses —Geoffrey de Leventhorpe ; William, son of Robert de Horton ; Adam del Apilyerde ; John Mortimer, of Clayton, sen. ; and John Bailey, of Allerton.

It would thus appear that Thomas Sharp divided the manorship of Leventhorpe with John de Horton, but his possession was not of long continuance, for in the year 1402, according to another deed,

Thomas, son of John Scharpp, of Little Horton, released to Geoffrey, son of William de Leventhorp, all his right in the manor of Leventhorp, and of all lands in Thornton, in Bradforddale, which he lately had of the gift of the said William.

In records of the time of Ed. IV. (1461-83) we find the names of John Scharp and Christopher Scharp (son and heir of John) parties to a deed with John Hollins, of Clayton. This Christopher Sharp was assessed in 1520 upon £20 in goods (a large amount in those days), and paid 10s. By his will, dated 1530, he ordered his body to be buried in the " Kirkgarth of SS. Peter and Paul, Bradford." To the " hye altar " there " for tythes forgotten," he bequeathed the sum of 3s. 4d. ; to "kyrkwork," 3s. 4d. ; the rest to Alice, his wife. The witnesses to this will were Sir Thos. Ecop, Sir Tristram Horton, and James Sharp. The titled gentlemen were priests of the " hye-altar of St. Peter " at Bradford, the order to which they belonged not unfrequently officiating as witnesses to the wills of wealthy members of the church.

As to James Sharp, the last-named witness, considerable interest attaches to his identity from an antiquarian point of view, as upon his connection with the family under notice depends the relationship of Archbishop Sharp with the Horton family of the name. John James remarks upon this point that James Sharp was evidently a near relative, but the exact point of relationship had not been found. The family, however, do not claim descent through the Christopher Sharp named above, but from another Christopher, a man of large property in Horton, whose will was proved in 1543, and to which document the James Sharp just mentioned was also witness. He was probably the Christopher Sharp referred to in the muster roll of the West Riding, as contributing a "horse and harness," the other four being William Feild, Omfray Wood, John Lister, and John Ffourness.

The establishing of the connection of Archbishop Sharp's family with the Sharps of Horton has engaged the attention of many genealogists, including Courthorpe, Rouge Croix Pursuivant of Arms, and we have, through the courtesy of Mr. F. S. Powell, had the benefit of his researches, the result of which will more appropriately appear in treating of the Archbishop's descent.

The existence of several branches within one township and the repetition of John, Thomas, and Christopher as Christian names, renders research somewhat perplexing, and of this multiplicity sufficient evidence exists. In 1606, from the copy of a deed before us, it appears that "Christopher Sharp, of Horton, clothier, gives and grants to Samuel Sharp, his son, one close called Nether Moor Close, containing one acre, which he purchased of Thomas Hodgson, Thomas Sharp, Robert Booth, and William Feild (and which was evidently a portion of the waste land conveyed in 1589 from the Lacy family to the persons named in the deed)—Signed —Thomas Sharp, John Hillhouse, Thomas Butterfield, and by me Thomas Sharp, the writer "—the latter being evidently a lawyer.

In the Subsidy Roll of May, 1608, Thomas Sharp, sen. and jun,, and John Sharp are each assessed for lands at 20s., and pay upon that assessment 2s. 8d. We have also an

Rambles Round Horton.

indenture before us made between Alice Sharp, of Scholemoor, late wife of Thomas Sharp, and others. The Scholemoor Sharps were somewhat influential at that period. Coming to more recent times we may close our extracts from taxation rolls by quoting from the land and property tax for Horton of the year 1704, laid at 4s. in the pound, in which Mrs. Sharp appears as a contributor to the extent of £4 17s. 6d., and Isaac Sharp for £3 11s. 3d. These individuals represented the two main branches into which the family had become divided, and which now centre in Mr. Francis Sharp Powell, the present representative of the Sharps of Horton.

As just intimated, the Sharp family were in two branches, the partition taking place upwards of 200 years ago, when Horton Old Hall (the residence of Mr. F. S. Powell) was built for the younger branch. Horton Hall, the adjoining residence, was the home of the elder branch, associated in recent times with the names of Madam Sharp and Mrs. Giles, and more recently with that of Mr. Hailstone. The two branches were of different religious and political tendencies—the elder branch being staunch Parliamentarians and Puritans; while the younger were Royalists and Episcopalians. Following the dictates both of convenience and propriety, we may therefore first make reference to Horton Hall and its former owners and occupants.

The Sharps, like most of the yeomen of these parts, combined the trade of clothier with that of cultivator of the soil. The result of this arrangement may be observed in the construction of residences of the period, which as a rule were roomy and substantially built, providing accommodation in the "house-body" or in an upper chamber for several pairs of rude wooden looms, the preparatory processes being managed by the women or young people of the family, while the male members alternately plied the loom and engaged in field work, as occasion demanded.

To this class we assume Thomas Sharp, whose will was dated 1607, to have belonged. He was the son of John Sharp (from whom also sprang the Sharps of Tong), whose father was the Christopher previously referred to as having died

G

in 1543, and who was a man of considerable means. Thomas Sharp profited by his inheritance, his father leaving him "one thing of the best of every kind of vessel accustomed to be 'occupied' at his house at Horton." By indenture dated 1589, he, with Thomas Hodgson, of Bolling, Robert Booth and William Feild, of Horton, had conveyed to them from Richard Lacy 250 acres of the unenclosed wastes of Horton and fourteen acres lately enclosed. By another indenture he purchased from Thomas Hodgson, of Bowling, a close called Bowling Mill Close for £88. In conjunction with his son John he also added to the estate South Croft, Leysteads, and Hollingreave land.

It was from this Thomas Sharp there sprang two sons, Thomas and John, who became the founders of the two main branches of the Sharp family. John, the younger brother, was a distinguished Royalist, having been in several battles on the side of Charles I., and who never suffered his beard to be shaved after his Royal master's execution at Whitehall. In 1629 he added to the Horton estate Kent Close, and purchased other land from Thomas Wood and Henry Walker, of Bradford. To his line, however, we must refer subsequently. His elder brother Thomas, who died in 1636, was the father of John Sharp, the noted Parliamentarian, having been born in 1604. He married Mary, the daughter of Robert Clarkson, of Fairgap, Bradford, and among their nine children were the Rev. Thomas Sharp, once vicar of Adel, and afterwards an ardent Nonconformist, and Abraham Sharp, the mathematician.

John Sharp, the Parliamentarian, was undoubtedly a prominent character during the Civil Wars. He was also a clothier, reference having been previously made to him in that capacity as the master of Joseph Lister, the historian of the siege of Bradford; but in all probability he was a merchant as well as manufacturer. His educational training, however, must have been above the average of the craft to which he belonged, as is evidenced by documents prepared by him still extant. His sympathies were strongly on the side of Parliament during the fierce struggle which prevailed during the Civil Wars, the results of which were apparent in the partial sacking of Bradford town. After the battle of Adwalton Moor and the siege of Bradford he followed the fortunes of General Fairfax, and was present at the engagements at Nantwich and Marston Moor. John Sharp, indeed, seems to have acted as private secretary to General Fairfax during the western campaign, evidence of which is furnished by a relic now in the possession of Mr. Hailstone, of Walton Hall. For his services he was presented by Parliament with a gold medal, having a figure of Fairfax on the obverse ; round the rim of the reverse " Post hac meliora " ; and in the centre the word " Meruisti." Besides his other duties John Sharp was the receiver of the rectorial tithes of Bradford parish for Sir John Maynard, and generally occupied a position of influence in the neighbourhood. He died respected by all his neighbours in 1672, the inventory of his possessions showing him to have acquired considerable wealth during his lifetime.

John Sharp by his will left his house and lands to his eldest son, the Rev. Thomas Sharp, brother of Abraham the mathematician, who rebuilt Horton Hall from a plan now in Mr. Powell's possession, which shows how he used up the timbers of the house then existing for the larger and more pretentious residence. Towards the close of 1675 he prepared an agreement with Nathan Sharp, of Wike, mason, for the building of " one piece of housing adjoining the now dwelling-house of Thomas Sharp, about 18 yds. or 19 yds. in length, $7\frac{1}{2}$ yds. in breadth, and about $6\frac{1}{2}$ yds. in height, at the square, and to pay for the same £46" (a very modest sum as building is now computed).

An inspection of this interesting relic of old Bradford shows the original building to have been completely encompassed by the newer erection, the ancient timber-built walls, once outside, being plainly visible now within the building. The old erection, judging by its appearance, seems to have been six " crooks " in length, a " crook " representing the span of the original roof timbers. The entrance-hall on the north side of the building is low and quaint in appearance, showing the ancient timber supports of very substantial character.

The original entrance was by an arched doorway, the arms of the Sharps being thereon. There was a courtyard, having on one side the blank wall of some outbuildings, and another courtyard, which were thrown together by Mr. Edward Hailstone to form one large court. The panelling on the north side of the hall has been brought forward. The space to the back, where a pillar was put up by Mr. Hailstone to support the ceiling, was originally two rooms, with a passage between, and there were folding-doors, one towards the hall, and the other the library. One space was called the "Tinello," the Italian expression for "servants' hall." The reception-rooms contained good work in oak, the wall decoration and ceiling reliefs being evidently of later date than 1680, the period when the old mansion was completed by Thomas Sharp.

A quaint and picturesque appearance is given to the frontage on the south side by the projecting porch, forming the base of a square tower. This formed part of the original structure, and was used by Abraham Sharp for his observatory, from whence his observations of the heavens were taken. The room known as Abraham Sharp's study had an internal railing, with a door and slide window, through which, it was said, meals were served to him while engaged in his studies. The railing was some years ago taken down to fit the room for use. The chamber over the washhouse outside was his workshop, and in the window are the original pieces of wood to which Sharp's lathe was attached. The sketch given of Horton Hall shows the observatory tower used by Abraham Sharp. A wing to the right has given place to a handsome modern residence.

This house, so famous for many stirring and interesting associations, was early resorted to by the Nonconformists of the period as a place of worship. A large room on the ground floor, afterwards used by Mr. Hailstone for a portion of his library, was licensed in 1672 by the Rev. Thomas Sharp, Abraham's elder brother, for preaching therein, and on the inside of the capacious window are scratched by his hand the initials **T. S.** During the occupancy of his father, John Sharp, the Parliamentarian, Horton Hall was frequently

Horton Hall.

resorted to by Oliver Heywood, in whose diaries there are frequent references to the visits paid by him. Two only must suffice :—

Decem. 3, 1666, went to Mr. John Sharpes at Little Horton, where Mr. Sharpe having appointed a meeting where he was to preach they put me upon that work in his roome.

Mar. 5, 1671, I was called to keep a private fast at Mr. Sharpe's in Little Horton. Much of the day was spent before I could get my hand to the work, worldly thoughts much prevailing, but afterwards while Joseph Lister was at prayer my heart was wonderfully melted and kept in a wonderful sweet frame.

The Joseph Lister referred to was doubtless the man who had served his apprenticeship to John Sharp, and was now on terms of Christian friendship with the family.

Thomas Sharp, who succeeded to the Horton estates upon the death of his father in 1672, received his education at the Bradford Grammar School, then a notable nursery of learning, and in 1649 entered Clare Hall, Cambridge, and became an excellent classical scholar and mathematician, acquiring the degree of Master of Arts. Entering holy orders in 1660, he afterwards became vicar of Adel, near Leeds. Calamy says—" He enjoyed the living only for a little while, for upon the Restoration, Dr. Hick, of Guiseley, challenged it as his." Mr. Sharp hereupon resigned, and could have had other preferment but for the Act of Uniformity, whereby he was silenced. He retired to his father's house at Horton, and married a daughter of Mr. Bagnall.

Upon the death of his father in 1672 the Rev. Thomas Sharp procured the licence for worship at Horton Hall, and there exercised the ministry with great acceptance to a large number of persons of like religious views with himself. His first wife dying he married Faith, a daughter of the Rev. James Sale, of Pudsey, by whom he had several children. He afterwards accepted the pastorate of the Independent Chapel at Morley, and subsequently that of Mill Hill Chapel, Leeds, where he removed, meanwhile continuing his house at Horton. He died at Leeds in 1693, leaving his widow, and a son and two daughters, viz., Dr. John Sharp ; Elizabeth, who married Robert Stansfield, a drysalter, and whose son, Robert by a second marriage, became owner by purchase of the Esholt estates; and a daughter who died young.

Dr. John Sharp was a man of great promise, but died at a premature age. He was born in 1674, and at twenty-three years of age proceeded to study physic at Leyden, as appears from a memorandum book in the possession of Mr. Powell. From this interesting relic we glean particulars of his journey to Holland, the outfit required for a medical student of his time, and other particulars. Thus, under date of 1697, we find the items :—

	£	s.	d.
Passing from Rotterdam to Leyden	6	3	0
Porter	0	1	0
Weekly reckoning	3	1	2
Sword belt	1	0	2
Buckles	0	2	4
Scissors Case	0	2	4
Pencil	0	0	4
Scissors	0	2	0
Wafers	0	0	6
A quire of Paper	0	0	6
Snuff-box and Snuff	0	2	2½
Wax Candles	0	2	0
Quills	0	0	5½
Spent at the Anatomy Class	0	4	0
To the Rector, for Matriculation	1	10	0
Weekly reckoning	3	4	0
Wash gloves	0	15	0
Teapot	0	3	2
Handkerchiefs	1	3	0

The date of his matriculation was the year 1699, when he was twenty-five years of age, as appears from entries in the memorandum book as follows, he having prior to that event made a journey to England :—

1699.—Tuesday, 7th of 6th, at 3 ok, set sayle from Hull towards Rotterdam. Staid at anchor 2 leagues from land.
Wednesday, at 4 o'clock, weighed anchor with wind S.W.

Under date 22nd October, 1699, is the form of his matriculation. Dr. John Sharp died in 1704, aged thirty years.

By his decease, Horton Hall became the property and residence of Abraham, the second son of John Sharp, the Parliamentarian. This distinguished man was born at Horton in 1651, in the building still associated with his name. He received his education at the Bradford Grammar School, which had been the seminary of his distinguished relative, Archbishop Sharp, Dr. Richardson, of Bierley, and others. The story of his life has been oft repeated, and but a brief reference need now be made. On leaving school he was bound apprentice to a mercer at York; but his mind was averse to trading, and his indentures were "broken" in order that he might give himself to scientific pursuits. At first he resided near Liverpool, but appears to have gone to London when nineteen years of age, in the position of bookkeeper to a merchant, and it was while filling this situation that he contracted a friendship with Flamsteed, the astronomer, who secured him as his assistant at Greenwich Observatory, then recently erected. At twenty-four years of age Abraham had made such progress in astronomical science that it is said he had constructed or regulated all the instruments used in the famous Greenwich Observatory. In 1694 he returned to Horton. During this period of nearly a quarter of a century he appears to have kept entries of every half-penny he expended, as is shown by memorandum books to which, through Mr. Powell's courtesy, we have had access, and this methodical habit he kept up after his return to Horton, and probably until his death at over ninety years of age. Unfortunately many of the celebrated mathematician's papers and astronomical memoranda and calculations have been destroyed, some being only thought fit for lighting fires, and hence it is doubtful whether the life-story of a very remarkable Hortonian is now available.

The handwriting in such memorandum books as have been preserved is of the most minute character, requiring the aid of a magnifying glass to thoroughly decipher the contents. In them we find many curious entries; mathematical calculations, entries relating to purchase of material for making scientific instruments, books, articles of wearing apparel, cost of living, &c., all mixed up together in the order apparently in which they were expended. Thus, under date of the year 1685, we cull the following items:—

	£	s.	d.
Boat hire to Greenwich	0	2	0
Phil. Transactions	2	9	0
Pd. for tying cravats	0	1	5
Washing 9d., spent 6d	0	1	3
Pd. for 12 doz. hair buttons	0	6	0
4 yds. Shalloon	0	15	0
Pd. for Transactions	0	18	0
A letter	0	0	8
Pair of Stockings	0	4	6
Brass wyer	0	3	9
Conquest of China	0	1	6
Dressing hat	0	0	6
A dictionary	0	1	6
Lens	0	2	2
A pair of brass Compasses	0	3	0
3 Ground Wheels	0	3	6
Boat hire to Greenwich	0	1	3
Gellibrand's Trigonometry	0	10	0
Ink horn	0	0	4
4 glasses for a six-foot	0	10	0
Pratts' Architecture	0	6	6
Paid for a hone	0	1	6
Pd. for Arcad. Princ.	0	6	0
Clear Varnish—6 bottles	0	2	7
2 pieces Lignum Vitae	1	18	0
2 rolls of brass wyre, 27lb. 5oz., at 18d.	2	0	6
Gloves and tying cravat	0	5	6
Gold Thread	0	0	8
Loadstone	0	6	0

There are many other items relating to personal expenses, cost of living, &c.

Abraham Sharp returned to Little Horton in 1694, shortly after the death of his elder brother Thomas, and never left it afterwards for any lengthened period. He never married, but devoted his life to the study of astronomical subjects. His workshop was fitted with every description of astronomical instruments, all made by his own hands, a list of which made at his death, and the valuation, together with some of his account books, are in Mr. Hailstone's possession, as also his walking-stick, fitted with glasses as a telescope.

There is also a fine orrery in the museum at York, made by Abraham Sharp. His communications with Flamsteed were kept up at Horton, as is evidenced by the mention made of postage of letters from the great astronomer.

Mr. Sharp was very irregular at his meals, and remarkably sparing in his habits. A little square hole, something like a window, afforded communication between the room where he was generally employed in calculations, and another chamber or room in the house where a servant could enter, and before the hole he contrived a slide. The servant always placed his victuals, without speaking or making the least noise, and when he had a little leisure time he visited his cupboard to see what it afforded to satisfy his hunger and thirst. But it often happened that the breakfast, dinner, and supper remained untouched by him, and when the servant went to remove what was left the philosopher was found to have been so deeply engaged in his calculations that he had quite forgotten all about his meals. Mr. Sharp is said to have been "one of the most accurate computors ever known." It is to be regretted, however, that he devoted his talents to such futile efforts as "squaring the circle," constructing logarithms to *sixty-one* places of decimals, &c., instead of more practical work.

It is said that he lived the life of a recluse, rarely holding communication with any one. Two friends, however, had the privilege of his acquaintance, namely, Dr. Swaine, of Hall Ings, and a Mr. Dawson, who were admitted by the signal of rubbing a stone against a certain part of the outside of his rooms. Abraham Sharp attended the Presbyterian Chapel at Bradford, of which he was a member, and every Sunday he took care to be provided with plenty of halfpence, which he very charitably suffered to be taken out of his hand, held behind him during his walk to the chapel, by the poor people who followed. He never looked back or asked a single question.

Whatever the nature of his scientific studies, astronomical and mathematical, Abraham Sharp evidently kept a close eye upon the management of his estate and his household expenses, as is evidenced by the minute accounts he kept of every item of receipts and expenditure. Thus in the year 1710, under dates June, July, and September, we find such items as the following :—

	£	s.	d.
Pd. Thos. Myers for making my black coat	0	3	6
Ben Bartlett for dressing sister's leg, and salve	0	2	0
Robert Stansfield to be laid out for funeral exs.	38	0	0
Registering Sister's Will	0	5	8
At Chapel for quarter which sister left	0	10	0
David Rodes for shearing, 7 days	0	3	6
For a load of wheat	0	15	6

And under date 1712, the following details :—

	£	s.	d.
Paid Land tax for Brecon Hill	0	19	3
Land tax for Ferrand Close	0	13	4
½-yr. Land tax for Shibden Hall land and Howgate Farm	1	8	4
Earl Warren's rent for Shibden Hall (land)	0	8	0
Lord's rents for land in Sowerby	0	6	9
Uncle Abm. Sharp's interest	20	0	0
Abm. Jewett 1½ year for window tax	1	10	0
Wm. Raper, for monument in Church	11	15	0
8 load of lyme and leading stones for balcony	0	8	0
Joseph Carr, for plastering 8 yards	0	8	0
8 stroak hair to Mr. Swain	0	2	8
100 slates to John Booth, and leading	0	6	6
Wm. Ellis for his work	0	13	0

On the other side of the account for the last-named year we obtain some insight into the sources of Abraham Sharp's income, as follows :—

	£	s.	d.
Rd. of John Horton for trees	0	9	8
Jos. Stansfield for his father's Whit-rents	6	8	0
Jos. Stansfield for Higher End rents	1	2	0
Rd. Ingham for Pudsey Mart	1	11	6
Henry Atkinson for a calf	0	15	0
Robt. Myers last ½ yr.'s rent	1	11	6
John Dobson, ½ yr.'s rent	1	17	2
Thos. Craven, ½ yr.'s rent	4	12	0
John Burrow, ½ yr.'s	1	18	0
Abr. Sharp board, one year £8 0 0			
For Near and Far Langsides, whole year	10	13	0
Abm. Firth, ½ yr.'s rent	5	4	6
For a red cow and calf	5	7	6
Of uncle Josiah for a red cow and calf	5	16	0
Of Abm. Jewett for blind horse "Hugh"	2	2	0

The total income for the year 1712, as shown in the account, is £205 13s. 0d.

Notwithstanding his irregular habits, night watches, and laborious studies, Abraham Sharp lived to reach the 91st year of his age, and died in July, 1742. There is a monument to his memory in the chancel of Bradford Parish Church. In his will he bequeathed a house to the minister of the "Dissenters' Meeting Chapel, Bradford."

Abraham Sharp having died a bachelor, the Horton estates of his branch of the family were enjoyed by his grandniece Faith, the daughter of Robert Stansfield, the latter having married Abraham's niece Elizabeth. There were six sons and two daughters of this marriage, but only Faith survived. She married, in 1722, Richard Gilpin Sawrey, of Horton, a magistrate, and died in 1767 without issue, this branch of the Sharp family therefore ending with her death. By her will Mrs. Sawrey bequeathed to Hannah Gilpin, the daughter of William Gilpin, formerly of Whitehaven, and then residing with her, the mansion at Horton wherein she dwelt, with all her other messuages situate in Bradford, Great and Little Horton, Burley, Wheatley, Guiseley, and Farsley, &c. Hannah Gilpin took the name of Sharp, and in 1769, two years after coming to the Horton estates, entered into matrimony with Mr. Charles Swaine Booth, the son of the Rev. Charles Booth, of Bradford.

Reference has previously been made to the influential family of Swaine, of Horton. The family had also a Bradford branch, which occupied a good house standing at one time in Hall Ings. Here Dr. Swaine resided, and here, according to an extract from the *Halifax Journal* of April, 1759, there died a Miss Swaine, "whose virtue and charity made her death greatly lamented." She left her property to her nephew, Charles Booth, barrister-at-law, who hereupon added the name of Swaine to his own, which was that of a family of considerable standing in Horton so far back as 1608. His father, the Rev. Charles Booth, married a daughter of Mr. William Swaine, of Bradford, whose monument is in Bradford Parish Church. Charles Swaine Booth therefore acquired the property of both the Bradford Swaines and the

Booths. Swaine Street was named after him. By his marriage with Hannah Gilpin Sharp he acquired further property and influence, and in compliment to his wife added the name of Sharp, and for many years resided at Horton Hall. During his lifetime the new portion now fronting to Horton Lane was added, a wing of the old residence built by the Rev. Thomas Sharp being removed for the purpose.

Charles Swaine Booth Sharp died without issue in 1805, leaving his widow, Hannah Gilpin, or better known as Madam Sharp. He left the property coming to him from the Swaines and the Booths, after bequeathing certain legacies and confirming the settlement made upon his marriage, to his sisters, Beatrix Rishton, widow, and Sarah Booth, widow, and after them to his nephew, the Rev. Godfrey Wright, of Hooton Pagnall, and his heirs. His widow, Mrs. Hannah Gilpin Sharp, died in May, 1823.

By her will Madam Sharp bequeathed the mansion at Horton, with all her estates in Bradford and elsewhere, to her nephew, Captain Thomas Gilpin, and his male heirs, and in default of issue to her niece, Ann Kitchen, widow of Major Kitchen, in the service of the East India Company, and her heirs; and in default to the daughters of Captain Gilpin, conditionally upon their residing at Horton. Captain Gilpin, after enjoying the estates three years only, died at Madeira in the year 1826, without having been married, whereupon Ann Kitchen came to the property, and married in 1828 Mr. Edward Giles, a clerk in Somerset House, for her second husband, who died in 1832, leaving an infant son, Edmund, heir to the Horton estates.

This son Edmund went to Australia, being enamoured of sea life, but never returned, as he only lived three days after landing in the far-off colony. He was twenty-five years of age. Mrs. Haines, of London, then came into possession, she being the daughter of Mrs. Giles by her first marriage. In 1839 an Act was passed for disposing of the Giles estate at Horton, owing to the great increase of buildings and manufactories in the immediate vicinity. The property extended over many portions of Horton, including that fringing both sides of Horton Lane, where it was intersected by the estate of Colonel Fitzgerald, formerly belonging to Samuel Lister.

The next tenant of Horton Hall was Mr. John Wood, the philanthropic manufacturer, and after him Mr. Samuel Hailstone, attorney. Mrs. Giles, however, had a portion of Horton Hall reserved for her own residence after Mr. Hailstone took it, and resided there a short time every year. Joshua Smith, an old servant of Madam Sharp, was the caretaker. The occupancy of the hall was continued by Mr. Edward Hailstone, after the death of his father, until his removal to Walton Hall in 1870, and it is now the residence of Mr. Ezra Waugh Hammond.

Horton Hall and grounds were bought by Mr. F. S. Powell in 1871 from Giles's trustees, and again form part of the Sharp estate.

CHAPTER X.

Horton Old Hall—The Sharp Family—Their Ancient Possessions—John Sharp, the Royalist—Lieutenant Isaac Sharp—The Stapletons—The Bridges—The Powells—Francis Sharp Powell.

Continuing our notice of the Sharp family of Horton, we now refer to the younger branch, whose seat for probably 250 years has been that known as Horton Old Hall, the residence of Mr. Francis Sharp Powell.

In tracing Mr. Powell's descent as a representative of the Sharp family, we are materially assisted by the Sharp pedigree, drawn for Mr. Powell by Mr. Courthorpe, of the College of Arms. That pedigree is rendered very complete from the time of Christopher Sharp, of Horton, who died a Roman Catholic, in 1543. He left a son John, father of Thomas Sharp, who died in 1607, and was the immediate progenitor of the stock from whence sprang the two main branches of the Sharp family of Horton.

In a previous article we quoted from documents showing a Thomas and a John Sharp to have been parties to transfers of land in Horton in the years 1365 and 1390. In the absence of registers of the period it may not be possible to connect the Sharps just referred to with Christopher Sharp, who died in 1543, but from the continuous occurrence of the name of Sharp as follows, viz. :—1390, Thomas; 1402, Thomas; 1461, John; 1483. Christopher; and 1530, Christopher — it may reasonably be assumed that the Christopher above named was a member of the family whose history we are tracing, and that the family had a common origin.

Thomas Sharp, who died in 1607, was evidently a man of considerable means. He is described as a yeoman and clothier. In October of 1589 he had conveyed to him, along with Thomas Hodgson, Robert Booth, and Wm. Feild, 250 acres of the unenclosed wastes at Horton, and fourteen acres lately enclosed, by Richard Lacy and John, his son. These Lacies were of the Cromwellbotham family of that name, and

were lords of the manor of Horton, having acquired the
Leventhorpe interest in the manor by marriage. Thos. Sharp
also added considerably to the estate left him by his father—
which comprised " one thing of the best of any kind of
vessel accustomed to be 'occupied' in his house at Horton "
—by purchasing various portions of the landed property in
Horton held by the family of Wood. Mr. John James, in
his account of the Horton families of an early period, stated
that John Sharp, the father of Thomas, was assessed in 1545
upon £20 value in goods, " which was the only assessment to
that amount in Horton, except that on Humphrey Wood,
who paid the same," and that in the assessment of 1552 he
was assessed for £16 in goods, " the largest assessment in
Horton, except that of Thomas Wood, who was charged the
same."

Through the courtesy of Mr. Powell we have had access
to many ancient deeds showing the large extent of land held
by the Wood family in Horton at one time, which was
without doubt acquired from the Lacies of Cromwellbotham,
as Rosamund, the wife of Thomas Wood, was a daughter of
John Lacy, living in 1558. We have before us a copy of
feoffment, dated 1558, from " John Lacy and Richard his son
to Thos. Woode and Rosamund his wife of one messuage and
five oxgangs of land in Little Horton, at the yearly rent of
£2 13s. 4d., payable at Pentecost and Martinmas." In 1591
a friendly suit was instituted, wherein Thomas Wood and
Rosamund his wife were plaintiffs, and John Lacy defendant,
in respect to " one messuage, six crofts, two gardens, sixty
acres of land, forty acres of meadow, and forty acres of
pasture in Horton." In 1572 John Lacy, of Leventhorpe,
conveyed to Thos. Wood " three parcels of land lately taken
from the waste, rendering knight's service, suit of court at
Horton, and an annual rent of one red rose."

Other examples might be given furnishing testimony to
the standing of the Wood family in Horton at the period
referred to ; it may, however, be equally interesting to note
how and to whom their estates became transferred, for it is
certain that the family has been of no repute in the township
for more than two centuries.

It was about the close of the sixteenth century, then, that for some cause the Woods disposed of their Horton lands, as about that period numerous conveyances are dated, a few examples of which may be given :—

1592.—Indenture made 8th day of January, between Thos. Wood, of Askwith, yeoman, Rosamund, his wife, and John Wood, son and heir apparent, on the one part, and Jasper Brighthouse, or Brighouse, of Bradford, yeoman, of the other part, whereby, in consideration of the sum of threescore and ten pounds of lawful English money paid to them by the said Jasper Brighthouse, the said Thomas, Rosamund, and John Wood convey to him all those three closes of land called the Hollingreave lands, *alias* Spittle Roods, Cross Butts, and Souther Half-acres, situate and being in Horton in Bradford-dale, now in the tenure of the said Jasper Brighthouse, &c.

Witnesses—William Hallsteade, John Lacie, Henry Packet, Samuel Tailer, William Currer, Thomas Tailer, attorney,

1601.—Conveyance from Thomas Wood and his wife Rosamund to Thomas Sharp, sen., and John, his son, of a messuage with outbuildings (in three tenements), lands, &c., all in Horton, in the tenure of Richard Booth, Robert Balme, and William Booth (except three closes called the Langside), and also of the two Southcrofts, Ackers, Leysteads, and Northcroft, and of several yearly rents as follows :—viz., 30s. and a boyne hen out of a cottage and lands at Haycliffe ; another of 12d. out of Hollingreave Lands ; another out of a close called Broad-dole ; and another out of a close called Huetson Yeard, *alias* Hutcheon Yeard, all in Horton.

Other deeds might be cited showing transfers from Thomas Wood and his wife about the same period, thus : In 1592, conveyance of the Intack Close and a close called Two Lands, to Thos. Hunter ; 1601, conveyance of messuage in Horton and close of land called the Bent, to Chris. Sharp and Samuel his son ; 1601, conveyance of three closes of land called Far Langsides to Robert Heaton.

In endeavouring to trace the various properties alluded to, documentary evidence is afforded that nearly the whole passed into the hands of the Thomas Sharp named above, confirming the statement that he was a man of considerable means. Thus in 1606, John Sharp, his son and heir, contemplated marriage with Susan, a daughter of Richard Waterhouse, of Shelf. In consideration of that marriage, Thomas Sharp re-leased to his son, by indenture dated June 15, 1606, "all the messuage, lands, &c., purchased by him of Thomas Wood, of Askwith, and of John Wood, his son and heir. Also all that close called the Intack, or Bowling Mill close, late in the tenure of William Law, and purchased by Thomas Sharp of Thomas Hodgson, late of Bolling, deceased; also the Hollingreave lands, and the third part of a close called the Haycliffe, and in a place called Nethermore; and also the third part of a close of land lately enclosed from the common of Horton on the north and east side of a hill called Haycliffe, and in a place called Over Moor." On his part Richard Waterhouse, the father of the intended bride, agreed to assign to John Sharp, his intended son-in-law, "all that messuage in Shelf wherein he dwelt," also the sum of £150, &c., upon the consummation of the marriage. The attorney who drew up the necessary documents was Abraham Lister, of Bolling. Thomas Sharp had already made over to his son the two Southcrofts, the Northcroft, the Ackers, the Leysteads, and the Southern Half-acres, all in Horton.

The frequent references to enclosures made from the "wastes" of Horton afford good ground for fixing the date when the main portion of the township was common land, and the recurrence of terms like the "Two Lands," "Broaddole," "Cross Butts," "Southern Half-acres," &c., is equally suggestive of a period prior to the age of enclosures, when such lands were held in common, *i.e.*, "Common Fields." These common fields were generally of three descriptions, for the unvarying round of growing winter corn, spring corn, and fallow. They were respectively divided into oxgangs, evenly scattered over every field, in order to give more facility for the system of ploughing then in vogue, and for other desirable purposes. There was likewise the common meadow, while other portions of the township were laid out in pasture, as an appendant to the common field land, each oxgang having a right to a limited number of "gates" for cows and working oxen. The "Common Fields" were distributed over the township. Hence we derive the terms Southfield (Southfield Lane), Northfield, Westfield, &c. Almost every township "round about Bradford" furnishes evidence of this remote period, either in the present appearance of the land or the names which still remain.

We have also mention of the ancient forms of rent and services rendered by the holders of lands. Thus, three parcels of land taken from the "waste" rendered "Knight's service, suit of Court at Horton, and an annual rent of one red rose." Thomas Sharp's purchase of the North Crofts, the Leysteads, &c., was charged with the yearly rent of "30s. and one boyne hen," &c. The payment of a red rose, "in the time of roses," was a common form of acknowledgment where the title was not of the clearest. "Boynes" (*alias* "boons") were services rendered, so many days' ploughing or reaping, and called "plough-boons" and "sickle boons." "Hens" were often reserved as a species of rent in kind to be paid, generally, at Shrove-tide. The custom was a survival of the Anglo-Saxon "gafol," a tribute. The subject of these old customs suggested by the above terms although digressive is interesting, and may be alluded to at a future opportunity.

John Sharp, who thus became endowed with a considerable portion of his father's possessions, was only a younger son, there being two brothers older than himself, viz., Isaac, who died at a comparatively early age and was named in his father's will, and Thomas, the eldest brother, who died in 1636. The latter, who succeeded to the family mansion at Horton (that known as Horton Hall), became the father of John Sharp, the noted Parliamentarian and Puritan, whose career and that of his family, which included the Rev. Thos. Sharp, the Nonconformist preacher, and Abraham Sharp, the astronomer and mathematician, were traced in a previous article.

John Sharp, whose line we must now take up, was as ardent a Royalist and as distinguished on the King's side as his nephew became on that espoused by Parliament. He was in several battles on the side of Charles I., during one of which he received a severe contusion on the head with a battle axe. Notwithstanding, he lived to over seventy years of age, although he was wont to say that but for the awkward blow on his cranium he might have lived to be an "old man." So distressed was John the Royalist at the fate of his Royal master, that it is said he never suffered his beard to be shaven

Rambles Round Horton.

or his hair to be cut after the execution of Charles I. at Whitehall. The headpiece worn by him in the Civil Wars is preserved among the family heirlooms at Horton Old Hall, along with armour, swords, &c.; also the helmet and armour worn by Isaac Sharp, his son, a lieutenant in the Train Bands; a cannon ball picked up after the siege of Bradford, and other relics of that momentous period. It is from this branch of the Sharp family that Mr. F. S. Powell is descended.

John Sharp's interest in the affairs of his household, however, must have been actively maintained, notwithstanding his zealous partisanship. During his lifetime he added considerably to the family estates—as we find from the family deeds in the possession of Mr. Powell—in addition to the property inherited by him from his father. Among his purchases were two closes called Burnet Graves and Storbrokes, lying in Great Horton, from Elizabeth Bayrstow, of Barkerend; and Kent Close, in Little Horton, from Henry Walker, of Bradford. John, the Royalist, died in 1658, leaving two sons, Isaac and Thomas, the latter of South Kirkby.

Isaac Sharp, the eldest son, born in 1613, lived at Horton into the next century. He married Elizabeth Rhodes, of Mirfield. He was also an active partisan on the King's side, and received a commission as lieutenant in the Train Bands of Agbrigg and Morley, his company comprising 120 men. This document, signed by Buckingham, is dated May 22, 1653, and is in Mr. Powell's possession.

It is assumed that this branch of the family were resident in a house not above a stone's throw from that occupied by the elder branch, and it was left to Lieutenant Sharp to establish his family in a residence entitled to be ranked as a mansion of the period, namely, that in which Mr. Powell resides, and which was built upon the site of the older structure. There are several dates about the premises, showing the various stages of progress. Over a door in the building now used as estate offices on the western side of the courtyard is the date 1665. Over the entrance door on the south side of the hall is the date 1674; and over the fireplace in the south-west chamber the date 1675, with the initials I.S.—S.S. There is also a Latin motto of doubtful construction, as follows—*Mementem tu est mortallis*, and probably intended to remind all future occupiers that they were but mortal. The initials are said to be those of Isaac Sharp and his wife; but do not accord with the Christian name of the wife, Elizabeth (who was living at the time), except upon the assumption that some familiar cognomen was adopted by the carver. Lieutenant Sharp lived to the ripe old age of ninety-two, having survived all the troubles of the Civil War and the reigns of the second Charles, of James the Second, of William, Prince of Orange, and Mary, his wife; and he witnessed the accession of Queen Anne.

At his death in 1705, Lieutenant Sharp was succeeded by his son, also called Isaac, who inherited all his father's lands, and married in 1705 Elizabeth Wood, of Bramley. One of his sisters married the Rev. Matthew Smith, of Mixenden, and another Wm. Young, of Bradford, cutler. He died in 1743, but probate of his will was not obtained until 1761, a recital of which shows that he devised all his lands to Richard Gilpin Sawrey, of Horton, and John Smith, clerk, of Mixenden, in trust for the benefit of his daughter Dorothy, wife of Francis Stapleton; then to her daughter Elizabeth (married to Francis Bridges), and next to his granddaughter, Mary Stapleton. His estate was charged with an annual payment of 20s. to the preachers at Mixenden and Horton Chapels, "so long as Dissenting ministers shall be there."

Isaac Sharp is said by John James to have rebuilt the east end of the mansion at Horton; and, if so, he also contemplated the rebuilding of the house, judging by the following extract:—"All my goods I give (except the wood lying in the barn and the stones prepared for rebuilding the dwelling-house in which I live, to each devisee of my real estate as shall rebuild the same) to my daughter Dorothy, whom I constitute my executrix." The witnesses to the will were John Rhodes, clothier; James Hall, yeoman; and John Northrop, schoolmaster. Attested by Richard Wainman, attorney, and John Siddall, his clerk.

Isaac Sharp was the last of the male line of his branch of the family, and it is somewhat singular that the male line in the elder branch had ceased to exist within twelve months of his death, namely, in 1742, by the decease of Abraham Sharp, the mathematician.

In the recital of the terms of the will of the last Isaac Sharp there occurred two names brought newly upon the scene, the owners whereof were destined to play an important part in the family history which we are attempting to pourtray. The names in question were those of Stapleton and Bridges. Contemporary with these, however, was that of Powell, the respective representatives being Francis Stapleton, of Little Horton, born 1703; the Rev. Wm. Bridges, rector of Castleford in 1696 ; and Thos. Powell, of Bawdsley, co. Montgomery.

The Stapletons were living at Felliskirk, Yorkshire, in 1599, and one Francis gravitated towards Bradford as a drysalter, and married a daughter of Thomas Lister, of Manningham, a major under General Fairfax. Of this marriage was a son Francis, born in 1703, who married Dorothy, the surviving heiress of Isaac Sharp, above referred to. Meanwhile Thomas Bridges, of Leeds, son of the Rev. Wm. Bridges, married a daughter of the first Francis Stapleton, and their son, Francis Bridges, of Leeds and Horton, married the eldest daughter and co-heiress of the second Francis Stapleton and Dorothy Sharp. In this manner were the family interests of the Sharps, the Stapletons, and the Bridges bound together.

The eldest child of Francis Bridges and his wife (there being also several others, including Francis Sharp Bridges, afterwards of Horton Old Hall) was married to the Rev. Thos. Wade, of Bierley, and afterwards of Tottington, Lancashire ; and their sole surviving daughter and heiress, Anne, became the wife of the Rev. Benjamin Powell, of Bellingham Lodge, Wigan, a grandson of John Powell, of Bawdsley. The Rev. B. Powell died in 1861, aged sixty-nine, and his wife in 1873 at the same age. They had a family of eleven children, of whom there survive Mr. Francis Sharp Powell, the Rev. Thos, Wade Powell, of St. John's College, Cambridge, and four daughters, two of whom are married and have families.

Mr. Francis Sharp Bridges, as the only surviving son of Francis Bridges, of Leeds and Horton, succeeded not only to his father's Leeds estates, but to those at Horton belonging to the Sharp family. On his father's side he came of an old and respectable Leeds family. Thomas Bridges, his grandfather, who died in 1735, and who married Elizabeth Stapleton, was a noted antiquary and the intimate friend of Thoresby, the author of the "Ducatus Leodensis." Dr. Whitaker's estimate of him may be gathered from the following extract from a second edition of the "Ducatus," edited by the doctor, who, in his comment upon the inscription found in St. John's Cemetery, Leeds, says:—"It contains a memorial of a true antiquary, to whose activity and exactness in recording the transactions of this town (Leeds) and parish for a series of years the editor of 'Thoresby' has been greatly indebted." Thomas Bridges also gathered the most valuable collection of ancient medals which the town of Leeds had to boast since that of Thoresby. His son, Mr. Francis Bridges, was also of an antiquarian and literary turn, and was a great collector of coins, besides having got together a valuable library, containing examples of the earliest printed books, and many MS. volumes.

This collection of coins and books, it may be added, is in the possession of Mr. Powell, at Horton Old Hall. The cabinet in which the medals and coins are contained is in itself a treasure, the lock being surmounted by a bronze shield, said to have formed the lid of a snuff-box possessed by Charles I. at his execution. There is also a crescent-shaped bronze surmounting the shield, containing an antique design.

From certain entries in the rent roll of Francis Bridges, it would appear that in 1788 part of the Old Hall was let to John Wood, also the barn, outbuildings, the Laith Croft, Low Croft, New Croft, Far Burnet Graves, and Far Leysteads, at a rental of £34 per annum. John Wood died in 1795. Another part of the mansion, with cellar under Wood's part, was let to the Rev. John Dean, minister at the Unitarian Chapel. Mr. Francis Bridges, residing principally at Leeds, only retained a portion of the mansion in his own occupation. He died in 1795.

Rambles Round Horton.

The son of Mr. Francis Bridges, namely, Mr. Francis Sharp Bridges, resided at Horton Old Hall during the course of a long life. He was a bachelor, and lived singularly retired, his principal outward excursion being when he went to dine weekly with his two sisters at Hallfield House, Manningham Lane. Although very wealthy, he employed no servants beyond an antiquated housekeeper, named Mallinson, and a kitchen girl, keeping neither horses nor cattle on his homestead. His tall, erect, and portly figure; his white cravat, deep-frilled shirt, set off by a square-headed amber brooch, are remembered by many, as he took his "constitutional" on Horton Green, measured by the frontage of his residence. Mr. Bridges died in 1844, aged seventy-eight years.

Under his will the Horton estates are inherited by his nephew, Mr. Francis Sharp Powell, M.A., in addition to large properties in Lancashire left him by his father. Mr. Powell was born in 1827, his father, the Rev. Benjamin Powell, being at the time of his birth incumbent of St. George's Church, Wigan. Mr. Powell received his early education at Wigan Grammar School, and partly at Sedbergh Grammar School, an institution in which he has ever since maintained a lively interest, and in its management has, more than any one else, been the means of effecting an improvement. To such an extent has this been recognised that for some time he has been at the head of the board of governors. From Sedbergh Mr. Powell entered St. John's College, Cambridge; was elected a fellow in 1851; and graduated M.A. in 1853. In the same year he was called to the bar of the Inner Temple, and went the Northern Circuit two or three years, but his inclination was towards a political career. He has sat four times in Parliament in the Conservative interest, namely, for his native borough of Wigan, for Cambridge, and for the Northern Division of the West Riding. In recognition of his faithful services to his party, Mr. Powell had an excellent portrait of himself presented to him in October, 1884, by gentlemen connected with the Northern Division of Yorkshire.

Mr. Powell, however, is not exclusively a politician. His services are ever at the call of those whose aim is the promotion of philanthropy, educational advancement, religious propaganda, or social and sanitary reform. As a devoted Churchman he has given largely of his wealth to church extension and endowment in Bradford and the neighbourhood. He has expended upwards of £30,000 upon the erection of All Saints' Church, Horton Green, the schools, and the vicarage. As an example of ecclesiastical architecture of its period this church stands pre-eminently above any other in the town or immediate neighbourhood. He has also assisted in the erection of nine of the churches of Bradford projected by the society for promoting the building of ten churches, besides helping materially towards the erection of schools. He is a frequent contributor towards the deliberations of the Church Congress and Social Science Association, and an ardent advocate of the promotion of education, elementary, religious, and technical, being upon the councils of several colleges and institutions having these ends in view.

Mr. Powell married, in 1858, Annie, daughter of Mr. M. Gregson, of Liverpool, but has no family. The arms of the family are—Azure, a pheon argent, within a bordure or, charged with eight torteuxes. Crest, an eagle's head, erased azure ducally gorged or, holding in his mouth a pheon argent.

Horton Old Hall, a view of which is given as the frontispiece to this volume, is the residence of Mr. Powell while in Yorkshire, and is a substantial and characteristic example of the period of its erection, namely, that of the reign of Charles II. It is evident, however, from the existence of several branches of the Sharp family of Horton, that there were other residences belonging to them, that known as the "Old House at Home," at Holme Top, being probably one of them.

Horton Old Hall, however, as a residence of the family, is the only one preserving its continuity of connection, and in the hands of its recent possessors it has been preserved in excellent condition. It has two frontages, one towards All Saints' Church, and another overlooking the open fields townwards. As previously remarked, its position is admirable from a residential point of view, notwithstanding the encroachments of modern dwellings on various sides. The arrangements of the hall are those usually found in similar examples of the domestic architecture of the period, and comprise central hall open to the roof, with oaken gallery admitting to the retiring rooms above, and eastern and western wings, containing comfortable apartments such as are not always found in modern residences. The hall or "house-body" is wainscotted in oak of beautiful colour, and contains the armour and other relics previously alluded to, also a small collection of family portraits, including those of Abraham Sharp, the mathematician; Archdeacon Sharp, the son of the Archbishop; and others. The oak furniture of the hall is also in harmony with its surroundings.

In an adjoining apartment there is a fine portrait of Hogarth, painted by himself; an antique specimen of needlework and embroidery, probably three centuries old; and many articles of *vertu*, bespeaking the taste of the owner. The library is on the upper floor, upon the corridor of which there is a triptych taken from a Spanish monastery, and in its way one of the treasures of the house. It is divided into three folding leaves, containing compartments depicting various scenes in the life of our Lord, in illuminated colours of medieval workmanship. The library, from an antiquarian and bibliographic point of view, is really valuable, containing as it does collections of works representing the earlier printing age, ancient MSS. in Gothic characters, rescued from monastic archives on the Continent, besides several valuable early English manuscripts.

An adjoining bedroom contains a massive and richly-carved oak bedstead, which, tradition has it, once rested the limbs of the Protector during his brief residence at Horton Hall (the home of the Parliamentarian branch of the family). So far as we are aware, however, there is no record of old Noll ever having honoured Bradford by his presence; but it is an ungracious act to discredit old traditions, and we tell the story "as 'twas told to us."

We may add that Mr. Powell possesses many of the antiquarian tastes of his immediate predecessors at the Old Hall, but his more active interest in current topics prevents his prosecuting the study of archæology.

CHAPTER XI.

John Sharp, Archbishop of York—His Descent—His Early Years—His Promotion—His Family—Granville Sharp the Philanthropist—Wm. Sharp, Surgeon—Dr. Sharp, F.R.S.

This paper we propose to devote to that branch of the Sharp family with which John Sharp, D.D., Archbishop of York, is usually associated, and from whom sprang two archdeacons of Northumberland, Granville Sharp, the celebrated philanthropist, and others who have lived honourably amongst us. No apology should be needed for thus extending this record of a family which, although its members may not have been instrumental in introducing or extending the trade and commerce of Bradford, has nevertheless produced those who have served their country in the cause of religion and philanthropy, in the walks of medical science, and in literature.

At the outset, however, we are confronted with a difficulty which has prevented others who have made the attempt from clearly establishing the connection between the Archbishop's branch and that of the two families whose history we have already traced. The difficulty appears to commence with the question of the relationship of James Sharp, witness to the will of Christopher Sharp, in 1530, and of Christopher Sharp, whose will is dated 1543. Although the point has not been clearly defined by the College of Arms, this James Sharp is supposed to have been a brother or near relative of Chris. Sharp, and father of James Sharp (grandfather of the Archbishop), as he died before 1557, leaving his son James, of Horton, clothier, who, according to Hopkinson's MS., lived in "a house late belonging to Kirkstall Abbey," and whose will is dated 1590. The matter is not one to interest the general reader, but to the genealogist it is a question which will stimulate much research until the moot point is satisfactorily set at rest.

From James Sharp, whose will is dated 1590, sprang John of Woodhouse and Parkhouse, Bierley; James, of Woodhouse; also Thomas, Grace, and Isaac. At present,

Rambles Round Horton. 123

however, we follow the line of the second son, James, who had with other issue James, of Woodhouse, who died in 1690, the progenitor of the Sharps of Gildersome, afterwards of Bradford ; and Thomas, of Bradford, born in 1606, and whose will was dated 1671.

This younger son, Thomas, followed the trade of a drysalter and oil dealer in Bradford. It is noticeable that the business of drysalter, or "salter" by abbreviation, was common in Bradford in those early days, and must have been a source of profit, as several families, the Stansfields and others, derived from it considerable wealth. The house in which Thomas Sharp resided and in which his eldest son, John, afterwards Archbishop of York and Metropolitan of England, was born, was situated upon the site of the building adjoining the Unicorn Inn, in Ivegate, on the western or upper side.

Within the recollection of old Bradfordians, the original building stood with its antique gables fronting to that busy thoroughfare, which, it is needless to add, is one of the most ancient streets in Bradford. The original appearance, however, is now unrecognisable, owing to the house having been fronted with shop premises. The building behind contained many of its original features, until it was removed within the present year to give place to a new erection.

Thomas Sharp, the drysalter, married Dorothy, daughter of John Weddall, rector of Widdington, Yorks, and her brother John settled in Bradford as a solicitor, if he did not learn his profession here. His office was in Church Bank or Stott Hill. The name of "John Weddall, attorney," is familiar to any rummager of old legal documents relating not only to Bradford, but to a wide district round about, indicating that his practice was an extensive one. He died in London suddenly and mysteriously, it was said, in the year 1672.

In the Rev. Oliver Heywood's diary occurs the following mention of Mr. Weddall :—

June, 1672.—Mr. Weddall, of Bradford, who hath been as great an attorney as any in the country, and was raised to a great estate of late, had built a sumptuous new house near the church, and had many men's businesses upon his hands. We were at dinner lately at Mr. Milner's funeral. Speaking of death, he said complimentally, " It will surely come," &c. I advised him not to go into his new house too soon. He answered " No, not till Michaelmas." He had been exceeding intent upon it, it must forward, was almost finished, he went up to the town, came into London on Monday, June 17, or Tuesday, but he dyed on Thursday, June 20, 1672. Some say he was seized upon by a palsy, others that he had been at a tavern and got hurt with drinking, but he is gone, and his wife takes on very heavily. They are left in a labyrinth of trouble, not knowing how things stand. He purposed that should be the last time of his going to London—so it proved.

Besides the future Archbishop, Thomas Sharp and Dorothy his wife had several children, viz. :—Hannah, Thomas, James, and Joshua. Their only daughter married John Richardson, of Birks Hall, attorney-at-law. James resided at Bradford in competence; and Joshua received knighthood in London.

The Archbishop's father and mother were religious and hospitable people, but were of a different way of thinking upon the disputes of those days. Thomas Sharp was inclined to Puritanism, and much favoured the Parliamentarian party, being himself in great favour with Lord Fairfax, who made his head-quarters at the house in Ivegate when in these parts. Among other expressions of his favour, the general is said to have offered a commission to his host, which probably might have been accepted had not his wife, who was a strenuous Royalist, stoutly opposed the proposal.

From his parents the future Archbishop early received those religious impressions which were never effaced. He was sent at an early age to the Bradford Grammar School, and while there his father had him taught a system of shorthand for the purpose of taking down every Sunday the sermons he heard at the Parish Church, and these he was called upon to repeat to the family each Sunday evening. This peculiar acquirement the Archbishop turned to good account in his maturer years. He was never at any other school than that of his native town, and he made such progress that at fifteen years of age his father determined to send him direct to the University and maintain him there for seven years. He was accordingly admitted to Christ College,

Cambridge, in April, 1660, just before the restoration of the King, his tutor being Abraham Brooksbank, afterwards vicar of Bradford.

While at Cambridge young Sharp was not idle, for in addition to classics and divinity he seemed to have made some progress in the study of chemistry and botany. In 1667 he left Cambridge owing to an attack of illness, and returned to his father's house at Bradford, to take the chance of preferment in some form. During his stay in Yorkshire the future Archbishop was a candidate for the curacy of Wibsey, but a more successful competitor obtained it. After being raised to the archiepiscopacy he invited the incumbent of Wibsey to dinner, and paid him the most marked attention as the providential cause of his own elevation. He presently afterwards received the appointment of domestic chaplain to Sir Heneage Finch, then Solicitor-General, who ever afterwards became his patron and friend.

Under his patron's roof, in Kensington House, young Sharp zealously continued his studies, and received valuable assistance from Sir Heneage Finch. In 1669 he took his M.A. degree, but again, owing to the closeness of his application to study, he was obliged to return to Bradford, and received benefit by the change. The opportunity occurred also of taking a last leave of his father, who was declining apace, and who died about a month after he left him, namely, in the year 1671. Returning to the home of Sir Heneage Finch, his patron, now Attorney-General, procured him the Archdeaconry of Berkshire, Mr. Sharp being then only twenty-eight years of age. His youth, indeed, caused him to accept the office with some diffidence, but for his encouragement his patron not only paid the expenses of his first visitation, but lent him his own servants and horses. Upon Sir Heneage Finch attaining the woolsack in 1673, his good offices towards his favourite chaplain were again exercised, and in the year 1675 he disposed of three preferments upon him, namely, by appointing him a prebend of Norwich, vicar of St. Bartholomew's, and rector of St. Giles's-in-the-Fields, all of which preferments were accompanied with further deeds of kindness.

It was as rector of St. Giles's that Dr. Sharp first won fame. During this period James II. had issued an order that the clergy should not preach on Popery, but the doctor notwithstanding preached his annual sermon, for which the King ordered the Bishop of London to suspend him. The Bishop refused, and this led to the seven bishops being sent to the Tower of London, and then to the abdication of James.

Towards the end of the spring of 1676 Dr. Sharp married Elizabeth, daughter of William Palmer, Esq., of Winthrop, in Lincolnshire, the marriage being solemnised by Dr. Tillotson, his intimate friend—another distinguished Yorkshireman who filled an archiepiscopal throne as Archbishop of Canterbury. Dr. Sharp's own elevation to the Archbishopric of York took place in 1691. By the influence of Lord Nottingham he had been promoted to the deanery of Canterbury in 1689, vacant by the elevation of his friend Tillotson, and in the summer of 1690 he visited Bradford, where his mother still resided. In May, 1691, the aged Archbishop of York, Lamplugh, died, and, by the joint influence of Lord Nottingham and Archbishop Tillotson, Dr. Sharp obtained the see. He was only in his forty-seventh year when he mounted the archiepiscopal throne of York.

Soon after his consecration he first drew up a short account of the most material things which had ever happened to him till that time, and which laid the foundation for the Archbishop's diary, from whence was drawn material for the " Life of Archbishop Sharp," written by his son Thomas, Archdeacon of Northumberland. Soon after the accession of Queen Anne, when the Archbishop began to have more business upon his hands, his memoranda grew more frequent and particular, and instead of the weekly account he kept a proper diary or journal, which from the year 1702 to 1713, the last eleven years of his life, makes up five volumes quarto, all written in his own shorthand.

Archbishop Sharp held the archiepiscopal see of York longer than any of his predecessors since the Reformation viz., above two and twenty years. During that long period the conscientious manner in which he discharged its duties has long ago become historical. Although we cannot here follow up his career, prominence may be given to two rules which at the outset he laid down for his own guidance—the first being that no one but a Yorkshire clergyman should hold a benefice in his gift ; his other rule was, never to meddle in the election of members of Parliament. In looking after his diocese and the clergy in it he has had no successor more industrious ; while as a preacher he was especially renowned. His published works are principally sermons, and at one time he was remarkably prolific. He was also an industrious collector of coins, and was a great friend of Ralph Thoresby, the antiquary. Archbishop Sharp died at Bath on February 2nd, 1713, in the 70th year of his age. He lies interred in the Cathedral at York, where a sumptuous monument is erected over his remains.

Of his marriage with Elizabeth Palmer the Archbishop had fourteen children, seven sons and seven daughters, of whom, however, two only of each sex survived him. Thomas, his younger son, was made Archdeacon of Northumberland in 1722, and was no less distinguished than the Archbishop had been for integrity, piety, and a conscientious discharge of his duty. His writings are very numerous. Among the most valuable is a life of the Archbishop, which includes a collection of many of his letters and other papers. He married Judith, youngest daughter of Sir George Wheler, a prebend of Durham, and died in 1758, having been the father of a numerous offspring, of whom five sons and three daughters arrived at maturity. His eldest son, John, succeeded to his father's principal dignities in the church, viz., as Prebendary of Durham and Archdeacon of Northumberland. He was also vicar of Hartburn, and perpetual curate of Bamburgh. He is distinguished in the records of British humanity at Bamburgh Castle in Northumberland—which as a charitable asylum has a history almost unparalleled in the kingdom.

Bamburgh Castle played an important part in the Wars of the Roses ; the battles of Towton and Hexham, together with the siege of Bamburgh Castle, which surrendered to King Edward IV., tending to place the crown more firmly on that monarch's head. Although of very ancient foundation, the castle acquired its present interest from its bequest by Lord Crewe, Bishop of Durham, along with considerable estates in Durham and Northumberland, for the purposes of benevolence, the augmentation of livings, the founding of schools, &c. The fund seems to have been faithfully disbursed by the trustees, but not upon any permanent system until Dr. John Sharp succeeded to his father's position as chief of the trustees, and took its affairs into his own management.

Bamburgh Castle is situated on an almost perpendicular rock close to the sea, accessible only on the south-east side on a spot where (according to the monkish historians) once stood the palace of the kings of Northumberland, built by Ida about the year 560, and part of the present ruins are supposed to be the remains of his work. The rock on which it is placed is 150 ft. above low-water mark, and after the structure had fallen to decay was famous only for the wreck of vessels and the helpless cry of forlorn mariners thrown on the coast. Some partial repairs had been undertaken for the purpose of holding the manor courts and of forming a temporary dwelling for a religious minister within the castle, when the view of its stately remains of ancient grandeur and of the distress and danger which surrounded them suggested to Dr. Sharp more enlarged designs and ideas of relief proportionate to the magnitude of the occasion. Plans were laid down and preparations made for roofing and clearing out the great tower or keep, and adapting its spacious contents to the service of several charitable establishments. The upper storey of the tower was formed into granaries, whence in times of scarcity corn was distributed to the indigent, without distinction, at a low price. The lower storey was divided into rooms for the manor court; schools for educating the children of the poor; a hospital with accommodation for incurables; a dispensary and a general surgery, with cold and warm baths for poor persons of all descriptions.

Dr. Sharp resided at Bamburgh several months in the year, and during his life expended a large part of his own property on the place. He died in April, 1792, having bequeathed an estate, his library, and other property for the preservation of the castle. At Bamburgh Castle are preserved many memorials of the Sharp family. There is a very fine portrait of Archdeacon Sharp, also his ancient Sedan chair; and in the church a fine monument of him by Chantrey.

William Sharp, another brother, was most eminent in his profession as surgeon in London, where he practised for thirty-seven years, and was also surgeon to St. Bartholomew's Hospital.

Granville Sharp, the most distinguished of the sons of Archdeacon Sharp, was born at Durham in 1735, and was intended for the London mercery trade. Passing over the details of his younger days, a short outline of his life ought to interest every Englishman. His great works may be classed under four principal heads, viz. :—The liberation of African slaves in England; the colonisation of Sierra Leone; the establishment of Episcopacy in America; and the abolition of the slave trade. To these may be added his attempt to reconcile the British colonies with England at the commencement of the American troubles. While his efforts were at various periods directed towards one or other of the above objects, his monument as a philanthropist is based upon the self-denying efforts put forth by him in the interests of the slave.

It has been customary to place the name of Clarkson and Wilberforce in the front rank in the movement leading to the abolition of slavery; but, without detracting from the good work done by them, it is simply a matter of history that Granville Sharp first struck the blow which severed the chain of the negro slave. Clarkson joined him, and the two together prepared the way and made it possible for Wilberforce to bring the subject before Parliament, and, with the assistance of William Pitt, obtain the desired Acts of Emancipation.

An instance of the length to which disrespect for human freedom had proceeded may be quoted from the newspapers of the period. Thus, in April, 1769, an advertisement appeared in the *London Gazetteer*, in which, among other "goods and chattels," mention was made of "a chesnut gelding, a Tim Whisky, and a *well made, good-tempered black*

I

boy." No wonder that such open dealing in human flesh should have aroused the better feelings of men of Granville Sharp's calibre. He had about ten trials during five years before Lord Mansfield, Lord Chief Justice of England, for setting free slaves in London, before he succeeded in getting a declaration from the judge that English laws knew nothing of slavery. When the action was brought against him for having "stolen goods" in his possession, Granville Sharp could not persuade a single barrister to take up his brief. All these learned gentlemen said he was in the wrong, and that the chief legal authority was against him. This was true enough, but it had only the effect of spurring the noble-minded man to further effort, one result being that he set to work to study the laws of England for himself in order to defend his own case. Granville Sharp succeeded in his first trial, and then persevered in bringing on a succession of trials by obtaining writs of *habeas corpus* against individual slave-holders; but it was not till after five years of personal fighting in the Court of King's Bench that he obtained a final judgment in his favour. Upon this, about 400 negroes were turned out into the streets by their masters, and in their emergency the whole body went to their liberator, Granville Sharp, who took care of them until he had secured the colony of Sierra Leone for a settlement and had seen them colonised, although this was not accomplished without involving considerable labour and embarassment upon the philanthropic promoter.

Granville Sharp's labours were equally conspicuous in other important points affecting the national character, which cannot at length be alluded to here. In addition to his national labours he was an active promoter of various religious, philanthropic, and literary institutions. He was also a voluminous writer of controversial literature, and was learned in languages. His death occurred in July, 1813, at the age of seventy-eight, and his remains lie at Fulham. A monument was, however, raised to his memory by the African Institution, and executed by Chantrey, in Poets' Corner, Westminster Abbey, which contains an inscription setting forth his many virtues.

Having so far as space permits referred to the more distinguished members of Archbishop Sharp's branch of his family, we turn with pleasure to the elder stock which, like the junior branch, traces its descent from James Sharp, of Horton, clothier, and Alice, his wife. As observed in noting the Archbishop's descent, James Sharp had a son James, of Woodhouse, in Bierley, the grandfather of Archbishop Sharp, whose son Thomas has been referred to as the Archbishop's father. An elder brother James also resided at Woodhouse, and died there in 1690. During his lifetime, therefore, he was a near neighbour of the celebrated Dr. Richardson, of Bierley Hall. Some discrepancy exists in the published pedigrees as to the issue of this James of Woodhouse, but there is little doubt as to his being the progenitor of the Sharps of Cutler Heights and Gildersome, from whom the Bradford Sharps were descended. Following the pedigree drawn for R. Hey Sharp, Esq., of York, we find that James Sharp's eldest son was living at Tong in 1684. Another son, named Abraham, was born in 1656, and resided at Cutler Heights. Abraham Sharp, of Cutler Heights, appears to have died without issue, his property being inherited by a fourth Abraham (for there was a succession of that name), who died unmarried in 1841. The property afterwards went to Samuel Sharp, architect, then of Leeds, his nephew.

John Sharp, of Tong, the eldest son of his father James, however, had a numerous following, his line being still continued, and with every prospect of its continuance. His son was William Sharp, of Bradford, whose only son having issue was John Sharp, of Gildersome, who married Hannah Milner, and died in 1753. His eldest son, John, born in 1737, married Sarah, daughter of Richard Hey, drysalter, of Pudsey, and sister of four brothers who all distinguished themselves, one being William Hey, F.R.S., of Leeds, surgeon; another, John Hey, D.D., Norrissian Professor of Divinity; a third, Samuel, M.A., President of Magdalen College, Cambridge; and the fourth Richard Hey, LL.D., of Hertingfordbury, Hertford.

We are now brought in contact with members of the Sharp family in whom Bradfordians have reason to feel an especial interest. William Sharp, the eminent Bradford surgeon, was the second son of John of Gildersome, having been pupil with his uncle, William Hey, of Leeds. He was born in 1769, and after having held the appointment of house surgeon of St. Bartholomew's Hospital, London, settled in Bradford in 1792, when in his twenty-fourth year. He soon became pre-eminently the surgeon of Bradford, then a pleasant little town of 5000 inhabitants, as well as of the district, a position which he held until his death, and he practised here for over forty years.

As a medical man and citizen Mr. Sharp was universally respected for his professional talents and amiable character. In addition to his medical duties Mr. Sharp was captain of the Bradford Volunteers, enrolled in expectation of an invasion by Buonaparte. He lived mostly in Kirkgate, in a gabled house at the bottom of Dale Street, but some time before his death erected a house in Manor Row, then at the "outskirts" of Bradford. Mr. Sharp died suddenly in November, 1833, aged sixty-four years. A monument was erected to his memory by subscriptions raised by his friends in Bradford. It is a marble sculpture representing a female figure in an attitude of sorrow, and for years occupied a position in the Bolling Chapel of the Bradford Parish Church. The monument has since been removed to the corridor of the Bradford Infirmary, where there is also a bust of the eminent surgeon.

William Sharp had several brothers—John, who married Mary Powell, of Whitkirk, and died *s.p.* in 1806; Richard, of Gildersome, who married Mary, a daughter of John Turton, Esq., of Gildersome, and died in 1810; Abraham, the youngest, who died unmarried in 1841; and Samuel, vicar of Wakefield, who died in 1855, and had two sons, both living, namely, the Rev. John Sharp, M.A., vicar of Horbury, which living he has held for over fifty years; and the Rev. William Sharp, M.A., of Marcham Rectory, Boston.

Richard Sharp, of Gildersome, had three sons, who all attained to prominent positions in life, namely, Richard Hey Sharp, architect, of York, who died in 1853, aged sixty years; William Sharp, M.D., F.R.S., F.G.S., formerly of Bradford, and now living at Horton House, Rugby; and Samuel Sharp, of Leeds, architect, who died in 1874, aged sixty-six years.

The only survivor of Richard Sharp's children, and the representative of the elder branch of James Sharp, of Woodhouse, is, therefore, Dr. William Sharp, of Rugby.

The record of this gentleman's connection with a notable Bradford family will doubtless be regarded with equal interest to that of his distinguished uncle, William Sharp, the elder, whose pupil he was, and to whose practice he succeeded on the death of his uncle in 1833. At that period, too, his uncle's residence in Manor Row became his, and there he continued to reside. During the winter of 1838-9 Mr. Sharp delivered in the Exchange Rooms a course of lectures on natural philosophy, which excited considerable attention, and led to the formation of the Bradford Philosophical Society, an account of which is given in James's "History of Bradford," and of which Mr. Sharp was unanimously elected president. While Mr. Sharp had before him the laudable object of exciting attention to the pursuits of the higher branches of science, he had mainly in view the inauguration of "local museums," that formed in Bradford being the first of its kind in the kingdom. Afterwards a paper read by him at the meeting of the British Association, held at Birmingham in 1839, was so well received that it may be said to have had no small share in the now general formation of local museums.

Mr. Sharp enjoyed the reputation of a skilful practitioner, having successfully performed lithotomy five times. He is the author of a medical work entitled "Practical Observations on Injuries to the Head," besides other writings on medical subjects. For thirteen years he was surgeon to the Bradford Infirmary. In 1843 Mr. Sharp disposed of his practice to Mr. R. H. Meade, who also became tenant of his house in Manor Row, and went to reside at Rugby, in Warwickshire, where he became a physician by two degrees of M.D. His attachment to this neighbourhood, however, is sufficiently indicated by the name given to the house in which he resides. In 1840 Dr. Sharp was elected a Fellow of the Royal Society. He is not now in practice, but soon after settling at Rugby pursued an investigation into Hahnemann's system of medicine, which has gone on until the present time, with the result that while not owning himself a disciple of

Hahnemann, Dr. Sharp has found by a practical and experimental inquiry into his method what may prove to be a truly scientific basis for therapeutics—the healing of diseases by medicine.

Dr. Sharp married Anne, a daughter of Saml. Hailstone, Esq., attorney, who died in 1834, and for his second wife Emma, daughter of the Rev. John Scott, M.A., of St. Mary's, Hull. The remains of his first wife and her daughter lie in the family vault in the Bradford Parish Church, where there is a monument. Of his family three sons and one daughter survive.

The reason for Dr. Sharp's selection of Rugby as a place of residence was the education of his sons at the famous school of Rugby, where the late Archbishop of Canterbury (Dr. Tait) was then head master. To him Dr. Sharp proposed in 1849 the introduction of the teaching of physical science into the school curriculum. That proposal was adopted, and Dr. Sharp had the pleasure of being the first to begin such teaching in any public school. His eldest son, John, after taking his degree at Oxford, was ordained in 1861 by Dr. Tait (then Bishop of London), and went out as "Rugby Fox Master," to assist Mr. Robert Noble in his High School (for high-caste natives) at Masulipatam, South India. Mr. Noble dying in 1865, Mr. Sharp became principal until he was driven home by ill-health in 1878. He married Elizabeth, daughter of Dr. Maclean, of Oban, and has several children.

Dr. Sharp's second son, William Hey Sharp, M.A., has recently been made a canon of the cathedral of Sydney, New South Wales, by Bishop Barry, Primate of Australia. He is head of the Church of England portion of the University of Sydney; and married Mary Edith Pattison, daughter of Archdeacon Farr, of Adelaide. A third son, Granville Sharp, M.A., is assistant master of Marlborough College, Wiltshire.

CHAPTER XII.

Little Horton Green—All Saints' Church—The Old Workhouse—"Skinny Booth" —Frank Ackroyd—The Moulson Family—Abraham Balme—Edmund Riley— Benjamin Kaye.

For a little while longer we must linger at Horton Green, noticing in this topographical ramble what may appear of interest. Unquestionably the grandest pile that has been erected under the auspices of the Bradford Church Building Society is All Saints' Church, Horton Green. Both the site and the cost of the erection have been provided at the sole expense of the founder, F. S. Powell, Esq.

This church, one of the choicest specimens of Decorated Gothic architecture to be found in the North of England, was built from designs by Messrs. Mallinson & Healey, of Bradford, Mr. Israel Thornton being the contractor for the whole of the works. The edifice is in the form of a Latin cross, with nave, side aisles, transepts, and chancel, the length of the church internally being about 137 feet. Pillars with clustered shafts and admirably-carved capitals of flowers and leaves divide the side aisles from the nave. The tower, with spire, is of semi-hexagon design, and rises to a great height. The windows are filled with stained glass of great beauty. Marble steps lead to the altar, and the stalls for the choir, the reading-desk, and pulpit are elaborately and beautifully carved. Taken altogether, All Saints' Church stands unrivalled in these parts for architectural beauty and internal arrangement. The corner-stone was laid on November 23, 1861, and the edifice was consecrated in March, 1864, having cost upwards of £15,000.

Until the erection of All Saints' Church the ground upon which it stands formed part of the wastes of Horton, and in the township survey of 1802 is called Little Horton Green, without owner's name, the area being estimated at 6a. 2r. 3p. The shaft of a coal-pit was after the above date sunk upon the site of the church, the coal being worked by David Armitage. The ground was, however, claimed by Mr.

Francis S. Bridges, of the Old Hall, as part of his share of the wastes, and was enclosed.

The first building erected upon the Green was the township Workhouse, after the previous one, which stood in what is now Horton Park, had been vacated. For many years the building (still standing) was used for housing the poor of Horton. The introduction of the New Poor Law, however, necessitated a change in the arrangements, an after-effect being the erection of the stupendous pile called the Bradford Workhouse, upon a large open space formerly the park of Horton Hall. After the building on the Green became no longer necessary, it was converted into dwellings. One of the first tenants, we believe, was Mr. Tom Mitchell, father of Mr. Abraham Mitchell, of Bowling Parks. Mr. William Pullan followed, and lived there for forty-five years, his son Robert succeeding him. Another portion was taken by Mrs. Milner, who, with Miss Hauptmann, an unmarried sister, resided there some time.

The appearance of Horton Green, with the exceptions just named, has undergone less alteration than probably any other portion of the residential parts of Horton, and it still remains a pleasant quarter of the great borough. Formerly there stood upon the upper side of the Green a large plane tree, whose umbrageous shade,

> For talking age and whispering lovers made,

answered well its purpose for several generations of Hortonians, while but a slender stretch of the imagination is required to picture the "village train from labour free" assembling round it for sport and recreation such as were usual in the "good old days." Gardens, orchards, old-fashioned dwellings of the better class, and homesteads, where the labours of the husbandman were combined with that of handloom weaving, constituted the primitive surroundings of this picturesque hamlet.

There were formerly many freeholds on the Green, principally held by the Sharps, the Listers, the Swaines, the Balmes, and the Dentons. We incline to the belief that in more remote times the Booth family had possessions, if not a residence, on the Green. This opinion is founded on an indenture bearing date April, 1603, wherein Thomas Booth, of Little Horton, clothier, assigns to Richard Booth, of Horton, clothier, his brother, a lease of " all that messuage in Horton," occupied by the latter, with several closes of land bought from Thomas Wood, temp. 33rd Elizabeth. By another indenture, dated 1654, John Booth, yeoman, of Horton, conveys to Henry Pollard, clothier, a house and closes of land adjoining the lands of Thomas Swaine. The whole of the property abutting on Horton Green, however, has now been acquired by Mr. Francis Sharp Powell, who has expended a considerable sum in improving the surroundings.

In addition to the families named as owners there have been several tenants of long standing on the Green, whose names are intimately associated with the locality. Taking their residences in the order in which they stood on the north side of Horton Green we look in at the old house next to Horton Old Hall, associated in times past with the name of John Booth. In 1802 the property belonged to James Swaine, Booth being the tenant. " Skinny Booth " was the familiar title bestowed upon this representative of the Booth family, but he bore no relation to the Booths above referred to. The appellation it would seem was justified, as Booth was a man of most penurious propensities. It is said that his constant Sunday morning amusement was to bring out his golden guineas, pile them up on a table, and then knock them down again to see how far they would spread themselves out ! After his death the house in which he lived was found to be in a sad state of neglect. It is a large, rambling building of the early seventeenth century period, and although without family, Booth occupied the whole. Most of the rooms, however, were fastened up, some of them not having been entered for years. When broken into the walls and ceilings were found to be thickly festooned with cobwebs, and the formerly whitewashed walls contained charcoaled scrawls of sums of arithmetic, the names of persons owing him money, and " Skinny " Booth's remarks upon the sin of not paying twenty shillings in the pound ! John Booth was a farmer upon a small scale, but he must have amassed wealth by other means.

Just behind Booth's house lived David Stephenson, for twenty years steward to Mr. Bridges, who afterwards built Stephenson Fold, Horton. It was his daughter, the present Mrs. Wm. Draper, who, as servant to Mr. Bridges, so courageously withstood a gang of burglars that broke into the Old Hall on a Sunday night in October, 1843. That was a period when burglaries were very common in the neighbourhood. The Stephensons were very old inhabitants of Horton Green. One of their houses, inhabited by John Stephenson, was owned by Mary Balme, a descendant of the family of that name to which reference has previously been made. Edward Balme and John Balme subsequently became owners of the property.

The little brick house adjoining John Booth's was built by the Denton family, a member of which, named Samuel Denton, married a sister of Samuel Cordingley, the steward for the Bridges estate after David Stephenson. His son, Mr. John Denton, is at present steward for Mr. F. S. Powell.

The substantially-built house situated nearer to Laistridge Lane, and long occupied by Alderman William Moulson, has doubtless an interesting history attaching to it, if stones and oak panelling were communicative subjects. There is no inscription either within or without the house, but the period of its erection might be placed at fully two centuries ago. In the Horton plan of 1802 the owner was Mrs. Hodsden, of Horton House, an almost certain indication that it had been the property and was perhaps a residence of the Lister family of Horton, whose property Mrs. Hodsden (previously the wife of Samuel Lister, Esq., the last of the name at Horton) inherited.

Mrs. Hodsden's tenant in 1802 was Francis Ackroyd. He was the head of a family which has done much towards developing commercial industry in the neighbourhood. Old Frank (colloquially "Frenk") was a worsted-piece maker, and a member of the Independent congregation at Horton Lane. He followed his trade at Horton Green in the fashion common to the period, giving out work to neighbouring workpeople, until he removed to a house on the site of which the Neptune Inn, Bridge Street, was afterwards erected. Originally, however, we believe the Ackroyd family came from the neighbourhood of Otley, in Wharfedale.

Frank Ackroyd had a numerous family of sons, all of them men of some standing in commercial circles. Of these were Joseph, Thomas, William, Francis, Cowling, and Robert Stables Ackroyd. It is unnecessary to follow the fortunes of the several sons. Suffice it that the second son Thomas had, in the year 1817, erected for his occupation Mirypond Mill, at Horton Bank Top, by Mr. E. C. Lister, of Manningham, and there he continued the worsted manufacture until he established the business at Birkenshaw Mills since carried on by his sons. William, the third son of old Frank, went to Otley, where he also founded a large manufacturing establishment. Cowling Ackroyd was a prominent Hortonian for many years, as we have had occasion to remark, he having succeeded the Knights, of Great Horton, an equally notable family. Robert Stables Ackroyd built the original Fieldhead Mill, now the property of Alderman I. Smith.

Thomas Booth succeeded old Frank Ackroyd at his Horton Green residence in the early part of the century. Booth was also a piecemaker, and the large room of the old house was occupied with handlooms, the "clickatty-clack" of which was so familiar a sound in those days. A portion of the house, however, was occupied by Thomas Waddington, whose daughter Booth married. A brother of Isaac Pitman, whose system of shorthand has since become of such repute, was a schoolmaster at Little Horton, and lodged at Thomas Booth's, finally marrying his daughter. He also taught shorthand, then known as "stenographic sound hand."

Since the year 1848, however, the substantial old residence in question has been wholly occupied by Alderman William Moulson. The Moulsons have been connected with the township of Horton since about the commencement of the century. Originally they came from Emley, near Huddersfield. From the first until now they have been connected with the stone trade, either as quarrymen or builders, and in that capacity have necessarily had a considerable share in the construction of Bradford town. The first generation consisted of three brothers—William, David, and George. They were fair specimens of the type of Yorkshiremen left by our Saxon progenitors. William and David lived in Planetree Fold, a cluster of dwellings which has been swept out of existence by railway operations; the former subsequently building and becoming the landlord of the Black Bull Inn at Little Horton. George was unfortunately killed in a coalpit, and his son John lost his life in 1825 during the erection of the extension to Rand's Mill which overlooks the burial-ground of old Horton Lane Chapel. The family is still strongly represented in Horton.

There is a tolerably good house standing at the end of the Green, with a barn attached, which has also its associations. At present, and for many years back, it has been the residence of Mrs. Clark, a daughter of Abraham Balme, formerly assistant-overseer of Horton, and a well-known townsman. Judging by the inscribed stone over the doorway the date of the erection of this house was 1755, and the initials are **F. S.** There is also the chevron of the arms of Sharp upon the stone. The erection must, therefore, be ascribed to Faith Sawrey, the last lineal descendant of the elder branch of the Sharp family.

The property, of course, passed to her successors, as is confirmed by an indenture of lease made in 1789 between Charles Swaine Booth Sharp, of Horton Hall, in favour of Benjamin Kaye, cotton manufacturer and farmer, of "all that messuage, &c., where Samuel Swaine did lately dwell; also of certain closes called Gooselands" (now forming part of Horton Park). In 1807 Madam Sharp, widow of the above, renewed the lease to Benjamin Kaye, who was succeeded by Abraham Balme, his nephew.

The cotton manufacture, it would appear, was a considerable industry in Horton about the beginning of the present century, and Mr. Kaye was one of the largest dealers in the trade. His workshops, since made into cottages, still adjoin his former residence on Horton Green. He afterwards removed his business to Allerton Hall, where it was conducted on a larger scale, his waggons being always upon the road between that place and Manchester, then as now the chief market for cotton.

Rambles Round Horton. 141

His nephew, Abraham Balme, succeeded to the premises at Horton Green, and was also a cotton-piece maker on a somewhat extensive scale. He was a native of Wilsden Hill, but when quite a youth came to Horton to learn the business with his uncle. On the cotton trade declining, Mr. Balme took up the making of worsted, but developed abilities for parochial work which were for many years of service to the township of Horton. As assistant overseer and in similar capacities he enjoyed well merited respect, and on his retirement was succeeded in the former position by Mr. Thomas Myers.

The three-storeyed house opposite Abraham Balme's was built by Samuel Swaine for his own residence, and in which he carried on the cotton trade ; and in one portion John Riley also made cotton pieces on a smaller scale. Two of his sons were Joseph Riley and Edmund Riley, previously referred to as assistants to Joseph Hinchliffe, of Horton House Academy, and afterwards schoolmasters upon their own account. Edmund Riley published in 1859 a small volume of poems, comprising " Picciola, or the Prison Flower," and a versified rendering of " The Lord's Prayer." The little volume also contains an Allegory in prose. Although faulty in composition, the poems afford indication of a lofty imagination and an aspiration beyond the power of poetic expression vouchsafed to the author. Mr. Riley also published some very nicely written " Juvenile Tales," one of which is founded on the story of " Fair Becca," the scene of which he gives as Brackenhall Green.

Another old resident of Horton Green was John Blamires, who resided at the farm near the end of Laistridge Lane. He was also a farmer and piece maker, and was the first steward employed upon the Bridges' Estate. Thomas Duckitt succeeded Blamires upon this farm, and occupied it for many years. Still another well-known figure on the Green was that of Robert Heaton, whose garden and orchard were pleasant resorts in past times. Many other incidents might doubtless be added in connection with some former inhabitants here resident, but we must pass on to notice other places.

CHAPTER XIII.

The Old Red Lion—Holme Top—The "Old House at Home"—Horton Park—Horton Villa—The Cousen Family—Wm. Richardson—Todwell—Quaker Lane—The Old Black Horse—The Hammond Family—Chapel Green—The Thorntons.

In immediate proximity to Horton Green stands the Old Red Lion Inn—but not the building now known by that name, as the original inn was of the humblest description, consisting of one or two low rooms, with plenty of space around and in front of it. In this condition it remained at the beginning of the present century. The owner at that early period was a Mr. Glenton, and the landlady, Mary White. The building shortly afterwards had a storey added to it, and so remained until the licence was transferred to the present building, which is situate a little higher up Horton Lane. Mr. Joseph Baxter then became the landlord, and his widow married Robert Dunn, who was "mine host" in 1837. Mrs. Dunn afterwards removed to the Bermondsey Hotel, in Cannon Street, Bradford, and at the latter place her name is associated with the introduction of the music-hall element upon the London plan into Bradford.

The good house at the lower corner of Holme Top Lane was built by Mr. Jos. Barrans, farmer, horse dealer, and piece maker. Barrans was a man of some substance, and belonged to all the land upon which Holme Top Mills and other property adjoining have been erected. The house at Holme Top was afterwards purchased by Mr. Richard Denton, who resided there, he being succeeded by Mr. Thomas Ackroyd, of Mirypond Mill, Bank Top.

The house lower down Holme Top Lane was the residence of "Dick Smith," who despite his familiar appellation was in his time the largest worsted spinner in Bradford. Mr. John Wood (of Wood & Walker's), Mr. Thomas Clayton, Mr. Wm. Cousen, and Mr. Thomas Aked, men of some standing in the early Bradford trade, all learnt their business with Mr. Smith, who afterwards removed his residence to Lower Burnet Field by an exchange with John

Stowell. As previously intimated, "Dick Smith Mill" formed the nucleus of the present extensive manufactory owned by Messrs. Mitchell Bros., situate at the foot of Old Bowling Lane.

In the very old house at the upper corner of Holme Top Lane lived John Clayton, and here by dint of patient plodding and industry he brought up a family of thirteen children. John was a small piece maker and kept combers, and might have been termed in a fair way of business, as he flourished at a period when a pair of looms and a "pot o' four" for as many woolcombers constituted a respectable stock-in-trade. He was one of the first to introduce mule spinning by hand into Bradford, and in this capacity employed a few hands. His sons were Joseph, William, James, Thomas, and John Clayton, the two latter being both well-known woolstaplers of Bradford. James Clayton was somewhat eccentric, but an intelligent man. He was a good mathematician and meteorologist, upon which latter subject he wrote and published several pamphlets which are now very scarce, besides many articles in the magazines of the day. An earlier member of the same family gave the name to Clayton Lane by the erection of a substantial house bearing the initials J. C., and the date 1776.

Clayton's house at Holme Top is probably one of the most ancient dwellings left in Horton. In deeds dated 1757 the building is called The Holme Top, and at that period was the property of Joshua Stansfield, stuff maker, who carried on his business there, besides owning three cottages adjoining, tenanted by William Laycock, John Moulson, and Henry Blackburn. Stansfield also owned closes of land known as Bowling Mill Close, the South Field, the Ing, &c. Joshua Stansfield was probably of the family of Robert Stansfield, who married a daughter of the Rev. Thomas Sharp, of Horton Hall, as evidence exists that the Bowling Close field formed part of the Sharp estate, and was disposed of by Mr. Powell to the late Sir Henry W. Ripley. The old house is now the property of Mr. Michael Smith, and is about to be cleared away.

On the opposite side of Horton Lane, however, there still remains a building of antique construction, and of considerable interest on that account, which is well known as the "Old House at Home." It stands some little distance back from the Lane, having an extensive frontage, with garden and open space in front. There is also a projecting porch, bearing the following inscription :—

```
I.   S.
 1669
```

The windows are mullioned, and the interior of the house bears evident indication of its having been the residence of a gentleman. There is a stupendous fireplace in the kitchen.

Tradition has generally ascribed the erection of this remnant of past times to Isaac Sharp, the younger brother of Thomas Sharp, of Horton Hall, and that it was what was termed the "dower" house of the family. It is probably the building alluded to in Thomas Sharp's will, dated 1693, described as "his house and land at Holme Top," which were bequeathed to his son John when he came of age. If this hypothesis be correct, it becomes a question difficult of explanation why the property should have passed into the hands of the Listers of Manningham. In 1753 the land surrounding it belonged to Robert Stansfield, drysalter, who married Miss Sharp, and was farmed by Jacob Hudson, who lived at the house. Jacob afterwards purchased the old homestead known as the "Skinhouse."

In the hands of Mrs. Lister, however, the property was during the township survey of 1802, John Jowett being then the occupier; and it was purchased by Mr. Powell some years ago of Mr. John Cunliffe Kaye, brother of Mr. S. C. Lister. One of the former occupants of the "Old House at Home" was Tom Firth, a carrier. William Jowett and John Crabtree, of Shipley, also farmed the land afterwards, but for some years the building has been divided, one portion being occupied by Mr. Benjamin Sugden as an inn bearing the above "homely" sign.

Directly opposite to this house is the Horton Moravian Chapel, a neat little structure, of comparatively recent erection. The chapel was opened on December 28, 1838, at a cost of about £700, one of the most active promoters having been the late Joseph Hinchliffe, of Horton House Academy. Although involving what would be considered nowadays a very moderate responsibility where the erection of a place of

The "Old Hous at Home," Little Horton.

worship is concerned, it was by no means a small undertaking that the Horton Moravians entered upon ; but they were supported by gentlemen like Mr. Henry Leah and others, and came through the ordeal. The neighbourhood at that time had a growing population, but comparatively neglected in the provision of places of worship. Additional school-rooms have since been erected in the rear. The history of Horton Moravianism, however, dates from a much earlier period than the year 1838, the original place of meeting having been in Paternoster Lane, Great Horton, to which reference will subsequently be made.

Holme Top Mill was built by John and Squire Stowell in 1835. The two brothers had previously been in partnership with Thomas, John, and Francis Mitchell at a little factory in Manchester Road ; when Mr. Tom Mitchell retired and went into partnership with Mr. Geo. Turner at "Dick Smith Mill," which after Mr. Smith's death had stood empty a while. Holme Top Mills were afterwards occupied and became the property of the late Alderman S. Smith, of Melbourne Place, and his brother Michael, and of late years have been let off to tenants.

Holme Top has given birth to at least one family of more than ordinary note. Nathaniel Hulme, M.D. and F.R.S., and Joseph Hulme, M.D., were both born at Holme Top. They were the sons of Mr. Samuel Hulme, some time minister at Kipping, Thornton. Joseph Hulme was educated for the ministry, but afterwards studied medicine, and practised at Halifax, where he died in 1806, in his ninety-second year, a skilful physician and very rich man. His brother Nathaniel was born in 1732, and graduated at Edinburgh in 1765. He became physician to the Charterhouse, one of the most desirable preferments in the profession, and was admitted a Fellow of the Royal Society in 1794. His death occurred in 1807, having been caused by a fall from the top of the staircase in his house to the basement.

What is now called Horton Villa, the residence of Mr. John Harper Mitchell, was at one time the abode of a family which has produced members of more than ordinary ability in the artistic world. James Cousen, formerly a woollen draper in Ivegate, lived there in the early part of the century, succeeding James Mann, the former owner, who had married his daughter. Cousen afterwards resided at Boldshay Hall and at Miryshay, where he joined the firm of Rawson, Clayton & Cousen, coal merchants, and died at Miryshay in 1844, leaving a family of six sons and two daughters. Of his sons several were engaged in the Bradford trade, while others became eminent in art work.

John Cousen, who was born in 1804, was articled when about fifteen years of age to the celebrated John Scott, the animal engraver. During his pupilage he evinced considerable talent, and at its close was engaged by the Messrs. Finden to assist them in the various publications then illustrated by them; but after three or four years spent in their service his beautiful work in landscape engraving attracted the attention of other publishers, from whom he accepted commissions on his own account. He engraved many charming plates after Turner, Stanfield, David Roberts, and others, his "Mercury and Hersé," after Turner, the "*Victory* towed into Gibraltar," and "The Morning After the Wreck," after Stanfield, are among his most important works. He also engraved the frontispiece of the "History of Bradford," drawn by his brother Charles, and a few other local works. In all his work he displayed a refined taste and artistic feeling such as have not been exceeded by any other engraver of his time, his most exquisite taste being perhaps best displayed in his small book plates after Turner, which are full of artistic feeling and playful execution. Mr. Cousen was very retiring and unassuming in his habits and manners, and was much esteemed by those who had an opportunity of knowing him. In consequence of poor health he retired from the practice of his art about twenty years ago, and died at South Norwood, Surrey, on December 26, 1880, in his seventy-seventh year.

Charles Cousen was born in 1813, and was a pupil of his brother John. He also acquired a considerable portion of his brother's excellence besides exhibiting characteristics of his own, combining to some extent figure with landscape engraving. He is still engaged in the pursuit of his art, the last surviving member of his family. The engraving of Bierley Hall in the "History of Bradford" is from his pencil, in addition to the drawing of the frontispiece already referred to.

William, the oldest son of James Cousen, was a manufacturer, and in 1819, in conjunction with his father, he completed the erection of Cross Lane Mill, Great Horton, commenced by Eli Sudderds, which he occupied for some years. He married for his second wife Phœbe, only daughter of Samuel Blamires, jun., and built a house near the mill for his residence. By this marriage Mr. Cousen acquired the property of this branch of the Blamires family. His son by his first marriage is the present Mr. James Cousen, lord of the manor of Horton. All the Cousen family were remarkable for their stature, and their father used to say that he had "six-and-thirty feet of lads."

It may be added that Horton Villa, which is quite a modern title, was for some time the residence of Mr. W. Chapman Haigh. The adjoining farmhouse was inhabited by Mr. William Richardson, professor of natural philosophy and an accredited lecturer of the Society of Arts. For many years Mr. Richardson was identified with this neighbourhood as a scientific lecturer, and in his especial walk it may be said that he has left no successor in this part of the country. He was a self-taught man, having had but the humblest chances in early life, and took an especial delight in instilling into others a love of scientific knowledge. He had consequently many disciples, who revered him as a father. In addition to his ability in the art of instruction, Mr. Richardson was a practical workman, having made all his own scientific apparatus, besides others sent to all parts of the kingdom. He was also a fluent exponent of dramatic literature, and a rich conversationalist on most subjects. Mr. Richardson was a native of Brookfoot, near Brighouse, and died at Southowram, in June, 1878, aged seventy-three years.

In immediate proximity to Horton Villa is the spacious ground of the Bradford Cricket and Athletic Club, situate in Park Avenue, which in capacity and appointments is not surpassed by any similar ground in England. The land belongs to Mr. F. S. Powell, from whom a lease of fourteen years was obtained in February, 1879. This lease, however, only referred to about eight and a-half acres, but in February, 1884, an additional one and a-half acres were taken in, making the present area of the ground about ten acres. The ground is divided into cricket and football sections, with large pavilions, grand stands, and other appointments. The procuring of this ground points to a very critical period in the history of cricket in Bradford. When the Bradford Old Cricket Club were obliged in 1875 to give up possession of the field in Horton Road (their predecessors having in like manner been ousted from a former ground now the site of Claremont), they knew not where to look for another suitable spot. Fortunately, by the friendly co-operation of Mr. F. S. Powell, the present site at Park Avenue was obtained, and it is not too much to state that, by the successes of the cricket and football sections of the club combined, " Park Avenue " is a *locale* known favourably throughout England. It should be added that the promoters are much indebted to Mr. J. Harper Mitchell for generously giving up a portion of his grounds in order that the quantity of land required, both for the original and subsequent requirements of the club, might be obtained.

Horton Park was opened in May, 1878. In extent this popular resort for recreation is about forty acres, and included in it is a spacious cricket ground, detached from the Park. Including the laying-out, &c., it has cost the ratepayers of Bradford about £42,000. The site was obtained by throwing together a number of fields forming separate properties, and some negotiation was requisite in order to bring the whole together in park-like form. Several fields constituting an area of seventeen acres, and comprising Low Close Farm, were purchased from the Bower family for £3000. The Well Close House Estate, comprising twelve acres, was purchased from Noble's trustees for £10,212. A purchase, comprising over seven acres, was made from Mr. Thos. Firth for £7068 ; and a further sum of £6480 was paid to Mr. Gamble for about seven acres of land. In conducting these negotiations, and in carrying forward the movement generally, it will be by no means invidious to mention the name of Alderman John Hardaker as a principal. Although not opened until the year 1878, the initiatory proceedings in connection with Horton Park were taken at the Council meeting held in May, 1870, when it was decided to purchase Manningham Park, and on the same occasion a promise was extorted from the Council that similar parks should also be provided for Horton and Bowling. On the occasion referred to, a powerful appeal was made for public recreation grounds by the late Alderman Mark Dawson, who with great appropriateness quoted the Cowperian lines—

> A breath of unadulterate air,
> The glimpse of a green pasture, how they cheer
> The citizen, and brace his languid frame.

Horton Park is 630 feet above sea level, and 300 feet above the level of Market Street. It is needless to state that as a place of public resort the park is largely frequented; the display of greenhouse and other flowers being during the season a great attraction. Mr. Michael Lander has been the head gardener from the formation.

The next object attracting attention is the building known as Mount Carmel Chapel, opposite the entrance to Horton Villa, erected in 1836, by John Parkinson, for the Gospel Pilgrims. Mr. Parkinson was one of the old Bradford booksellers, a business in which he was engaged for nearly fifty years. After leaving Little Horton he removed to Hull, and thence to Colne, in Lancashire, where he still continued the business until his death in 1860. On his removal to Hull Mr. Parkinson joined the Primitive Methodist Society, amongst whom he laboured as a local preacher until his decease. Mount Carmel Chapel, however, has had an unfortunate history, having been degraded into a workshop and for other purposes. It has now reverted to uses more in harmony with its former design, having become a mission-room of All Saints' Church.

On the opposite side of the lane leading from Park Lane may be seen a portion of the buildings formerly used as a coal-staith by the Low Moor Company. In the days when railways were unknown, and coal was generally carted from a

Rambles Round Horton.

distance for domestic use as well as for the requirements of the rising worsted trade, the coal-staiths of the Bowling and Low Moor Companies were a convenience, as the stores were brought comparatively near the consumer by means of tramways or waggon-roads. Such a tramway brought Low Moor coal from the pits at Brownroyd Hill and Wibsey to Little Horton, and from thence it was carted to all parts of the town by the company's vehicles. The stables of the company were consequently extensive. The agent in charge was Paul Bairstow, who lived upon the spot, and was a great man in the neighbourhood, with which his family had been long associated. Briggella Mills, the property of Messrs. John Briggs & Sons, occupy a portion of the site of the old staith and tramroad.

Tod (or Toad) Well Farm, opposite, is an old homestead, associated with the Knight family. In 1753, John Knight was the owner and occupier ; and in 1800, Isaac Knight, his son, a carrier and farmer, the progenitors of the Knights of Great Horton. William Cass, constable and overseer of Little Horton, for many years lived in the lane leading to Todwell. A very old house, belonging to the elder Sharp's estate, is situate just above Todwell, the land being farmed by Joseph Bennett. Immediately above comes the Delph Hole or Barley Fold, the site of which was waste ground in the township survey of 1802. Abutting upon it was Clough House, the residence of James Clough, quarry owner, who built a number of the cottage houses in the neighbourhood. He died in 1871, at ninety years of age. The maltkiln in Barley Fold is associated with the name of Jonas Jowett, maltster, also of those of Stockhill and Green. The extraordinary feat of building a house in a day and sleeping in it at night, in order to acquire a title, was accomplished on this bit of waste ground.

Skirting Todwell Farm is Quaker Lane, which by sundry bends emerges in Southfield Lane. Although little more than an occupation road it is probably one of the oldest bypaths in Horton, and from its retired position was chosen as an appropriate place of burial by the early Bradford members of the Society of Friends. From an examination of the society's burial registers, it would appear that the first interment at the Quaker Lane burial ground was made in the year 1656, and was that of one Thomas Judson. Between that period and 1699 twenty-six interments took place in the above ground, the last being that of the body of John Appleyard, of Bowling.

The following is a list of some of the names of Quakers buried at Horton, with the dates of interment, viz. :—1656, Thos. Judson ; 1658, Richd. Thornton ; 1660, Grace, wife of Jas. Marshall, Bradford ; 1664, Esther, wife of Robt. Birkby ; Thos. Kitchen, Bradford ; Dorothy, wife of John Verity, Wibsey ; 1665, the wife of Zachary Yewdall ; 1667, Jeremy, son of Wm. Croasdale, Bradford ; 1668, Sarah, wife of Jonas Bond ; Hannah, daughter of William Cook ; Mabel, wife of Moses Sykes ; 1669, Susannah Judson ; Thos. Hird, Bradford ; 1670, Elizabeth, daughter of John Winn ; 1671, Mary Hillas ; 1673, Mary Verity, Thos. Parker, Thos. Kitchen, and Jacob Winn ; 1681, Martha, daughter of John Jowett ; 1683, John Verity, Wibsey ; 1684, Robt. Birkby, Wibsey ; 1692, John Jowett, Bowling ; 1696, Ann, wife of John Appleyard ; 1697, Sarah, wife of Isaiah Verity ; 1699, Paul, son of John Harwood, Bradford ; Edward Wood, Great Horton ; John Appleyard the elder, Bowling. Elizabeth Winn was the daughter of John Winn, the persecuted Quaker preacher.

The first interment at the Quaker burial ground at Goodmansend was that of Matthew Wright, who gave the ground, and, strange to say, was the first to be laid in it. That was in the year 1672, so that Quaker burials at Horton were continued for some time after the Goodmansend ground had come into use. It is even said that within the recollection of old inhabitants of Horton living at the beginning of this century interments were occasionally made, and they were understood to be the bodies of suicides, buried at midnight. However, the ground belonged to the Quakers in 1830, and was purchased from them by John Hardy, a small quarryman, who erected his present house upon the site. In making the excavations he found abundant evidence of the sacred uses to which it had been devoted.

Continuing our ramble to the top of Horton Lane we pass the Old Black Horse Inn, famous in the days of

"Wibsey weddings" during the time when there were many colliers in the district. The landlady at that day was Pal Hammond, or "Hawmond," who when the orgies of her customers were at their height often asserted her authority in a manner to astonish even the rough collier lads. Pal was a match for her customers otherwise than physically. Being "plain of speech" and an adept in her native Doric, she was not backward in giving any one a "bit of her mind" when occasion required. Nevertheless, Pal was a good-hearted woman, and was admirably suited to her position. She had a fine old oak bedstead in the parlour, elaborately carved, the envy of many, and for the use of which an extra charge was made to newly-married couples who spent the commencement of the honeymoon at the Black Horse. In the days of Chartism this inn was used by the patrols of special constables during their midnight rambles in search of men drilling. The usual meeting hour was one a.m., when warm ale and oatcake were in readiness, and acceptably partaken of, it being rough work patrolling the high lands during winter time.

The family of Hawmond is of very old standing in Horton. As early as 1379 two members of the family appear in the poll-tax of Richard II. That they were landholders, and as such acquired grants of land from the adjoining wastes, is evident from the following and other documents, viz. :—

December 11, 1510.--Oswald Leventhorp, son and heir of Robert Leventhorp, lord of Horton, grants to Gilbert Hawmond one piece of land 2½ acres, lying on the moors of Little Horton, to wit, on the south side by land belonging to Chris. Rawson, and on the east side of the land of Wm. Field, of Great Horton. To hold the same on his payment of 10d. in silver at the' Feasts of St. Martin and Pentecost, in equal portions. Witnesses, Richd. Tempest, Esq., Thos. Gelles, John Field.

1538. Indenture between Richd. Wilkinson, of Bradford, clothier, and Miles Hawmond, of Little Horton, yeoman, whereby the latter conveyed to Wilkinson thirty-three roods of arable land in the Netherfield of Horton, and Kyrswellcliff in the township of Little Horton, in the tenure of the said Miles Hawmond and Thos. Byrkby.

In Sir John Maynard's valuation of the tythes of Horton in 1656, Jonas Hammond is credited with two oxgangs of land. In 1708, by indenture, William Hawmond, of Little Horton, joiner, for the sum of £20 mortgaged to Abraham Sharp, the mathematician, " all that field called the Flatt, containing 2½ days' work, then in the occupation of Jonathan Rhodes, and adjoining to lands late the inheritance of Mr. Thos. Sharp on the south and east, upon land belonging to Mr. Samuel Lister on the north, and on the lane leading from Bradford to Halifax on the west, paying yearly to Wm. Hawmond the rental of one red rose in the tyme of roses (if the same be demanded), and no more or other rent." From the description given above, the Flatt close adjoined the old Black Horse Inn, which was probably an hostelry at that time. The Hammonds of Bradford are of this family, among the present representatives being Mr. Benj. Hammond, whose generous gifts to his relatives recently found expression in a substantial form ; also his nephew, Mr. Ezra Waugh Hammond, of Horton Hall.

In the rate-books of 1839 certain fields at Brownroyd are called by the following Wibsey-like names:—Back o't House, Top o't Hill, and Maiden Brigg Slack. Brownroyd Fold has been long the abode of the family of Greenwood, Paul Greenwood residing there in 1800, and he succeeded his father. The property, however, belonged to Mr. Joseph Stocks, who disposed of it to the Low Moor Company. The Greenwoods were farmers, scavengers, and horsekeepers, leading much coal for the above company. The family had also farms at Miryshay and Calverley. Paul was a Moravian, and generally entertained the preachers who came from Fulneck to officiate at Chapel Fold, at Brownroyd Hill, and at Paternoster Lane, Great Horton. His well-known figure was regularly present at both places, and after becoming stricken with blindness he was frequently led to his favourite places of worship. Paul's son John succeeded him at Brownroyd Fold, and the family is still resident there.

The neighbourhood of Chapel Green and Thornton Lane would doubtless furnish material for continuing this paper if well explored. We have, however, already alluded to the interesting subject of the first Presbyterian meeting-house situate at Chapel Green. A very old homestead in Thornton Lane called Thorns has recently been pulled down. The property belonged to Hutton's trustees, and formed part of Lady Hewley's Charity land, the proceeds of which were distributed among several Dissenting congregations in the neighbourhood, among them being those at Kipping and Eccleshill. Mrs. Clark, a daughter of one of the Thorntons, resided at Thorns Farm for some time.

Chapel House, still standing, bears an initial stone denoting it to have also been a residence of the Thorntons, a favourite Christian name of this family being Jeremiah. The will of Jeremiah Thornton, of Little Horton, was proved in April, 1749, his son being Wm. Thornton, who purchased in 1755 a close of land called Thornton Ing of Wm. Dixon, of Bowling. His son, Jeremiah Thornton, was a man of substance in the latter part of the last century, and was a stuffmaker. He died in 1780, leaving three sons, Jeremiah, John, and Joseph, all stuffmakers. He left property in Horton, Bowling, and Bradford, comprising a messuage in Horton, occupied by William Stonehouse and Marmaduke Pighills, and four closes of land, called the Ing, the Horse Close, the Far Close, and the Moore Close; also messuages in Bowling, with closes called the Castle Hill and Thornton Ing, and coal mines. John Bakes and William Shaw were old tenants of Chapel House, which is generally associated with the site of the old Presbyterian Meeting-house. Several old cottages, called Lincey Fields, situate in Thornton Lane, were pulled down some years ago.

CHAPTER XIV.

Southfield Lane—The Open Field System of Land Tenure—Haycliffe Hill—The Old Bradford Waterworks—Beldon Hill—Horton Bank Top—Hollingwood Lane—Horton Bank Bottom.

The neighbourhood of Southfield Lane and Haycliffe Hill is not without its interest. Although but sparsely populated, compared with some portions of the township, it has been the abode of Horton families of long standing, albeit they may have been little known outside their several circles. For the most part they belonged to the small yeoman class, farming bits of poor land and eking out a subsistence by the aid of the spinning wheel or shuttle. The remaining population comprised colliers employed in the pits of the neighbourhood, who resided in one-storeyed cottages of the humblest exterior appearance, but which gave an amount of shelter and warmth in that high-lying region that was sought for in vain in two-storeyed or "chaymer-height" houses.

Southfield Lane, otherwise called Saughfield or Southgate, has evidently derived its name from the custom prevailing in ancient times, when land was held and tilled in common, namely, the "open-field system," illustrated in a recent paper read by Mr. Lister, of Shibden Hall, before the members of the Bradford Historical Society. Of the existence of this primitive mode of tenure Mr. Lister found conclusive evidence in the neighbouring township of Wibsey. Under this system the cultivated land was situate in various parts of a township, known as the North-field, the South-field, &c., and was divided into narrow strips or "lands," of an acre, half-acre, or rood in extent, parted from each other by green balks of unploughed turf. When instead of being arable they were strips of meadow, they bore the name of "doles." A fieldway or "gate" admitted to the common field, and in those portions which were in pasture there was also the right to "gates" for feeding oxen. Corners of fields not shapely enough to be divided were called "butts."

Rambles Round Horton.

In old deeds frequent mention is made of the South-field of Horton. Thus, by indenture bearing date March, 1619, Thomas Cook, of Bradford, yeoman, sells to Wm. Booth, sen., clothier, of Horton, and Wm. Booth, jun., his son and heir, " all those three closes called the South-field, in Horton, now in the tenure of Elizabeth Gledhill." In like manner we read of Two Lands, Nine Lands, the Southern Half-acres, Broad-dole, Cross-butts, &c., several of which have reference to land in Horton " on the north and east side of a hill called Haycliffe." Probably a knowledge of the names of closes of land in the neighbourhood of Haycliffe or Southfield Lane would supply additional testimony of the existence of the open-field system in Horton as well as in Wibsey.

At Close Top Farm, Southfield Lane, John Smith, grandfather of the present occupier, employed many hand woolcombers, and made tops for the trade around Great Horton. Cragg Farm belonged in 1800 to Mr. Gorton, having been previously a portion of the Brooksbank estate, and was occupied by Samuel White, who not only followed the occupation of farming, but was the shoemaker for the district. The land upon which New Harrogate is built formerly belonged to this farm. Benjamin Knight, the cotton spinner, bought the property of Mr. Gorton, and on his bankruptcy the late Mr. George Hadfield, once a candidate for the Parliamentary representation of Bradford, took possession of Cragg Farm, it was said, for the legal expenses incurred by Knight. A portion of the land has turned out valuable, the Bradford Brick and Tile Company having opened it out for brickworks.

Haycliffe Lane has been for generations the residence of a branch of the Swaine family previously alluded to, who were owners of small portions of land adjoining their tenements. In the survey of 1839 occur the names of William Swaine, Joseph Swaine, and John Swaine ; also of Kalema Gledhill, Samuel Wilson, Samuel Haigh, F. S. Bridges, and Hird, Dawson & Hardy. Messrs. Jos. Stocks, John Tommis, John Booth, and Joseph Nichols were previous owners of land at Haycliffe. Some of the houses on Haycliffe Hill were rebuilt about the year 1839. The little

Wesleyan Reform Chapel in Haycliffe Lane only dates from the year 1875.

It may not be generally known to the present generation of Bradfordians that the first waterworks company of Bradford obtained its supply from Haycliffe Hill. The old watercourse indeed is still running, and supplies several properties yet. The company's water was obtained from a "sough," or coal drain, in the hill, and was conveyed in a goit to the field behind the "Old House at Home," where there was a trough, and from thence the water was conveyed in lead pipes to a small reservoir situate near "Judy Barrett's" shop in Westgate.

From a plan of the works drawn for the proprietors in 1753 by John Smith, of Manningham, we gather that the fountain-head of the supply was situate in Squire Leedes's land at Haycliffe; that the water passed through Joseph Stocks's land, occupied by John Nicholls; was brought down through Robert Stansfield's land at the corner of Southfield (or Saughfield) Lane End, through lands owned by Samuel Lister extending from Southfield Lane to Todwell Farm, where the company's water again entered Stansfield's land at Horton Green. Continuing past Richard Gilpin Sawrey's grounds at Horton Hall, the pipes were taken in a line with an old occupation road which skirted the side of what was formerly known as Hailstone's Park, crossed the bottom of Melbourne Place, and emerged in Horton Road near the site of the present Vicarage. From that point the water-pipes dipped towards the valley, crossed the beck and goit, and thence were carried forward to John Street, Westgate, where the reservoir was placed.

The supply, however, was only scanty, and much contention arose, not only along the line of route, in consequence of the attempts made to divert or impound the water in a dry time, but also at the Westgate terminus. At this point there was a tap for supplying those in the neighbourhood, and frequent "rows" occurred in determining the question—"Whose turn next?"

In 1790 the proprietors, consisting of Richard Sclater, James Smith, John Hardy, Sarah Ward, and John Crosley, became incorporated by Act of Parliament, but not without much opposition from an influential section of the community, whose interests were said to be jeopardised by what were called the " unreasonable and oppressive " clauses of the Act. The original undertakers of the works being in 1790 all dead, their shares were transferred to other parties. The two shares of Squire Leedes were, under his bankruptcy, sold by his assignees to Mr. John Hardy for £39 per share, and that gentleman was the principal promoter of the application to Parliament. There were only ten shares in the undertaking, three being held by Richard Sclater, and three by James Smith. Sarah Ward had one, John Crosley one, and John Hardy two. The application was opposed on the part of the inhabitants by Benjamin Ferrand, Samuel Lister, Isaac Hollings, George Barber, Dawson Humble, Francis Bridges, and Richard Hodsden ; but the Act was passed. The subsequent history of the Bradford Waterworks has no immediate connection with the history of Horton.

A large quantity of coal was obtained between the years 1830 and 1841 from the hillsides extending from Haycliffe along Beldon Hill to Cliffe Valley, much of it having been carted for the supply of the mills and dyehouses around Horton and in the neighbourhood of Thornton Road. The coal on Pickles Hill, Crag Hill, Crag Valley, and on the upper side of Cliffe Mill was better-bed coal, and was worked by Squire Tordoff and George Mortimer, who also got the coal in a very large field, called Moor Field, betwixt Pickles Lane and Crag Valley, and most of the coal on the Haycliffe side of Beldon Hill. The coal around Haycliffe Hill was worked by Joseph Knight, and was that known as " black bed," the ironstone having been got out by the Bowling Ironworks Company many years before.

Joshua Slingsby, Robert Britcliffe, Abraham Brewer, Abraham Bolton, Charles North, and Messrs. Ramsden and Co. have also got coal under several fields in the same neighbourhood. " Better bed " coal sold in 1840 at 7s. per ton. After the coal which would pay for getting had been removed, the pit hills were levelled by test labour during the depressed times of 1847-8.

A portion of the land about Beldon Hill at one time belonged to the Booth family, previously alluded to as large landowners in Horton. There was also a William Beldon, who owned and farmed his own land, but it would appear that the hill derived its name from Benny Beldon, his predecessor, who also owned and farmed a few closes. The old name for Beldon Hill was Upper Haycliffe, and Haycliffe Hill was called Lower Haycliffe.

An old farmhouse on Beldon Hill, divided into two tenements, and now the property of Mr. Wm. Ramsden, is worth inspection as affording a sample of the squat, substantial erections intended to withstand the elements in exposed positions. One portion is occupied by Mina Wilkinson, and another by old Benny Priestley. In "old Benny's" comfortable domicile will be found a singular combination of old-time and modern luxuries—to wit, a fine carved oak bedstead, fully three centuries old, and a splendid trichord pianoforte of most approved construction, upon which the best of classical and sacred music is played to a select but appreciative audience on certain days. The little garden plot in front also contains one of the best collections of pansies to be found in the neighbourhood, the great altitude notwithstanding.

The Priestleys have lived a very long time upon Beldon Hill and Pickles Hill, there being several families of this name. The Tordoffs, Wilkinsons, and Shepherds have also resided upon these hills for generations. It may be noted, too, that the denizens of these high-lying parts of Horton are very clannish—a peculiarity which may be found more or less in Hortonians generally.

The public gardens on Beldon Hill have been a favourite resort for over forty years. They were first laid out by Richard Townend—musical instrument maker, whose shop formerly adjoined the Old Foundry in Tyrrel Street—and were kept by him for nearly ten years, but have been occupied by the present tenant for thirty years. They are generally known over the country side as "Tom Hardy Gardens." The views from the gardens are very fine and the air is especially bracing.

Rambles Round Horton.

There is a higher altitude than Beldon Hill, however, in Horton, namely, Reevy Beacon Hill, which is 975ft. above sea level. Being in the line of connection with Beacon Hill at Halifax and Beamsley Beacon, near Addingham, there is little doubt that it derived its name from the uses to which this elevated spot was put in the disturbed times of the Scottish invaders, intimation of whose approach was made by means of beacon fires lit upon the most suitable elevations that could be found.

Holdsworth is a very old name in connection with these parts. From the subsidy roll, dated May, 1608, it appears that Georgius Holdsworth was taxed for lands held by him in Horton, of the annual value of 20s., for which he paid 2s. 8d. We have before us a receipt, dated June, 1687, given by Alice Holdsworth, daughter of Richard Holdsworth, deceased, of Shelf, to Matthew Holdsworth, of Reevy, and Gilbert Brooksbank, yeoman, of Horton (doubtless executors under the will of her father) for her "childe-portion" and the legacies bequeathed her by her father. It was a Jeremiah Holdsworth, who occupied Miss Thornton's land in the immediate locality, that gave the name to "Jer Lane."

In Beacon Lane once stood a number of low cottages called Miry Pond, from the nature of the ground. Hence came the name of Miry Pond Mill, now owned by Messrs. Thomas Priestley & Co., but first erected for Mr. Thomas Ackroyd, to whom reference has been made.

At Nettleton Fold, in Jer Lane, are two old houses, the initials on one being I. S. L., and dated 1711; on the other R. T., 1701. The owner of the first named was in 1800 William Oliver, and the tenant William Nettleton. The property was bought by Mr. Ellis Cunliffe Lister, and has passed into the possession of Mr. William Ramsden, who has acquired much property by purchase in the locality. Miss Thornton was the owner of the one erected in 1701, where Joshua Smith lived, and where Francis Barraclough has resided for over half a century. Jer Lane Old School was erected by subscription in the year 1822, for the use of the neighbourhood, and was conducted for many years until his death by an able mathematician and master, John Benn who

L

was entirely self-taught. Many persons who have risen to influence in the neighbourhood were indebted to Mr. Benn for their education. The Horton Bank Top School, erected by the Congregationalists in 1881, has superseded the old school for religious services, while the excellent Board School at Horton Bank, opened in August, 1874, supplies elementary education.

From an old survey and other documents we gather that the Jowett family, of Horton, were considerable owners of land and tenements in the higher parts of Horton during the latter half of last century. About 1760 Jeremiah Jowett, by his last will, bequeathed to his younger son, James, " all that messuage, with outbuildings and lands, &c., belonging thereto, in the occupation of William Topham, and all those two cottages in the occupation of John Ellis and Samuel Mires, paying unto Jonas Jowett, his eldest son, the sum of forty pounds within one year after the decease of the testator." Jeremy Jowett, the first of the family settling in Horton, originally came from Buttershaw, in North Bierley. His sons were Jonas o' Jeremy's, who lived at Beldon Hill; John Jowett, of Bank Bottom, whose grandson, Joshua, died in his eighty-fifth year, in Stephenson Fold, in 1885, having resided in that dwelling for seventy years. Charles Jowett, of Bank Bottom, was also a son of old Jeremy. All the family were handloom weavers.

At the corner of Cooper Lane there once stood several very old houses, with large gardens attached, owned and occupied by a family named Lister. The present buildings were erected on the site. Miss Thornton owned the Hare and Hounds Inn, kept in 1800 by Charles Parker, and he was succeeded by William Tordoff, who was the landlord for many years. Below the Hare and Hounds there were two old farmhouses, since removed, one owned by John Holdsworth, the other by Samuel Waterhouse, or " Watress."

Near the top of Hollingwood Lane there is a place called "Cockpit Hill," from the circumstance of its having been a place of resort for cockfighting. Another meeting-place for the same purpose was at Beacon Hill. Upon one of the cottages at Cockpit Hill are the initials $_T$ ^{H} $_M$, and the date 1781. It was the residence of one of the Holdsworths already noticed. Further down Horton Bank there is a sundial over a grocer's shop kept for a long time by William Swaine, inscribed T. H. (for Holdsworth, and the date 1827. The motto is—"Time flieth swiftly away." Tradition has it that Hollingwood Lane obtained its name from the holly hedges which once abounded in the neighbourhood. The Horton legend of "Fair Becca," whose unfortunate history lingers in the immediate locality, affords evidence in corroboration, as the story goes that "she would come ageean while 'holly grew green.'" If holly was once so plentiful in Hollingwood Lane it must have fallen a prey to an impregnated atmosphere, or more likely to the whittling knives of "knor-and-spell" players, who spared no holly bush large enough to afford material for their "knors." The following indentures testify to the name of Hollingwood being of very long standing :—

1623. Thos. Hollings by deed poll granted to John Midgley all his interest in the close of land called Hollinwood, estimated at four acres, situate in Horton, adjoining upon one great close called Clayton Pasture on the west, by lands in the occupation of Gregory Fox on the east, by the lands of Edd. Brooksbank on the south.

ROBT. ILLINGWORTH, Attorney.

1681.—Indenture between John Mortimer, of Hollinwood, and Richd. Mortimer, of Bolling, his brother, wherein John conveys to his sons John and Richard all his interest in a close of land called Hollinwood.

JOSHUA STANSFIELD, } Witnesses.
ISAAC BROADLEY,

The Drop Farm belonged at the beginning of the century to Richard Holmes, John Wilkinson being the tenant. His family had lived there a long time. The farm has now dropped out of existence, the site being occupied by Horton Bank Reservoir. The last tenant was named Birkby.

In the upper part of Horton and about Tanner Hill and Hollingwood Lane the Fox family owned and occupied property. In 1738 a close of land was called "Gregory Fox Close," in the then occupation of John Ramsden. One Gregory Fox lived at the roadside cottage in Pasture Lane, where Tanner Beck joins Bulgreave Beck. His son was named William Fox.

At Tanner Hill Farm, or Hollin House, the initials A. N. and G. N. existed, the date being 1666. The house was rebuilt in 1711 by some owner whose initials were J. H. probably answering for John Haley. In 1801 Jonathan Fox was the owner, and Samuel Holmes the occupier. The premises were afterwards occupied by Abm. Bairstow and John Holmes. Two old houses have been pulled down at Tanner Hill recently, the date of one of them being 1560. It is said that a tannery existed here at one time, and hence came the name. Paddock Dyehouse was founded by Abm. Bairstow, of Hill End, who was a character in Horton in his day. His son John, and son-in-law, John Holroyd, carried on the works, and afterwards Holroyd and Buckle, until the erection of Horton Dyeworks. Of two farms at Hill End, one belonged to Jonas Jowett, the other to Joseph Wardman. Joseph Cawthra and Saml. White were once occupiers, afterwards Wm. Fox and Abm. Bairstow became the owners.

Paradise Farm belonged to John Haley, a calico weaver, who attained his ninetieth year. It was purchased from Mr. Joshua Pollard and Mr. Paley, of Bowling Ironworks. David Mortimer, a respected townsman and octogenarian, has since acquired the property, and still resides upon it. Solitary, the name of an adjoining farmstead, formed part of the Ashton dole land, Daniel Dracup being for a long time the occupier.

What is known as Horton Bank, or the New Road, from Bank Bottom to Bank Top, was formed about the year 1807. The old road still exists, although in a much inproved condition to that in which it was when a portion of the highway and coachroad from Bradford to Halifax. In the olden times, when the Highflyer and Defiance coaches were pulled up the steep ascent by four and sometimes by six horses, it was in a shocking state. The road was very narrow, not permitting of more than one vehicle going along at a time. It was indented by deep ruts, and horses have been known to fall dead with the exertion required to pull up the coaches. It was not so bad for pack-horses, accustomed to highways which in these days of highway authorities would not be tolerated.

About half way up the Old Road there stood an old hostelry, called the Three Blue Bells, said to have been the oldest inn within many miles. The building consisted of two wings and a central portion, and doubtless afforded all the accommodation required for man and beast. The last landlord who kept it as an inn was Robert Fox. The licence was afterwards removed to the house belonging to the Blamires family, a little higher up the road; subsequently to the lane end, where it was known as the Dog and Gun, and was kept by David Armitage, a noted sportsman. It afterwards became the Crown Inn. The premises known as the old hostelry in Old Road still stand, but in a very dilapidated condition, and, with the farm land adjoining, belong to Mr. F. S. Powell.

The old homestead at Bank Bottom appears to date back to about the year 1600, and at one period must have been a residence of some standing in Horton. In 1763 Joseph Pollard bequeathed the property to his son Joseph, but he does not appear to have resided there, as he was a corn miller, and lived at Shuttleworth Hall, Fairweather Green. He was, however, an extensive property owner in Horton. In 1781 Joseph Pollard sold it to Joshua Crabtree, of Shipley, Samuel Swaine being at that time the occupier.

In 1787 Dr. Joshua Walker appears to have acquired the property. Dr. Walker was for twenty-five years physician to the Leeds Infirmary, but was a native of Bradford, residing in Wakefield Road. By his will, dated 1813, he bequeathed the property to Edward Jowett, of Eltofts, Leeds, James Swaine being at that period the tenant. James Swaine belonged to the old Horton family of the name, and lived to a very great age. It is said that while in his ninety-sixth year he followed the plough. He died about 1820 in his ninety-seventh year. His sons were—James, of Haycliffe Hill; Gilbert, landlord of the George and Dragon Inn; and John, who had a son, William Swaine, a grocer in New Road. Another brother of old James was named Samuel.

In 1837 the Bank Bottom farm became vested in Mary Leatham, daughter of Dr. Walker, and Edward Jowett, of Leeds. After James Swaine the farm was occupied by Isaac

Waddington, John Gaunt, and William Watson, the property having been acquired by William Murgatroyd, of the Heights. From the latter it was purchased by the present owner, Mr. John Ramsden.

Pickles Hill derived its name from a man named Pickles, a horse jobber, who lived at a farmhouse since pulled down, but which stood on the site of the new farmstead built by Messrs. Ramsden.

CHAPTER XV.

Horton Magna—The Blamires Family—John Wade—Hew Clews—"Fair Becca"—
The Horton "Guytrash"—Bracken Hall—The Ramsden Family—Horton Old
Corn Mill—The Beanlands—Hodgson Old Hall.

A glance at an old plan of Horton Magna, as Great Horton was styled in olden times, would show that very few houses existed there at the beginning of the present century. Beyond a few dwellings built anyhow on Upper and Lower Green, at Old Todley (the site of Broadbent's Mill), at Salt Pie and Town End, and detached tenements, generally fringing the sides of the high road from Bradford to Halifax, there were few buildings. Several lanes and "folds" branched from the main road, but not a single street, except that formed by the "row" of houses, latterly known as "Knight's Fold," then belonging to Mary Brooksbank. From the end of Southfield Lane, and continuing for some distance, there was a large space of common land called "Great Horton Green," including what is now known as Low Fold, which was approached on the north side by Paternoster Lane, probably one of the most ancient thoroughfares in Horton. An almost equally large open space was known as the Upper Green. How it has come about that the open spaces of common land in question have become covered with dwellings is a problem we cannot solve.

Standing near the highway, and at a short distance from Cliffe Mills, is one of the best examples of the farming class of homestead in Horton, that known as Blamires' Farm, or "Luke's." It was the homestead of one of the most numerous and respectable families of Horton, although latterly the property has passed into the hands of Mr. William Ramsden. The earliest reference we find to the Blamires family is in the township rolls of North Bierley, where they were numerously represented as early as 1660. A hundred years later, while still retaining property in North Bierley, the family would appear to have become settled in Horton, as is proved by the will of Joseph Blaymires, of

Horton, dated 1760, who devised to his grandson, Joseph Blaymires, "all that messuage, with several closes of land in Wibsey, in the occupation of Jeremy Blaymires, his son, and two other messuages in Wibsey inhabited by Samuel Wood and Rachel Blaymires," with annuities to his son Jeremy and his daughters Martha, wife of Samuel Kellitt, Mary, wife of John Stocks, Ann, wife of John Wilkinson, and Grace, wife of John Thornton. By agreement dated February, 1759, the above Joseph Blaymires leased to Samuel Kellitt, of Wibsey, a dwelling-house, situate in Wibsey, and four closes of land for the term of three years, at a yearly rental of £6 10s.

Our next evidence is that of the will of Luke Blamires, butcher, of Horton, dated 1789, wherein he bequeathed to his sons, Joseph, Samuel, and William, the messuages, lands, &c., in his possession in Horton, conditional on their paying to Martha Driver, his daughter, the sum of £10 per year during her lifetime, and the sum of £200 to her children. Luke Blamires died in 1794, aged eighty-one.

His sons, however, appear to have become owners of property by their own industry, as by deed of conveyance dated 1780, Joseph Pollard, of Fairweather Green, re-leased to William Blamires, of Horton, four messuages in Horton, formerly occupied by Jonas Blamires, John Smith, John Smithies, and Wm. Crosley, and at the date of transfer by John Blamires, Wm. Mires, John Crosley, and Isaac Wilkinson, also one close of land called The Croft, for the sum of £250. In October, 1791, also, John Loxley, clothdresser, of Wakefield, conveyed Gledhill Croft to Joseph Blamires, butcher, of Great Horton.

Samuel, second son of old Luke Blamires, kept the King's Arms Inn, in Great Horton, besides being a butcher, and died in 1818. His sons were Samuel and John. John was a butcher and cattle dealer, and at one time kept the Granby Inn at Queenshead (now Queensbury), afterwards removing to the Packhorse Inn at Bradford. Samuel lived in Cross Lane, Horton. It was his daughter, Sally Blamires, who many years ago gallantly repulsed a gang of **burglars** who attempted to break into the house in Cross Lane. Mr. William Cousen married another daughter of Samuel

Blamires, named Phœbe, and by the marriage obtained much property.

William Blamires, youngest son of old Luke, seems to have been the most substantial member of the family. Like his father and brothers, William was also a butcher, and at one time had his shop in Kirkgate, Bradford. He also possessed the family peculiarity, that of being somewhat "close-fisted" and intent on gain, and the story is told of him that, when hard driven by a bargaining customer over a joint of beef, he would point a skewer in the direction of the old Piece Hall, remarking at the time, "I don't get *that* at it!" Unsuspecting purchasers naturally supposed that by his action William meant the skewer, while in reality he had in mind the Piece Hall building!

By dint of much hard work, however, William Blamires acquired considerable land in the upper portion of Horton, his residence being the old homestead referred to, owned by his father Luke, and his grandfather. He died in 1829, aged eighty years. By his will, dated 1827, he bequeathed the old homestead and six closes of land to his eldest son John. To Luke, his second son, a messuage in Old Road, with several fields adjoining. To his son Timothy (who had the reputation of being the strongest man in Horton), five cottages at Hew Clews and two closes of land. To his daughter Lydia, wife of Thomas Myers, he bequeathed Low Fold Croft and four cottages; and to Elizabeth, an unmarried daughter, two closes of land. Through its descendants the Blamires family is still well represented in Horton.

High Street is also associated with the family of Wade, of whom one member is deserving of honourable mention in these records. John Wade was a good type of the Horton character, plodding and industrious, firm in principle, public-spirited, and a pattern of uprightness in all his dealings. He was a native of Paradise Green, where he was born in 1799, the son of humble parents. By dint of steady industry and thrift, however, he became in 1829, when a young man, a small employer of hand-loom labour, in the making of all-wool plainbacks, shalloons, &c., the staple articles of the then Bradford trade. He afterwards employed steam power, at

Dracup's Mill, Cliffe Lane, but ultimately got into the wool trade, which he continued until his death. For nearly fifty years he was one of the most regular attenders at Bradford market, and few men could better trace the development of the worsted trade from its infancy to maturity. Notwithstanding his attention to business, he was one of the most active men in the affairs of Horton, having a particular aptitude for public business. He served as churchwarden for many years at Bell Chapel, and also filled the position of poor-law guardian, and town councillor. The contest in Nov., 1850, in which Mr. Wade was opposed by Mr. Samuel Dracup, is still remembered as one of unusual keenness. He also dispensed the Ashton Dole for a period of ten years. Although warmly attached to the Episcopal form of worship, Mr. Wade was a thorough Liberal, and never flinched from upholding his views. His death occurred on January 6, 1876, in the seventy-seventh year of his age.

Hew Clews, in Cliffe Lane, is a name recalling several points of interest to Hortonians. As to the correctness of the spelling we have only conjecture to guide us. It may be either Hew, Ewe, Yew, or Heugh with equal correctness, although the form given above is generally adopted. "Clew," from the Saxon *Cleow*, is usually understood to be either a ball of twine, a guide, or a direction. At any rate, the little colony of Hew Clews is a distinctive part of Horton, and probably among the oldest settlers upon it was the family of Myers, formerly spelt Mires. A female of this name, whose daughter married John Shepherd, attained her 102nd year, having been born at Hew Clews. William Blamires had acquired this property as early as the beginning of the present century. John Hanson and his family farmed Hew Clews Farm for above a hundred years, the property belonging to Richard Hodgson, of Whetley.

Stories are told of the natives of Hew Clews and Ben Hill, of a character not in accordance with accepted notions of civilisation. It is said, for instance, that for about half a dozen cottages which stood on Ben Hill there was only one oven, which was used in common, and that a solitary spoon served alike the six families. Another story is told of

Sammy Rouse, who, having slept all day, aroused his spouse with the exclamation, "Sharah, t'world's coming tuv an end, for t'sun's risen t'wreng side o' t'hahse!"

The most popular legend in connection with Hew Clews, however, is associated with the story of "Fair Becca," who came to an untimely end at the hands of her sweetheart. This heartless swain lived at Hanson Farm, "Fair Becca" residing in one of the old cottages which until recently stood opposite the entrance to Cliffe Mill. As the legend goes, the sweetheart appeared one morning before Rebecca's cottage mounted as for a journey. Dismounting, he told her to array herself in bridal apparel, as he intended taking her to the kirk to be married. Rebecca delightedly obeyed, and was soon equipped, when they rode away in the direction of Wilsden, she mounting behind him on the double saddle ´the fashion of the period,. He then put his plan into execution. Near a lonely lane they had to traverse at Old Allen were some old disused pits, and, riding to one of the most remote, he told his companion to prepare for death, as he was going to throw her down. Rebecca pleaded for mercy, but he, disregarding her entreaties, galloped round the pit, and tried to throw her off the horse; Rebecca clinging to him desperately, he had to ride round three times ere he could effect his purpose, his victim shrieking at every attempt. The third time he succeeded in flinging her into the pit. When the deed was accomplished the murderer seems to have suffered pangs of remorse. Before he died he made a full confession of his crime, and the corpse of Rebecca was found, fearfully mangled, at the bottom of the pit.

Long, long afterwards the spirit-form of "Fair Becca" was said to wander in the neighbourhood of Hew Clews and Hollingwood Lane, in confirmation of her dying words, that " she would come ageean as long as holly grew green." Her name was a great scare in Horton, as may be imagined : but although the legend was religiously believed to be true, " old inhabitants " generally were slow to affirm that they had ever seen her. Latterly, her non-appearance is accounted for by the fact that she had been " flayed away " by the whirr of the machinery at Cliffe Mills.

The Horton "Guytrash" was another boggard in our young days, and generally took the form of a "great black dog," with horrid eyes. Horton Lane, Legrams Lane, and Bowling Lane, now Manchester Road, seemed to be particularly chosen as favourable places for its ramblings, and many are the tales told of this "Guytrash" being seen there. The late Edmund Riley, of Horton Green, used to tell the story of a well-known and staunch Independent of the old school, who resided at Horton, and was going home one night about the "witching hour," when, as he was passing the gates of Horton Hall, he was startled in his meditations by something jumping at his heels. He looked round, and, sure enough, there was the "great black dog." He made his way home, as fast as he could, and when he got there either fainted or was near doing so. The next morning he was told that Mr. Sharp (who inhabited Horton Hall) had died just about the time he was passing and saw the "Guytrash." In its ramblings the "Guytrash" was said to go about with chains rattling round it, and sometimes without; but as it has never been heard of since the town was incorporated, it is supposed to have become jealous of the policemen, and so has left the neighbourhood for ever.

Bracken Hall and Holly Bank, situate in Hollingwood Lane and Cliffe Lane, are the modern-built residences of Mr. Wm. Ramsden and Mr. John Ramsden, the energetic proprietors of Cliffe Mills. The former occupies the site of a farmhouse long tenanted by John Bennett and his family, and alluded to in the will of the Rev. Thos. Sharp, of Horton Hall, dated 1693, as "all my house and lands at Breckin Hill, Great Horton," which he bequeathed to his daughter, Elizabeth. The property belonged to the Giles family, successors of the Sharps, until purchased by Mr. William Ramsden. Holly Bank is an entirely new residence standing in an elevated position, and, like Bracken Hall, is surrounded by thriving plantations.

The name of the Ramsden family will long be honourably associated with the commercial history of Horton from the enterprise displayed by the present representatives, who from a humble beginning have built up an extensive business concern, and have become considerable property owners in Horton. The family sprang from Upper Green, where John Ramsden, grandfather of Messrs. William and John Ramsden, was a plodding, industrious carpenter and dealer in timber. His sons were Thomas, Joseph, Jonathan, and James, all of whom were engaged in similar avocations at Great Horton. Since their acquisition of the Cliffe Mill property Messrs. Ramsden have much enlarged the premises, which are now among the most extensive in the neighbourhood.

There are grounds for assuming that so early as 1311 there was a soke corn mill at Horton, as the Lord of Horton in those early times amerced some of his tenants for grinding their corn at the mill at Bradford. In the Hopkinson MS. it is recorded that Thomas Foxcroft held Horton Mill of the lord of the manor. Thomas Foxcroft, of Kebroyd, Sowerby, died 7th September, 36 Henry VIII. (1545), seised of one messuage and forty acres of land, meadow, and pasture, and of one "water mill" in Great Horton, and of a fee farm or annual rent of 46s. 4d. out of certain lands and tenements in "Lytle Bollyng," which were held of John Lacey, of Cromwellbotham, by knight service and rent of 6s. Richard Foxcroft was his son and heir.

The descent of the manor from the Lacies to the later branch of the Horton family has been previously traced. When Sir Watts Horton died, and the manor fell to Captain Rhyss, the manorial property was brought to the hammer in 1858, Mr. Wm. Cousen purchasing the lordship, including the building known as the Manor House, the pinfold, the "lord's rents," &c., and Mr. Samuel Dracup the old corn mill, farm, and water rights connected therewith. Upon an outbuilding of the mill there were the initials I.C.M., and the date 1668. The old mill has been partially rebuilt. The water-wheel supplied from the adjoining dam is also comparatively modern, although doubtless occupying its old position. There were several roads from Horton and Clayton down to the old corn mill, one of which is still known in the neighbourhood as the "Cat Steps."

Long before the manorial property left the hands of the Hortons, Joseph Beanland was the tenant of Horton old corn mill. He was a corn miller and colliery proprietor at Fairweather Green, and belonged to a Heaton family. Joseph Beanland was a man of some enterprise. In addition to running the old mill he erected for the purposes of his business a corn mill at Beckside, besides a worsted mill in Cliffe Lane for his sons-in-law, Samuel Hellewell, Joseph Wilkinson, and Edward Knight. Robert Fox was the miller at the old mill under Beanland for many years.

Joseph Beanland had a son John, who assisted him at the old corn mill, and when he married succeeded his father, the old man going back to reside at Shuttleworth Hall. The affairs of the Beanland family were unfortunately thrown into Chancery, resulting in much of their property being sold at a sacrifice. Beckside Corn Mill, with three closes of land, barn and about a dozen cottages, although not Beanland's property, shared a similar fate, having been purchased for an "old song" by Samuel Dracup, after the mill had stood unoccupied for some time, and after being considerably enlarged and adapted to the worsted manufacturing business was let to Messrs. John & Robert Turner and others. Messrs. W. & J. Pilling formerly occupied the corn mill, in addition to Sams Mill.

At a short distance from Beckside Mill there stood upon the brow of the neighbouring hillside two very ancient tenements, which have only recently been taken down. One of the houses stood at the bottom of Pleasant Street, and was known as Hodgson Old Hall. The other was situate beneath the Wesleyan Chapel burial-ground near to Cow-wells. Both were of very antique construction, with high pitched gables, massive chimneys, long, low mullioned windows, and oaken doors and panelling. The initial stone removed from the old house at Cow-wells has been built into the embankment wall close by, and contains the letters **T. S.**, and the date 1620.

For upwards of a century this house was occupied by a family named Smithies. The initial **S.**, however, had reference to the owner named Sugden, as is borne out by an indenture dated May 3, 1697, reciting that "whereas Robert Sugden, of Horton, by his will dated November 9, 1686,

Rambles Round Horton. 175

Old Corn Mill, Beckside.

devised to Isaac Hollings, of Horton, and Thomas Pighills, yeoman, all that messuage in Horton in the occupation of Grace Smithies, in trust to be disposed of for the benefit of his children." In discharge of this obligation the trustees sold the messuage, &c., to Robert Swayne. The indenture is witnessed by Robert Swayne and Samuel Swayne. The inscription upon Hodgson Old Hall contained the initials T S A and the date 1654. It is said that John Wesley preached from the horse-steps that formerly stood in front of the house. This building belonged to the Swaine family, Susannah Swaine being set down as the owner in the township survey of 1801, and John Hodgson as the occupier. Hodgson was a bachelor, and had for many years another bachelor named Robert King residing with him. Both were of a careful turn, as is evidenced by the fact that whenever old Hodgson had a load of coals to deliver Robert King followed behind to pick up any stray "cobbling" that fell from the cart. The property at the period of its demolition belonged to Mr. W. H. Fox, of Skipton.

CHAPTER XVI.

The Brooksbanks of Horton—Gilbert Brooksbank—The Charnocks—Old Todley—Harris Court Mill—Cowling Ackroyd—J. J. Broadbent—"Spectacle" Wood—Doctor Thomas—Edward Cockerham—Hunt Yard—The Legend of the Wild Boar—Low Green—Hall Yard.

One of the most important families in Horton Magna during the seventeenth century was that of Brooksbank. The name meets the eye continually in the records of the period, and the Christian name of Gilbert appears to have been a favourite one in the family, as it was continued during several generations. In the Subsidy Roll of 1608, Gilbert Brooksbank was assessed upon lands in Horton of the annual value of 20s., the same man having in 1602 been complained of along with others for enclosing waste land in Horton. This offence was, however, by no means uncommon at the period. In 1675 a Gilbert Brooksbank, yeoman, of Horton, proved the last will of Richard Brooksbank, of Oxheys, Norwood Green, he retaining the document in his own possession under a bond of £40 to produce it to Sir Wm. Horton, lord of the manor, when required. It was doubtless this Gilbert who paid the hearth-tax, levied in 1666, for two hearths or fires at his homestead in Horton. Still continuing, we find a Gilbert Brooksbank assessed in the Horton land-tax of 1704, and paying the largest amount of any landowner in Horton township, the Sharps, Listers, or Mortimers not excepted.

The existence in Great Horton of several residences of more than ordinarily substantial appearance, all bearing the initials of Gilbert Brooksbank, testifies to the standing which the family bearing this name had in Horton, and, with other circumstances to be subsequently referred to, justifies a somewhat extended record of the family history.

The earliest of the Brooksbank houses in point of date is the building known as the old "Four Ashes Inn," situate at Primrose Hill, and now the residence of Mr. James Akeroyd. On the lintel of the house G. B. 1674 and on the outer porch the initial B, and the date 1743. The building long used as

M

a tanhouse by the beck side at Primrose Hill was also a residence of the Brooksbanks. Other two residences are standing in the upper part of Horton. That now tenanted by Mr. John Denton opposite to Broadbent's Mill, bears the inscription ——— G. B. 1746 ——— It is a good example of a gentleman's residence of the period, and at the date of its erection would form a prominent feature in Great Horton. It has latterly become the property of Mr. F. S. Powell, Mr. Denton being his agent. Closely adjoining is the King's Arms Inn, which bears the above initials and the date 1739.

The inference drawn from these facts will probably be that this substantial family, including a succession of Gilbert Brooksbanks, originally lived at Primrose Hill, and subsequently erected the two houses at Great Horton, the more pretentious building becoming the family residence. This inference is borne out by the will of Gilbert Brooksbank, of Great Horton, gent., proved in 1763, wherein he devised to his niece Rebecca, wife of Jonas Atkinson, clerk, late of Tong, the mansion at Great Horton, wherein he resided, and two tenements occupied by Timothy Stocks and John White; also four other dwelling-houses occupied by Joseph Sutcliffe, Jeremiah Robinson, Samuel Holdsworth, and Joseph Wilkinson. The will was attested by Gilbert Brooksbank, jun., and John Hill, a Bradford physician.

The subsequent disposition of the family mansion is shown in an indenture bearing date 1779, and reciting that whereas a marriage was proposed between Richard Gorton, of Salford, merchant, and Elizabeth, daughter of Rebecca Atkinson, "all that capital mansion at Great Horton, then in the occupation of Joseph Swaine, also three fields called the West Croft, the Moorfields, and the Stunsteads; also the messuage lately occupied by Timothy Stocks, and the three closes called Stoney Lands, Upper Stunstead, and Crooked Royd; also the large Cragg where the Quarry is, the Ing or Coal Pit Close," were released to John Hill and Samuel Lister in trust for the use of the young children of Richard Gorton and his wife Elizabeth.

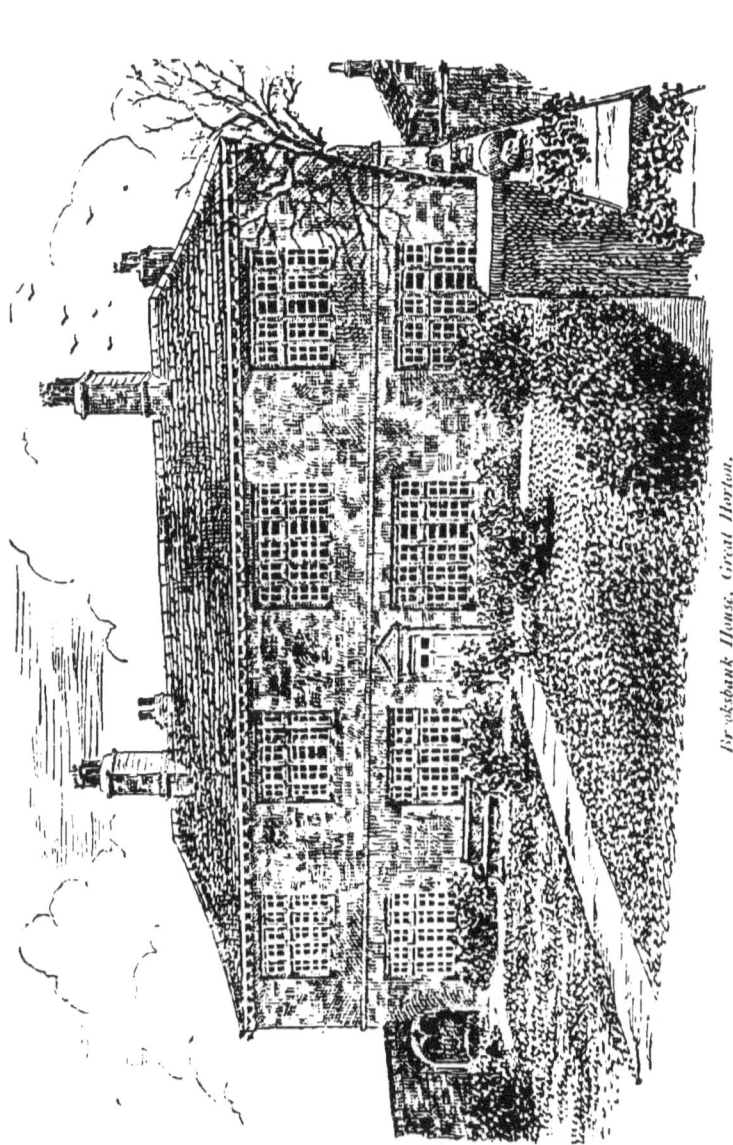

Birksbank House, Great Horton.

Residents of Great Horton will have no difficulty in identifying the closes named. The more complete description of the Brooksbank property comprised fourteen messuages, eight barns, eight stables, eight orchards, and 100 acres of land in Great Horton and Stanbury. Stephen Parkinson purchased Stoney Lands, and upon the site erected some of the houses at Summerseat Place.

Richard Gorton died intestate in 1816, leaving a son John and six other children ; and in July, 1821, by indenture bearing that date, his trustees sold to Benjamin Knight, cotton manufacturer, Great Horton, " all that mansion recently occupied by Joseph Swaine, also the West Croft, Stunsteads, &c.," for the sum of £2500, £2000 of which was borrowed on mortgage from Edward Ferrand, of St. Ives, John Gorton, and John Lambert, the two latter being trustees of the Gorton estate.

The ultimate proprietorship of the family residence of the Brooksbanks is bound up with the broken fortunes of Benjamin Knight and his brother John, who were made bankrupt in the year 1826, when the mansion and other hereditaments were seised by the Commissioners in Bankruptcy, and became the property, subject to the above mortgage, of Messrs. Chas. Harris and the partners of the Old Bank, who were the largest creditors upon the bankrupt estate. It would appear that the King's Arms property was sold in 1827 to Mrs. Trout, of Bradford, and ultimately came by will to the Rudd family, who sold it in 1878 to the Bradford Corporation for the purposes of street improvement for the sum of £5000.

The above recital, interesting and conclusive though it be, deals only with a portion of the property formerly belonging to the Brooksbanks. The family, as may have been gathered, was numerous, and, although for some reason the family mansion in the higher part of Horton passed from the male heirs as early as 1763, other possessions remained in the hands of the Brooksbanks. The family were also connected with the Barracloughs of Horton, and by marriage the latter were allied to the Charnocks, who have acquired much of the property formerly held by the Brooksbanks.

This we gather from an indenture dated June, 1797, reciting that a marriage was intended between Mary Barraclough, spinster, of Manningham, and James Charnock, incumbent of Haworth, and that the former "stood seised of the reversion expectant on the decease of Mary Brooksbank, the elder, widow, late wife of John Brooksbank, of Horton, gent., deceased, and Mary Brooksbank, the younger, widow of Joseph Brooksbank, late of Horton, gent., deceased," of certain messuages and lands described as "all that tenement situate at Horton Lane Side, with barn, &c.," and also "all those several closes of land belonging thereto, known as the Sherebrig Beck Close, the Lower Hall Brooks, the Tempest Field, Stonylands, &c., late in the tenure of John Brooksbank and Jonas Tommis, and also all the other hereditaments in Horton and elsewhere." The trustees under the marriage settlement were Thomas Hodgson, of Scholemoor, stuffmaker, and Wm. Smith, Bradford, grocer.

Mary Charnock died in July, 1809, leaving at her decease three children, namely, Thomas B. Charnock, Mary Hodgson Charnock, and Martha Hanson Charnock, to whom she bequeathed her property in three equal parts. Her husband, the Rev. Jas. Charnock, died in May, 1819. Mary Hodgson Charnock died in December, 1845, leaving her property in equal portions to her brother, T. B. Charnock, and her sister, Martha Hanson Charnock, who married in 1835 Mr. Thomas Horsfall, and went to reside at the Paper Hall, Barkerend, afterwards removing to Burley Hall. Thomas Brooksbank Charnock died in October, 1847, intestate, leaving a son, James Hanson Charnock. The Charnocks resided at the Mansion House, in Southfield Lane, after leaving Haworth. Thomas (locally known as Tommy) Barraclough, the father of Mrs. Charnock, married Mary, the only daughter of old Gilbert Brooksbank, of Tanhouse, and thus became the connecting link between the Brooksbanks and the Charnocks, who now hold their property. Unfortunately, the later members of the Brooksbank family were very improvident, the last of them, who died very poor, having, it is said, "swallowed five farms" during the course of an intemperate life.

The little colony of houses once known as Old Todley exists now only in name. The site of it is partly occupied by Messrs. J. J. Broadbent & Co.'s mill and the late Mr. Broadbent's residence, called Great Horton House. When Brooksbank House opposite was in its heyday it looked upon a few low cottages, a blacksmith's shop, and a little school-house, with burial ground attached, also a plot of vacant land. From the proximity of these buildings of high and low degree it is evident that Old Todley or Smithy Hill might be regarded as the centre of the village of Great Horton, a distinction which the site still retains.

From deeds in the possession of the Broadbent family it appears that the old school was built by the Wesleyans of Horton in the year 1766, the ground having been purchased for that purpose by Jonas Jowett and James Brayshaw. It remained as a day and Sunday school and preaching-room until the erection of Hunt Yard Wesleyan Chapel in the year 1814. The old school property and the land adjoining were sold in 1815 on behalf of the Wesleyan body to Messrs. John Knight & Co. by the following trustees, namely, Samuel White, James Helliwell, Thomas Stocks, Roger Milnes, Robert Turner, Eli Suddards, John Ramsden, and John Hall. Many interments having been made on the Todley site, the remains were removed to the burial ground adjoining the new chapel. The old school-room was afterwards used as a shuttle-making shop by Nathaniel Dracup, a noted bass singer. The smith's shop appears to have been in the occupancy of a man named John Abbott. Three of the cottages adjoining were occupied by James Aveyard, James Binns, and John Tommis, and on the side nearest to the Four Ashes was one cottage occupied by the Blagbrough family.

Reference has already been made to the earlier history of Messrs. Broadbent's Mill, erected in the early part of the century for the cotton manufacture by Messrs. J. & B. Knight, afterwards occupied by Mr. Cowling Ackroyd in the worsted business, and for about a quarter of the century by Mr. J. J. Broadbent. During the interval it has been respectively known as Knight's (or "Kneet") Mill, Cowling Mill, and Harris Court Mill, consequent on the property having come

Rambles Round Horton.

into the possession of Messrs. Harris, the bankers, on the bankruptcy of Messrs. Knight. The good house adjoining called Great Horton House, was originally erected by John Knight for his own residence, and was enlarged and much improved by Mr. J. J. Broadbent.

This gentleman was for many years connected with the staple trade of Bradford, and after his acquisition of the Harris Court Mill property was largely contributory to the welfare of the people of Great Horton, materially and socially. He was the son of Mr. John Broadbent, of the Canal Road Vitriol Works, Bradford. Prior to the removal of his business to Harris Court Mill Mr. J. J. Broadbent was at Atlas Works, Thornton Road, but as his business proved more and more successful he bought the Harris Court Mill property from Messrs. Harris, the bankers. He very much enlarged the mill premises, which at the present time form an extensive pile. Mr. Broadbent was a thoroughly practical business man, and was held in high esteem in commercial circles. He was of a retiring disposition, and took very little part in the political or municipal affairs of the town. For many years he attended St. John's Church, Great Horton, the building of which had been greatly helped forward by him, and he held the office of warden there for some time. In Great Horton he was highly esteemed both as an employer of labour and as a leading resident. Mr. Broadbent's death occurred in October, 1885, aged sixty-seven years.

The previous occupier of Great Horton House, Mr. Cowling Ackroyd, was a gentleman whose name was long associated with the trade of Bradford, while as a resident of Horton he occupied a very prominent position. He was one of the sons of old Frank Ackroyd, and commenced in the worsted business with his brother Thomas, at Mirypond Mill, prior to the latter's removal to Birkenshaw. Cowling Ackroyd then succeeded Messrs. Knight at Harris Court Mill, and for years was the leading man of the worsted trade of Great Horton, while at the same time an active townsman, and the leader in almost any movement, socially and politically. For a long period he enjoyed the title of the "King of Horton." He was an ardent Tory, and was the proposer of Mr. John

Hardy when that gentleman first contested Bradford in 1832, and again on the occasion when the present Lord Cranbrook (then Mr. Gathorne-Hardy) sought the suffrages of the Bradford electors in 1847. Mr. Ackroyd was at one time the parish constable for Horton, and was unsuccessful in a contest with Mr. Richard Denton for the office of councillor for the Great Horton Ward in 1848. He was, however, returned for the Bowling Ward in 1849. He was also a trustee of the Old Piece Hall, and a commissioner of taxes. In more recent times Mr. Ackroyd held an appointment on the Great Northern Railway. His death occurred in May, 1872, in the seventy-second year of his age.

Several old Horton families were located in the immediate neighbourhood of "Cowling Mill." John Clough kept a grocer's shop next to the mill, and nobody was better known and respected. His son William removed to Westgate, Bradford, and was a maltster there. Adjoining Clough's house was the residence of John Wood, familiarly known as "Spectacle Wood," to whom Great Horton was indebted for postal facilities, of which the village stood in great need half a century ago.

Mr. Wood was a native of Allerton, but migrated to Manningham as a schoolmaster, and in 1838 removed to Great Horton. One of his first engagements was to assist in the preparations made for celebrating the coronation of Her Majesty Queen Victoria, which event took place on the 28th day of June, and was observed in Great Horton as a day of general rejoicing. At that time postal affairs were managed with great laxity. All the letters were forwarded from Bradford twice a-week, the messenger being a man over seventy years of age, who could neither read or write, and who frequently remained drinking on the road until late in the day, deferring the delivery until the following morning. At Mr. Wood's initiation, however, a memorial praying for a daily delivery was successful, and subsequently a sub-post-office was established, Mr. Wood being elected sub-postmaster, and this position he held for twelve years. Mr. Wood afterwards became connected with various newspapers, and n that capacity was well known.

Another family named Haley, were for generations shop-keepers at the end of Southfield Lane, " Sally Haley's " being a household name in the neighbourhood, and a Jeremy Haley occupied the Mansion House before the Charnocks came to reside at it. Dr. Illingworth, afterwards of Bradford, occupied a room in this house, when commencing practice in the district ; and the Mansion House was subsequently occupied by the Misses Hinchliffe as a boarding school ; then by Mr. E. K. Fox, and the present tenant is Mr. John Buckle.

While gossiping about old Hortonians who resided in this neighbourhood we must make some reference to Abraham Thomas, or " Doctor Tom," as he was familiarly called, who was the village surgeon for over sixty years, and the only one in Horton for nearly forty. Dr. Thomas came from Hebden Bridge in 1822, and resided first in the old parsonage opposite Bell Chapel, afterwards removing to the end of Cross Lane, where he died in February, 1878, in his eightieth year. The doctor was one of the old school of surgeons, and bled for everything, but he had the wisdom to refrain from dosing with physic where fresh air was more suitable, and was in the habit of recommending a stroll upon Beacon Hill as the best thing possible. He had his peculiarities, however, among them being a love of money, although as a set-off he was moderate in his charges, and was never known to ask for a debt. He was a big, burly man, somewhat short-tempered, and not very particular in his choice of language. Apart from his medical standing, " Doctor Tom " played a somewhat prominent part in the affairs of Horton, and enjoyed considerable respect. He was a bachelor, and left several bachelor brothers, among whom he divided his great property while still alive. He was buried at Heptonstall, near his native village.

Edward Cockerham was also a man of some standing in Horton. He originally came from Leeds. His father was a carrier between Leeds, Bradford, Manchester, and other places, his waggons being well known as " Cockerham's waggons." The son came as an apprentice to Cowling Ackroyd, and remained several years after reaching manhood, afterwards acting as manager for Messrs. Priestman at Bradford, prior to his entering into partnership with Mr. Getz at Atlas Shed, Tumbling Hill. He lived at the house adjoining the Wesleyan Chapel, which was built by Samuel Blamires. Mr. Cockerham afterwards purchased Chapel House and resided there until his removal to Ashfield House, Bingley, where he died in 1883. He was an active churchwarden at Bell Chapel, and a kindly neighbour and friend.

The neighbourhood of Hunt Yard has been strangely altered since the commencement of the present century. When the old road from Bradford to Halifax by way of Silsbridge Lane, Green Lane, Toby Lane, Scarr Lane, was the chief highway, there was an open space at Hunt Yard, used in later times by the surveyors for a dross hill. Excepting an old hostelry there were only two or three low dwellings in Hunt Yard. According to the evidence of an inscribed stone still preserved, the old hostelry was erected in 1622, the sign being the "Robin Hood and Little John." The building was pulled down in 1800 for the erection of more modern dwellings. The original cellars, however, remain, and are arched, and in an underground recess there are several stone pillars which supported the old building. A portion of the original walling is above a yard in thickness. There used to be an old building connected with this hostelry called "Brick Castle," in which travellers were lodged; the beds of oak being built into the walls. Altogether, the "Robin Hood" was a noted house when the old Scarr Lane passed in front of it. It was at a "hen drinking" in this house, in which the murderer of "Fair Becca" took part, that her ghost, it is said, first appeared.

The most singular legend in connection with Hunt Yard, however, is one which has been told by Mr. James, in his "History of Bradford," and to which subsequent historians have been able to add little. The story runs thus:—That a wild boar once frequented a certain well in Cliff Wood to drink; that the beast was watched by a person who, having shot him dead, cut out his tongue, and repaired to court to claim the reward which had been offered to any one who would rid the neighbourhood of the presence of the beast. Presently after his departure from the well, another person came thither upon the same errand, and finding the beast dead, without any further examination he cut off his head and hastened away to the same place in expectation of the promised reward. Arriving before him who had been first at the well, and being introduced to His Majesty's presence, the head was examined, but was found without a tongue, concerning which the man, being interrogated, could give no satisfactory account. Whilst this was held in suspense, the other man was introduced with the tongue, claimed the promised reward, and unfolded the riddle by informing His Majesty how and by what means he killed the beast, and thus received the following grant, namely, a certain piece of land lying at Great Horton, known by the name of Hunt Yard, and for the tenure of which he and his heirs for ever should annually attend at the market place at Bradford on St. Martin's Day, in the forenoon, and there by the name of Rushworth hold a dog of the hunting kind whilst three blasts were blown on a horn, and utter these words following, expressed aloud, "Come, heir of Rushworth, come hold my dog whilst I blow three blasts of my horn to pay my Martinmas rent withal."

This tradition has been preserved for centuries. The famed John of Gaunt, lord of the Honor of Pontefract, it is said, added the blowing of the horn in order to make his progress through Bradford more imposing, and the original grant was made to John Northrop, of Manningham, who granted a portion of it to Rushworth, of Horton, for assisting in the horn-blowing ceremony. The horn went with the Hunt Yard property, and was handed down by its possessors for generations. At one time it was used to summon the manufacturers to market. By purchase of part of the Hunt Yard property it came into the possession of Mr. Richard Fawcett, who afterwards lived in Hunt Yard, where his son, the late Canon Fawcett, was born. Mr. Fawcett employed many handcombers in the neighbourhood, and for some time after his removal to Bradford continued the employment.

At the sale of Mr. Fawcett's estate the Hunt Yard property passed into the hands of Messrs. Harris, the bankers, and Messrs. Fox purchased it from them at the price, it is said, of £21 per house. The property now belongs to Mr. R. A. Fox. The famous horn, however, came into the possession of Mr. Jonathan Wright, whose trustees at his death sold it to the late Charles Rhodes, twho afterwards sold it to Dr. Outhwaite. Dr. Outhwaite, having given up his house in Bradford, did not feel himself justified in taking away this interesting relic, and, according to agreement, gave Mr. Rhodes the option of repurchasing it. This Mr. Rhodes did. Afterwards it came into the possession of the late Sir Titus Salt. Finally it has passed into the keeping of the Bradford Philosophical Society, and may be seen in their museum at the Technical College. Its length is about twenty-eight inches, and it is of a beautiful dapple-grey, tipped with silver. The silver tip is understood to have been added while the horn was in the keeping of Mr. Fawcett.

Whilst taking our topographical ramblings in Great Horton proper, we may add a sentence or two in reference to Low Green or Low Fold. The existence here of two or three very ancient houses, including the old Manor House, marks Low Green as one of the original settlements of Great Horton. Tradition has it that the ancient residence of the Horton family, formerly lords of the manor, was situate at Low Green, and some colour is lent to the assumption by an adjoining plot of ground being still called Hall Yard. With all deference to the tradition, however, it is more likely that the latter took its name from the family of Hall, which 200 years ago was one of some standing in that neighbourhood. Upon an old residence adjoining the King's Arms Inn, there are the initials H I M and the date 1697, while similar initials are inscribed upon a building at Low Green, with a subsequent date, 1722. As noted in a previous paper, James Hall was, in 1704, assessed in the property-tax for Horton at 20s., and he was also one of the collectors. He lived at what is called the Manor House, and owned land in front and at the back of his residence. He was a manufacturer, as well as a carrier from this district to London, conveying his own and other makers' goods to the Metropolis by means of bell or pack horses. He had a son John Hall, who lived at the same house afterwards, whose daughter Jane was married to Sammy Blamires, who kept the King's Arms Inn. By Mr. William Cousen's marriage with Phœbe, the daughter of Sammy Blamires, the Low Green property came into the hands of the Cousen family.

Another old residence of equal antiquity at Low Green was that occupied by Eli Suddards, a corn dealer, who commenced the erection of Cross Lane Mill, afterwards purchased and completed by Mr. William Cousen. Upon a house and the date 1657, but as situate near the mill, to its origin we have no is the inscription information. By the laying out of Horton Park several old homesteads have been absorbed. In one of them, called Low Close Farm, resided John Jennings, a well-known townsman, who succeeded James Wilson. The Hall Yard now forms the cricket ground of Horton Park.

CHAPTER XVII.

Lidget Green—Dr. Fawcett—Mount Pleasant School—Schole Moor—The Mortimer Family—The Midgleys—Schole Moor Cemetery—Birks Farm—Sams Mill.

There are doubtless several old portions of Great Horton, as for example Blacksmith Fold and Upper Green, which would yield abundant material for gossip, but we must hie away to Lidget Green and Schole Moor, which are not without features of interest.

Lidget or Lidgate Green has been supposed to be derived from the Saxon *Leodgate*, signifying a gate leading to the adjoining land, and we have abundant evidence that the land to the west was formerly waste or common land. In olden times Lidgate Green would be a quiet place upon the old road leading from Bradford to Halifax, the principal indication of its existence being a blacksmith's shop at the corner of the "Green," and two or three substantial farmsteads close at hand. To one of these the following extract from the Sessions Rolls of 1689 would doubtless apply, where we read:—" An assembly of dissenting Protestants in and about Bradford and Bradford-dale do make choice of the house of Richard Whitchurst, clerk, Lidgate, near Clayton."

From this extract we derive two facts, one being that two hundred years ago the place was called "Lidgate," and the other that under the provisions of the so-called Toleration Act, a little assembly at Lidget contributed to the foundation of Nonconformity in these parts by establishing a meeting-house. It would appear that the residents of Lidget Green in more recent times were intolerant of clerical imposts, the collector of vicar dues having been once stoned away at the risk of his life. Happily there has been no such martyr in recent times. We are unaware whether the great bonfire which upon each anniversary of Gunpowder Plot was set ablaze at Lidget Green had any political or religious significance, but it is certain that the residents of this hamlet have for generations held pronounced views on matters ecclesiastical and political, while local questions excite in them an equal amount of interest.

Lidget Green has given birth to a thrifty race of people, many families, such as the Rawnsleys, Bentleys, Cockcrofts Leaches, Dewhirsts, Holdsworths, and others having clung to the neighbourhood with loving pride. Their histories, however, we must pass over to notice that of one of the celebrities of the neighbourhood.

John Fawcett (afterwards the celebrated Dr. Fawcett) was born at Lidget Green in January, 1739. His father was Stephen Fawcett, a small farmer, and he leaving a numerous progeny, John was bound apprentice to a staymaker in Bradford. Although engaged from six in the morning to eight at night, the young man contrived to steal a few hours for study, and became a good linguist and Biblical scholar. His first religious impressions were received from the celebrated Whitfield, who preached in the Bradford Bowling Green to about ten thousand persons when young Fawcett was about sixteen years of age. He afterwards attended Haworth Church, where the Rev. William Grimshaw, the apostle of the North, officiated. In February, 1758, young Fawcett came before the Baptist Church at Bradford, and was baptised by the Rev. William Crabtree on the 11th of March. Having imbibed the doctrines of the Baptists, he still walked to Haworth to hear the Rev. James Hartley, the Baptist minister, preach; and in 1764 the latter was the means of pressing Mr. Fawcett to accept the pastorate of Wainsgate Chapel, near Hebden Bridge, where he laboured for many years. He afterwards established an academy at Ewood Hall, which attained considerable celebrity and brought him a handsome competence, and in 1811 the degree of D.D. was conferred upon him.

Dr. Fawcett's writings are numerous, his Commentary on the Bible being a text-book for all Biblical scholars, and he wrote many other valuable works, one of which, his "Essay on Anger," brought the author under the notice of George III. This was about the year 1802, when a dignitary of the Church, preaching before His Majesty, quoted a passage on the government of the passions, with which the Royal hearer was particularly pleased, and requested to know the name of the author quoted. This was given, and it was added that he was a minister in Yorkshire of the Baptist denomination. His Majesty wrote to Mr. Fawcett, and the book was sent, accompanied by a modest and respectful letter. The King having read it with great pleasure, expressed to Mr. Fawcett his wish to serve him in any way that might be agreeable. That gentleman, however, rested satisfied with expressing the high sense he entertained of the honour done him, without soliciting further favours. Some time afterwards, the son of one of Mr. Fawcett's members was convicted of forgery, and, sympathising with the afflicted parent, the minister determined to avail himself of his interest with the King, and wrote a very pathetic letter requesting the life of the young man. A reprieve was at once granted, to the great surprise of all who did not know the previous circumstances, but the full particulars of the event Dr. Fawcett considered himself bound by delicacy to conceal during the life of his benefactor. One of the doctor's sermons delivered at the Baptist Association in Bradford in 1810 produced a great effect. His death occurred in 1817; aged seventy-seven.

The building called Mount Pleasant Independent School may be regarded as a link connecting the present with the past. Although of humble appearance contrasted with such erections as the new Board school adjoining, or the numerous Sunday schools upon the elegant scale now prevailing, Mount Pleasant School did good service at a period when such institutions were much needed. Although, as we have shown, a small body of Dissenters had nearly two centuries ago done its part in establishing a meeting-house at the Green, no necessity had apparently arisen for the erection of a place of worship, and half a century ago there was neither church, chapel, nor school-house in the neighbourhood.

The pioneer in providing an acknowledged want was Mr. Joshua Rhodes Balme, of Crosley Hall. He first collected children in a cottage occupied by Sarah Silson, and the school was continued there until the cottage became too small to accommodate the numbers seeking admission. Subscriptions were then raised towards the erection of a school for instruction on Sundays and week days, and a plot of land was purchased from Messrs. John & Robert Turner, stone merchants, of Legrams, containing an area of 324 square yards, for the sum of £40 10s. The trustees contracting for the purchase were the Rev. J. G. Miall, Bradford; Rev. Thos. Hutton, Allerton; Henry Brown, Bradford, draper; Geo. Osborn, Bradford, woolstapler; Wm. Mackay, Manningham, tea dealer; John Wilkinson Balme, Allerton, coal proprietor; Wm. Smith, Legrams, worsted spinner; Samuel Rawnsley, Lidget Green, worsted manufacturer; Joseph Holdsworth, Lidget Green, worsted manufacturer; John Holdsworth, Paradise Green, stuff weaver; Thos. Hammond, Bradford, worsted manufacturer; Thomas Buck, Bradford, worsted spinner; Wm. Wyrill, Bradford, ironmonger; Robert Patterson, Bradford, stuff merchant; and John Dewhirst, Lidget Green, stuff weaver.

The building was opened in the year 1838, with about 120 scholars, Mr. Joshua Balme being the responsible head, assisted, as teachers, by his cousin, Mr. E. Balme, the Misses Holdsworth, Tiplady, Rawnsley, and others. Mr. Balme had had an academic training, and his heart was evidently in the work. He was, however, somewhat of a recluse, and had a little room fitted up in the attic of the school, in which he studied and slept, the dim light of his nightly lamp being often observed in the small hours of the morning. Mount Pleasant School was at first attached to Horton Lane Chapel, then to Salem Chapel, and afterwards to Lister Hills Chapel, with which it is now connected. In 1877 the building was completely remodelled at an expenditure of £600, chiefly through the liberality and endeavours of Mr. Robert Leach, an old scholar at the school, and one of the present trustees.

The National School at Lidget Green was opened in 1839, having been erected principally by subscription. The land for the site was given by Mr. Joshua Pollard, of Crow Trees. The architect of the building was Mr. Wm. Andrews, of Bradford.

Scholemoor (with which may be associated Paradise Green) is a hamlet of Horton adjoining to Lidget Green, and is supposed to have derived its name from having been moorland dotted with rude huts; *scholes* or *schales* denoting huts. That the commons or wastes of Horton lay in the vicinity, if not upon the actual site of the Scholemoor

Cemetery, the deeds handed over to the Corporation abundantly testify. These deeds extend backwards to the year 1520, and bring up the title to the most recent owners. The temptation to copy freely from such a wealth of material is undoubtedly great, but we must be content to indicate by a few extracts the line of owners since the land was "improved" from the waste.

While yet in this condition a family of the name of Thornton would appear to have been possessed of a messuage and lands at Scholemoor, but as they do not appear after about the year 1520, and were then described as of Byrtbe, in the county of York, their interest was probably bought up by the most important Scholemoor family on record, that of the Mortimers. In 1562 John Lacy, of Cromwellbotham, who had succeeded to the lordship of the Manor of Horton by marrying the heiress of the Leventhorpes, conveyed to John Mortimer, of Scholemoor, several parcels taken from the waste lands of Horton, and similar grants were made to William Ellison, of Horton, Thomas Littlewood, and Thomas Wood, rendering knight's service, suit of Court at Horton, and an annual rent of one red rose (an evident indication that the grantor could give no substantial title).

In Oct., 1589, Richard and John Lacy sold the moors and wastes of Horton, at that time said to comprise 250 acres, to Thomas Hodgson, of Bowling, yeoman, Thomas Sharp, Robert Booth, and William Field, of Horton. Accordingly we find several deeds, dated 1591, relating to grants made from the newly-acquired wastes, of which the following is an example, viz. :—

Mar. 31, 1591.—Thos. Hodgson, of Bowling, yeoman, Thos. Sharp, Robt. Booth, Wm. Field, of Horton, yeomen, granted to Edwd. Mortimer, of Horton, clothier, all those parcels of land, being portions of eight acres forming part of Horton common or moor, five acres being on the west side of the road *leading to the end of the mansion-house* of Ed. Mortimer, and abutting on the north side by the road leading from Clayton to Bradford. Another parcel of five roods abutting on the same road, and on the east side by land belonging to Benjamin Kennett, clerk ; and another parcel lying in the Upper Moor, being portions of land assigned to Edwd. Mortimer, Richard Clayton, John Hollings, Thos. Barraclough, and others. And also another parcel containing 1A. 1R., having a road over it, being the residue of the aforesaid eight acres, abutting on the lands of Ed. Mortimer, in Horton.

The mention of a "mansion-house" at that remote period naturally leads the antiquarian mind to wonder where it might be situate, and there can be little doubt that the residence in question was that which stood near the top of Scholemoor Cemetery when the land was acquired for burial purposes. The house was a substantial specimen of the class usually inhabited by the smaller gentry, having heavy overhanging eaves, and massive mullioned windows. A pair of huge pillars flanked the entrance gateway in front, a broad walk leading to the house. Several of the large trees surrounding the residence are now standing in the Cemetery.

The Mortimers evidently added to their possessions in other parts of the township, as is shown by deeds dealing with land at Hollinwood, to which place members of the family migrated from the paternal homestead. Particulars of the Scholemoor branch are given in the following summarised wills :—

Will of John Mortimer, of Scholemoor, dated 1658.

John Mortimer, yeoman, in his last will and testament, made May 12, 1658, devised to William Mortimer, his younger son, and his heirs, all that dwelling-house and barn, with one close of land belonging, then in the occupation of Matthew Sowden, and situate in Horton ; four closes called Milner Closes, and other closes in Horton, occupied by the said John Mortimer. To Elizabeth, Martha, Sarah, and Mary Mortimer, his daughters, he left one hundred pounds each. To his wife Mary he bequeathed a portion of his goods and chattels ; and to his eldest son John the residue of his estate.

Witnesses : Richard Booth, William Field, John Illingworth.

Will of John Mortimer, jun., of Scholemoor, dated 1678.

John Mortimer, yeoman, of Scholemoor, in his last will and testament, made December, 1678, provided that if the child then expectant should be a son, then he should inherit all his estate at Scholemoor ; and, if a daughter, he bequeathed to her the sum of three hundred pounds, and in that case devised his estates to his brother William, his heirs, &c., upon payment of the above bequest to his unborn daughter upon her attaining her majority. To his wife Elizabeth he made provision by a yearly allowance during her lifetime. To Elizabeth, Martha, Sarah, and Mary, his four sisters, he left the sum of one hundred pounds,

Witnesses : John Sagar, John Hodgson, David Midgley.

Rambles Round Horton.

In Sir John Maynard's valuation of the rectorial tythes of Horton, made in 1638, John Mortimer, of Scholemoor, is assessed at £21 on three oxgangs of land, and a John Mortimer is the only master miner named in the early registers of the Bradford Parish Church; while in the allotment of sittings at the church, made before 1705, Wm. Mortimer has the largest number allotted to him as a freeholder of Horton, namely, four and one-fourth, showing that William had succeeded to his brother John's estate (as bequeathed in the second will) failing a son being born to the inheritance. Indeed we have the receipt before us dated June, 1705, wherein his brother's wife Elizabeth acknowledges the half-yearly payment of £6 13s. 4d., "by virtue of the last will and testament of John Mortimer, my late husband."

The relation of the Mortimers to the Tempest family of Horton is indicated to some extent in the following extract from a deed referring to Shelf Hall, wherein by indenture dated

July 12, 1660.—Richard Mortymer, of Horton, in Bradford-dale, yeoman, in consideration of the sum of £19 6s., bargains to sell to Martha Best, of Landimere, Shelf, widow of Richard Best, and Michael Best, younger son of Richard Best late of the same, yeoman, deceased, the messuage called "the old house," &c., in Shelf, late the inheritance of Richard Tempest, of Horton, deceased, late uncle of Richard Mortymer deceased, who died without issue. The estate then came to Richard Mortymer, as cousin and next heir of the said Richard Tempest, (that is to say) son and heir of Sarah, late wife of William Mortymer, deceased, late father of said Richard Mortymer, and which said Sarah was sister and only heir of Richard Tempest.

Witnesses: Isaac Maude, Jas. Sagar, Will. Appleyard, John Learoyd.

About the beginning of the eighteenth century the Mortimer estate at Scholemoor appears to have become merged in that of the Midgleys, one of the four sisters named in John Mortimer's will having married a Midgley, who in 1706 administered to the personalty of her brother, William Mortimer. The Midgley family was of ancient descent at Headley, in Thornton, and was connected by marriage with many of the chief families in the neighbourhood. In the Bradford Parish Church there is a handsome mural monument

Rambles Round Horton.

in memory of John Midgley, of Scholemoor, who died in 1730, and of Bathsheba, his wife, daughter of John Hollings, of Crosley Hall, who died in 1736. The deceased gentleman was an attorney. The deeds conveying the Scholemoor estate to the Bradford Corporation describe the Midgleys as of Scholemoor, and presumably residing at the former mansion of the Mortimers.

About 1740 two maiden sisters of John Midgley, of Scholemoor, gentleman, named Mary and Martha, purchased the adjoining manor of Clayton for £1000. Mary Midgley became the first wife of Samuel Lister, Esq., of Horton, and, she dying in 1764 without issue, the manor became the property of her unmarried sister, Martha, who by her will dated 1778 devised the lordship of Clayton and all her estate to the Rev. Geo. Cooke, of Everton, and Mary his wife, who was a Hollings. The Rev. Henry Cooke, a son of the latter, succeeded to the Scholemoor estate, and in 1800 sold it to Mr. John Jarratt, of Bradford, who had land in the neighbourhood, the Scholemoor land being then in the tenancy of Richard Lumby, farmer. In 1814 Mr. Jarratt disposed of his interest to John Booth, farmer, of Denby, Allerton, who, by his will, dated 1826, bequeathed his estates at Clayton, Manningham, and Scholemoor to Joshua Robertshaw, of Swain Royd, and James and William Booth, both of Allerton, in trust for the use of his wife Mary, and Ann Lumby, his daughter, and her children.

The transfer of the Scholemoor estate to the Corporation was made in 1858 by Wm. Pickles, Wilsden; Dan Hopkin, Clifton; Jos. Woodhead, Cleckheaton; and Catherine Booth Woodhead, daughter of Samuel Lumby. Samuel and Richard Lumby, of Scholemoor, were brothers, the former residing in the homestead previously described as standing within the Cemetery grounds, and the latter in the farmstead situate near to the Cemetery gates. Both the brothers Lumby were very active townsmen during the early part of the present century. Richard was largely engaged in farming operations; Samuel, or "owd Sammy Lumby," as he was invariably called, was almost wholly engaged in town's business either as overseer or constable, and he was the leading churchwarden at

Bell Chapel. In 1857, when the Scholemoor estate came into the market, Mr. James Dixon, of Bradford, purchased two lots, upon the site of which he erected North Park Lodge, where he resides.

Scholemoor Cemetery stands in a beautiful position just beyond Lidget Green, the ground lying upon a gentle slope overlooking the Thornton Valley. An estate of more than thirty acres was purchased by the Corporation at a cost of £4750. Twenty acres have been laid out, ten acres being reserved in fields and meadows for future appropriation. The principal works were begun in the latter part of 1858, and were carried out under the direction of Mr. Gott, the borough surveyor, the registrar's house and the chapels having been erected from the designs of Mr. E. Milnes, architect. The cost of the site and the laying out was about £11,000

Springfield, the residence of Mr. Simeon Townend, is not very ancient, although it has been much altered in appearance. Formerly the ground upon which it stands, as well as the adjoining land, formed a part of the estate of the Pollards, of Crow Trees, afterwards bought by the Horsfalls. The house has been occupied successively by Joshua Dewhirst, John Hardaker, topmaker and farmer, John Sagar, Jo. Morris, solicitor; and others. Before Mr. Morris entered to it the land was said to be "too poor to summer a gooise," but under his care, and that of the succeeding occupier, it has been much improved.

Until recently the carriage way which divided the two portions of Scholemoor Cemetery led to a footpath which to the left went forward to Crosley Hall, and to the right led to Birks Farm, comprising two separate tenements. One occupied by James Pearson contains the inscription T H 1691 over the doorway and cut in the mantelpiece of an adjoining building the initials T H A and the date 1664. There is also a curious motto accompanying the latter inscription, as follows:—
"My son, fear the Lord and the King, and meddle not with them that are given to change." This portion of the homestead is in a ruinous condition, but was formerly owned and occupied by Thomas Hodgson, who is severally described

as a woolstapler and merchant. His family continued the occupation, a more recent Thomas Hodgson being one of the original trustees of Horton Lane Chapel, and described in the deeds of 1781 as a worsted stuff maker. He afterwards removed to a good house on the site of Messrs. D. Illingworth & Sons' Mill in Thornton Road. A long time ago this portion of Birks Farm was in the occupation of William Smith, and then of John Waugh, of Shuttleworth Hall, whose family combined clog-making with farming.

An adjoining house, but one not of so ancient an appearance, has for generations been in the occupation of the family of Bakes. Both properties until recently belonged to Mr. J. A. Jowett, as the descendant of the Hodgsons, but Bakes's Farm has lately been purchased by the Corporation for the purpose of improving the cemetery site.

The situation of Sams Mill marks it as the probable site of a very old corn mill, bordering the stream which, after receiving the waters of Bullgreave Beck, dividing Clayton from Horton, is afterwards known as Bradford Beck. The origin of the name of the mill is obscure, but the date of its foundation is probably given in an inscribed stone upon an inner wall, which originally was an outer wall, as follows :— T H 1690 with the words, "Sams Mill on Middle Broke," namely, that portion of the stream dividing Allerton and Clayton. The above date and initials, it will be observed, correspond with those upon the old house at Birks ; indeed, the mill was evidently erected by Thomas Hodgson, and afterwards passed to Dicky Hodgson, of Whetley, from whom the property has descended to its present owner, Mr. J. A. Jowett.

Of former millers we have only recent records. A century ago John Jennings, whose family were millers at Bowling Corn Mill, and lessees of the old Soke Mill, Bradford, was tenant of Sams Mill, and in April, 1789, was killed by the cogwheel of the mill. His widow married John Dalby, of Leventhorpe Mill and Crosley Hall, who succeeded to Sams Mill. After Dalby came Joseph Pilling, who had previously run Poole old mill. He lived at the house adjoining Sams Mill, where his sons William and Joseph were born. The latter were of an enterprising turn, as, in addition to running Sams Mill, they occupied Beckside Mill at Horton, and about forty years ago erected the premises in Manchester Road, now known as the Borough Mills (Messrs. J. Ellis & Co.).

James Pearson, of Leventhorpe Mill, followed the Pillings at Sams Mill, and has been the miller there now for forty years. By alterations and additions the old mill has been almost completely absorbed, and little is observable of the original structure. Many years ago, however, Mr. Pearson discovered an underground passage, which had apparently been long hidden from view, and of which the former tenant knew nothing, which had been probably a portion of the goit for the waste water. The old house adjoining has also received considerable additions.

In an old map of 1773 the adjoining land is named "Scoles-moor," and the bridge leading to it from Manningham, "Thief-ford Bridge." Thiefscore Lane, which has been greatly widened and otherwise improved, has been re-named Cemetery Road, and Scholemoor Lane altered to Necropolis Road.

CHAPTER XVIII.

Legrams Lane—The Bentleys—Horton Grange—Dr. Maud—The Turner Family—John Jackson and Stephen Fawcett Lister Hills—The West End Building Club—Tanhouse—Fieldhead Dyeworks—Samuel Smith—The " Happy Valley."

Legrams Lane is chiefly noticeable for the array of familiar names with which it has been associated. Indeed, to do justice to this part of the township an additional paper would be needed, but we must refrain.

One of the names calling for mention is that of Nathan Bentley. He was of a humble Horton family, and was brought up to handloom weaving. By marriage with a daughter of Mr. Joshua Bakes, of Horton, Mr. Bentley acquired property at Legrams, and in 1837 erected upon it Northside Mill, in which he successfully carried on the worsted business, being, next to Mr. Cowling Ackroyd, the largest manufacturer in Horton at one time. The business was afterwards conducted by his sons Edwin, William, Bakes, Nathan, and Henry Bentley, but was given up some years ago. Besides his commercial enterprise, Mr. Nathan Bentley had military leanings, and held a recruiting commission under Government. He was himself a man of commanding presence and of soldierlike bearing.

A more ancient family than the one last named resided in the substantial farmhouse opposite the entrance gates of Horton Grange, namely, that of Swaine. As already stated, it was from this homestead that Mr. John Rand the elder married his wife, the daughter of Samuel Swaine. The Woods, father and son, succeeded Swaine, and they have been followed by the Robertshaws. The farm, however, has for generations belonged to the Hodgson family, represented by Mr. J. A. Jowett. In an upper portion of the farmstead there is a fine plaster cast of the Royal arms, surmounted by the initials of Charles II. and the date 1660. At some period the apartment has probably been used as a justice-room.

Horton Grange has a twofold history, associated as it is with Dr. Maud, a member of an old Quaker family, and with the Turners, the latter being one of the most influential families in the township. Dr. William Maud was born in Bradford in 1765, his father, Timothy, being a surgeon there. His father's place of business was in Westgate, and to his practice William Maud succeeded, and became an exceedingly popular practitioner. He was amongst the first to give effect to Jenner's discovery of vaccination. He also established, with his partner, the firm of Maud & Wilson, druggists, in Sun Bridge, but in 1820 retired from practice, and went to reside at a large house which stood on the site of the Victoria Hotel in Bridge Street. He was an eminent member of the Society of Friends, and took great interest in the slave-trade question, the Bible Society, and Sunday schools, besides giving his professional advice gratis to poor people.

Mr. Maud removed from Bridge Street to Legrams, having for his residence an old house which stood on the site of Horton Grange. This house he much improved, and also planted the trees now surrounding the grounds.

About the year 1831 Mr. Maud withdrew altogether from town life, and retired to a small farm in Craven, which he took great pleasure in cultivating, and where he spent the remainder of his days. His death occurred in September, 1835, aged seventy-one. Benjamin Seebohm, of the firm of Hustler & Seebohm, woolstaplers, succeeded Dr. Maud at Legrams, but ultimately went to reside at Hitchin, where his family still live.

Horton Grange estate next became the property of Messrs. John & Robert Turner, stone merchants, whose quarries were also situate in Legrams. The old homestead of the Turners was that since acquired and enlarged by Mr. George Hodgson. The two brothers pulled down Dr. Maud's old residence and erected upon the site two houses, in which they resided, and upon the death of John the Grange was made into one residence for Robert, who was the father of Messrs. George, John, and Robert Turner, of Holme Top and Beckside Mills. Horton Grange is now the residence of Mr. George Turner, who has added to his estate much of the land in the vicinity. The Gothic villa in Legrams Lane was built for the widow of Mr. John Turner.

The Swaines and the Ramsbothams, families of importance in Bradford in the beginning of the century, were associated with Legrams, but ample reference was made to both families while treating of commercial matters in a previous chapter. The house, which is now the Willowfield Hotel, was the residence of Mr. H. R. Ramsbotham. Prior to his occupancy of it, a family named Smith, comprising two bachelor brothers and a sister, resided there. Lawrence Smith, whose residence was a little higher up Legrams Lane, farmed the land on which Princeville stands.

The building now occupied by Mr. George Robertshaw is one of the few farmsteads which retain their ancient appearance in this neighbourhood. Inscribed on the ample porch are the initials

B.
G. B.

and the date 1728. The main structure is evidently of a prior date. The leading initial, we believe, denotes the house to have been a residence of the Barraclough family, of Horton. The property had, however, been acquired by Dicky Hodgson, of Whetley, prior to 1800, at which period Isaac Wilkinson, a stuff-maker, was the occupant. John Rhodes, John Wilkinson, and George Robertshaw have since divided the occupation.

Tanhouse, probably the early residence of the Brooksbank family, was for forty years occupied by William Greenwood. Before him Joseph Freeman, tanner, occupied the premises. The new building, however, was erected as a residence for Tom Hirst, one of the Hirsts of Clayton, and sometime schoolmaster at the National School, Great Horton. The love of sport, however, was such a predominant feature in Tom Hirst's character that it is said he would any day leave his school to follow the hounds, and probably his scholars offered no objection to the holiday thus secured.

Before quitting Legrams a brief record of two of its celebrities, namely, the late John Jackson and Stephen Fawcett, may be inserted. Both occupied an humble sphere in life, and both were remarkable in their respective walks.

John Jackson, or the "old Chartist," as he was latterly styled, was a native of Harden, but when quite a lad came to Horton, where his father had obtained employment at

Knight's cotton mill. John himself worked at the padpost, and probably while at his occupation round the " pot o' four " he imbibed those political notions which distinguished his after life. He relinquished woolcombing, however, while yet a young man, and took to horticultural pursuits, for which he had a natural bent, and which he indulged so long as strength allowed him. Meanwhile Jackson was a close student of theology, of political economy, and of politics generally. He was one of the first Chartists, but he had no sympathy with " physical force," and strongly opposed many of the doctrines held by his colleagues. He, along with Mr. Squire Farrar, Mr. Wm. Richardson, and a few others, established the old Radical Reform Club in Bradford, out of which all subsequent organisations of a like character have sprung.

John Jackson was always ready with his pen to uphold his beliefs, and wrote many letters and pamphlets under the signature, " J. J.," his most notable pamphlet being that directed against Feargus O'Connor, entitled "The Demagogue Done Up." He was also a good conversationalist, being full of quaint humour. For more than half a century John Jackson lived at Legrams, and in the same cottage. His means, however, were very slender, and having lost his partner in life he gave up his modest mansion, and built himself a tiny hut in his garden allotment, and in this hermit fashion he lived up to within a few days of his death, which occurred at nearly eighty years of age, in March, 1875.

Stephen Fawcett was a man entitled to rank amongst the best of our local poets, and might have acquired an even more distinguished position had he not attempted too much. For forty years he wrote and published poems and lyrics descriptive of the natural scenery and legendary incidents connected with his native valley of the Wharfe, as well as on other topics, reverential, pathetic, grotesque, or tragic. His first essay was in 1837, when he published his " Wharfedale Lays and Legends " ; in 1842 his " Edwy and Elgiva " appeared ; and in 1872, by subscription, his " Bradford Legends." None of his literary ventures, however, brought him pecuniary gain — a penalty frequently attaching to literary effort.

Rambles Round Horton.

Stephen Fawcett was a man of voracious appetite for learning, and by his own efforts mastered Latin, French, and Italian, thus enabling him to consult authors in all three languages. It was within an hour of giving a discourse to a few friends in White Abbey, upon a passage from the Latin version of Swedenborg's *Adversaria*, in December, 1876, that he was found dead in a backyard in the neighbourhood. For some time previous he had been supported by the generosity of friends almost as poor as himself, and it is more than probable that he died from the lack of sufficient sustenance. Stephen Fawcett was a native of Burley, where he was born in 1806. At the time of his death, therefore, he had reached the allotted term of life.

Remembering the present populous character of Lister Hills, the statement would hardly be credited that in the year 1825 the inhabitants of that district were limited to the half-dozen families resident at Cuckoo Nest. It was so, however. There was no Lister Hills Road, nor Longside Lane, nor Richmond Road, nor Preston Street, giving access to the locality, this being alone supplied by Water Lane, leading to Silsbridge Lane, and a footpath in continuation of Shearbridge Road through the Fieldhead estate and over the beck to Manningham. The land principally belonged to Mrs. Giles, representing the old Sharp family, and Col. Fitzgerald, if we except the Fieldhead Estate, which belonged to Mr. Henry Oates, who had a residence opposite Shearbridge Road, then a narrow steep lane crossing the Horton Beck.

The origin of the name of Lister Hills is clear. The Fitzgeralds obtained the property by the marriage of Col. Fitzgerald with the daughter of Dr. Crowther, of Leeds, she being heir-at-law of Samuel Lister, of Horton House, gentleman. In the settlement drawn up in view of the marriage of Samuel Lister and his second wife Dorothy, in 1766, mention is made of closes of land in Horton called the Langsides, purchased by him of Benjamin Kennett, vicar of Bradford, and inherited by the latter from his grandfather, Mr. Stockdale; and also the Great and Little Laistridge, Tumbling Hill (then occupied by John Whitaker); and the Norcroft, purchased by Samuel Lister of Thomas Aked, but previously owned by Faith Sawrey (heiress of the Sharp estates). The bulk of the land in question comprised what is now known as Lister Hills, evidently derived from the name of Lister, of Horton House.

This view is confirmed by the ground plan of the Fitzgerald Estate, dated 1825, in which the names Upper and Lower Lister Hills occur. In the latter year a large portion of the Horton property of the Fitzgeralds was put into the market for sale as building land, and many blocks in Lister Hills were sold. Directly afterwards, however, came the great commercial crisis, bringing down the Wakefield Bank and other previously considered safe repositories, and as a consequence many of the speculators declined or were unable to take up their purchases. Nor was the difficulty got over easily, and not until the vendors had undertaken the laying out and construction of Norcroft Road, now Richmond Road, and Longside Lane, as an approach to the various building plots. For years afterwards very few dwelling-houses were put up on the estate, those in Lister Terrace, erected by Dr. Thomas Lister, being about the first.

In the year 1845, or twenty years subsequent to the opening up of the Fitzgerald Estate, an important building movement was instituted at Lister Hills, leading to the erection of Cobden Street, Bright Street, and Villiers Street. At that period building clubs were in their infancy, the Belgrave Place and one or two other clubs having just been started. Inspired by the growing desire to become landlords, carrying with it the privilege of a vote for the county, several working men put their savings together and founded the West End Building Society, and a suitable plot of land belonging to the Giles Estate of Horton Old Hall being available, they purchased the whole at the price of 2s. 6¾d. per yard. It may be added that the corner plot upon which the Waterloo Hotel stands, exchanged for a site selected by the West End Club, only cost 1s. 6d. per yard.

A critical moment, however, occurred in the early history of the West End Building Society which might have wrecked the hopes of its promoters. Their accumulated capital had reached £900, and had been invested in the Leeds and West

Rambles Round Horton.

Riding Union Bank, whose premises were in Bank Street, when a rumour reached the trustees of the society that the bank was in difficulties. In great distress the treasurer hastened with his bank book, arriving just in time to find the doors of the bank being closed to the public! The entire capital of the building club was invested in the bank, and affairs looked serious; but to the honour of the shareholders of the bank be it said that they paid every farthing of the club's deposit, not even reserving bank commission. At the commencement of the society's operations only a few straggling erections had appeared in Lister Hills, but the demand for shares was such that dwellings were put up as fast as share capital was available. The names given to the various streets were inspired by the great Corn-Law agitation, then at its height.

Practically, if not in order of priority, the opening up of the Fieldhead Estate led to the development of Lister Hills. This property, as previously stated, belonged to Mr. Henry Oates, a member of the Leeds family of that name. At the beginning of the century Mr. Oates was a somewhat prominent member of Bradford society, and was a partner in the Old Brewery. He was an active member of Chapel Lane Chapel, and of a very benevolent disposition. At any rate, he was a wealthy man, and lived at Fieldhead House, surrounding which he planted trees, adding quite a rural aspect to the suburban locality.

Upwards of half a century ago Mr. Oates disposed of his estate at Fieldhead to Mr. Robert Stables Ackroyd, of Great Horton, who erected upon a portion of it Fieldhead Mill, which he occupied. Another portion he sold to the firm of Messrs. Joseph Smith & Sons, comprising John and Thomas Smith, dyers, of Halifax, who commenced the erection of Fieldhead Dyeworks, opened in October, 1835. After a few years the senior partner and his son Thomas went out of the firm, and Mr. Samuel Smith joined his brothers at Bradford, under the style of Samuel Smith, Brothers & Co., the dyeworks at Halifax being still carried on. In 1843 a dissolution of partnership took place, and Mr. John Smith retired, when the firm traded as Messrs. Samuel Smith & Co., and under this title it has been carried on until the concern was transformed into a limited company in 1878, the directors being Mr. S. Milne Milne, Mr. C. Telford Smith, and Mr. William Binns.

It is unnecessary to add that the Fieldhead Dyeworks have been greatly enlarged since their formation, being now among the most extensive in the district. Field House was erected by Mr. John Smith, one of the early partners, and upon the late Mr. Samuel Smith coming to Bradford he took up his residence there. Fieldhead Mills were occupied by Messrs. Tremel & Co. after the death of Mr. R. S. Ackroyd, but were purchased by Mr. John Smith, father of Alderman Isaac Smith, who is now the owner and occupier. Mr. Archibald Neill some years ago purchased the residue of the Oates Estate, including Fieldhead House, and upon it he erected many dwelling-houses, including St. Andrew's Villas.

No topographic notice of Lister Hills would be complete without reference, however brief, to the character and enterprise of the late Samuel Smith, of Fieldhead Dyeworks. Of his commercial ability ample proof was furnished in the rapid increase of the dyeworks after he became the leading partner. He had not long been settled at Lister Hills before he began to afford evidence that his mind was not wholly absorbed in commercial affairs.

With a view to the development of the neighbourhood of the dyeworks he commenced the erection of dwelling-houses of an improved character in Preston Place, which was named after Mr. John Preston, of Bradford, woolstapler, and a cousin of Mrs. Smith, to whom he left some property. The street afterwards got the name of Preston Street. At the corner block Mr. Smith erected a building which was used as a chapel and school-room, and in which occasional oratorios were given under Mr. Smith's management. Preston Place School was completed in February, 1847, the organ being opened at the same time by Dr. Gauntlett.

Mr. Smith's love of music was intense, and his skill and judgment in musical matters were highly valued in quarters not restricted to this neighbourhood. He was the chief promoter of the erection of St. George's Hall, and was the

Rambles Round Horton.

chairman of the company for many years. It was during the first year of his mayoralty of Bradford, in 1851, that the foundation-stone of the hall was laid with Masonic honours. The Bradford Festival Choral Society was also established mainly through his influence, and as its president he gloried in the proud position to which the society attained. In public affairs Mr. Smith acquired equal prominence, he having been the first burgess called upon to sustain the office of Mayor of Bradford for three years in succession, namely, from November, 1851, to November, 1854. His death occurred at Cliffe Hill, Warley, in July, 1873, at the age of sixty-eight.

The church of St. Andrew, at Lister Hills, was erected in 1852 at a cost of £3000. The building was consecrated by the Bishop of Ripon on September 28, 1853. The tower has since been added. Lister Hills Independent Chapel dates its origin from the little preaching-room established by Mr. Samuel Smith, at Preston Place. The chapel was opened in 1854, and in its erection and subsequent well-being Mr. Smith took an active interest.

When the various wards of the borough were rearranged by the Town Council a short time ago, Lister Hills was made to include a very large portion of Little Horton, and the upper boundary was fixed at the centre of Trinity Road, Grafton Street, and Caledonia Street. Many people thought at that time that some entirely new name would have been better than an old one which represented a mere fraction of the newly formed area, Lister Hills proper being solely that part of the old hamlet and district of Little Horton lying between the stream called West Brook and the township of Manningham.

Ashfield, or the "Happy Valley," as it was termed from its being colonised by Quakers, was originally a portion of the Giles (or Sharp) estate, until the advantage of the site for residential purposes was recognised by John Armistead and Wm. Frazer Hoyland, two Bradford grocers, members of the Society of Friends. The situation was indeed very pleasant, all the land being open around Ashfield, with a clear stream running down the valley. Another company of Quaker builders erected residences in Westbrook Place, on the opposite

O

side of the valley, giving rise to the "happy" name by which for many years this immediate locality was known. James Ellis, also a Friend, erected West Lodge, now the residence of Alderman Nathan Drake, and in it he resided for some time. The "four ashes,"—a tree four stems of which grew from one root—and said to be about half way between Hull and Liverpool, once stood near to the top of Ashfield. It fell to the ground in November, 1835, completely blocking up the highway opposite.

CHAPTER XIX.

Religious Organisations—The Wesleyans—The Old School at Todley—Hunt Yard Chapel—The Old Bell Chapel - Rev. Samuel Redhead—Rev. J. C. Boddington—Rev. John Harrison Rev. G. M. Webb—St. John the Evangelist—Moravian Chapel, Paternoster Fold—Primitive Methodism—Wesley Place Chapel—The Congregationalists.

In "rambling" about Great Horton no mention was made of the religious organisations and several other matters, in order that the topographic survey upon which we set out might be presented in a connected form. The omission may now be supplied, and in so doing a chapter may be devoted to the religious societies of the place.

Among existing organisations the honour of first starting a school and place of worship in Great Horton belongs to the Wesleyans, who set about the erection of the small building at Old Todley (the present site of Broadbent's Mill), which, as previously stated, was completed in the year 1766. A class had been formed in Great Horton, however, long before this period.

In Stamp's "History of Methodism" we read that "amongst those who at this early period (1747) joined the ranks of Methodism was Nathaniel Dracup, of Great Horton; a steady, moral young man, then in his nineteenth year, who subsequently became one of the most exemplary and useful members of the Wesleyan Society." Dracup was a native of Idle, but early in life removed to Great Horton, and in all likelihood was the first Methodist in the then small village. He was the leader of the first class formed in Great Horton, and for many years previous to the erection of the school at Todley, the services were held beneath his roof. He died in 1798, aged sixty-nine, and was of course buried in the ground at Old Todley, but his remains were among those removed to Hunt Yard, when the oak coffin in which he lay was repolished by his son. Among the literary remains of Nathaniel Dracup is a touching "Elegy" written by him on the death of the celebrated Rev. Wm. Grimshaw, of Haworth, to whom he was devotedly attached.

Nathaniel Dracup, described as a "shuttlemaker, Great Horton," was a party to the deed of erection of the old Octagon Chapel at Bradford in the year 1765, and he was one of the society stewards, Bradford being at that early period regarded as a branch of the Birstall circuit. He had a son Nathaniel, also a son George, the father of Sammy Dracup, who, with his sons, were noted shuttlemakers and makers of jacquard engines when first introduced. The Dracups have been devoted Wesleyans throughout their history.

From the first "catalogue of the societies" in connection with the Bradford circuit, issued in 1781, we obtain the names of the class leaders and local preachers at Great Horton at that period, who were as follow:—John Murgatroyd, Nathaniel Dracup, John Hodgson, Richard Fawcett, Thos. Dobson, John Shutt, John Smith, James Wilkinson, John Haley, Jonathan Hudson, and James Throp. Including Clayton Heights and Brownroyd, there were at that period 175 members in the Great Horton Society.

In the year 1814, the old school at Todley becoming far too small to contain the increasing society and congregation, a new and spacious chapel (first called Hunt Yard Chapel), holding about 500 persons, was erected. Such was the desire, however, to occupy the new chapel, that service was held in it some months before its actual completion, and on Easter Tuesday, 1815, its formal opening took place, the Revs. Robert Newton and James Everett preaching on the occasion. The trust deed bears date May 1st, 1815, and is signed by the following persons as trustees, viz. :—Nathaniel Dracup, John Ramsden, Jonas Milnes, Eli Suddards, Joseph Wilkinson, Roger Milnes, John Suddards, John Fawcett, James Brooksbank, Thomas Stocks, William Holdsworth, William Nettleton, John Mason, George Dracup, Samuel Bentley, William Lee, and Thomas Ramsden. In 1820 a commodious school-room was erected on the chapel premises at a cost of £300. This was subsequently enlarged. In 1830 the land, originally on lease and subject to an annual rent of £16, was converted into freehold at an additional expense of £300, on which occasion the trust deed of the whole premises was renewed. This deed bears date November 17th, 1830. In 1834 the chapel premises were rendered still more complete by the erection of a preacher's house adjoining the chapel, its first occupant being the Rev. Benjamin Pearce. Annexed to the chapel was the burial-ground.

On the erection of the Church Sunday School at Horton in 1808, under the auspices of the Rev. John Crosse, vicar of Bradford, the Sabbath school which for many years had been held by the Methodists in their ancient school and preaching-room was transferred to the Church, and as a Methodist school was not revived till twelve years afterwards. But for this circumstance the Horton Wesleyan Sunday School might have claimed the precedence of well nigh every other in the West Riding. In 1842 the Great Horton circuit was formed of places mostly taken from that of Bradford West. Since that period the Great Horton Wesleyan Chapel has been much enlarged, and, with its accessories, forms one of the most valuable Conference properties in the county.

The memorial stone of the Wesleyan Day and Sunday Schools was laid by Thomas Farmer, Esq., of Arthington Hall, on the 30th day of August, 1859, and the schools were opened in the year 1860. The cost of the erection was about £3000, raised by subscriptions and a Government grant of £1050.

Many of the above particulars have been obtained from the historical notices of Wesleyan Methodism by the Rev. W. W. Stamp, which were compiled while that gentleman was stationed at Great Horton during the years 1838-40. The rev. gentleman may indeed be claimed as a Bradford man, having been born here in 1801, while his father, the Rev. John Stamp, was stationed in Bradford. The Rev. W. W. Stamp, was elected President of the Conference in 1860, and died in Liverpool in January, 1877.

The records of Methodism in Great Horton furnish many examples of devotion to the society, if space permitted us to enlarge upon the topic. Thomas Peel is said to have been the first subscriber to the new chapel at Hunt Yard. Nathan Bentley, with his large family of sons, was also a prominent figure, and the record, however incomplete, should contain the names of Ramsden, Blamires, Dracup, Jennings, White,

Myers, Shepherd, and Greenwood. In former times there was a "warmth" in the services of which the present congregation have little experience. The elder members have still a lively recollection of one "local," named James Carter, whose deep and powerful voice was often heard exhorting the people. Dick Throp had also one of the strongest voices in the village, and used it vehemently. Willie Thornton, a class leader, was nearly equal to him in lung power, and was greatly gifted in devotion. Other equally prominent Methodists were Job Robertshaw and W. Crabtree.

It was the custom in those days for Methodists to have preaching service every Sunday morning at five o'clock. James Carter, who was also a fine bugle player, would go an hour before that time to different corners of the village, and with some fine old psalm tune would arouse the people to early morning service. The anniversary, or "sitting-up," was also a great event. Financially, however, these occasions did not compare well with the present day. If £25 was raised it was thought a great sum; but after the Disruption in 1850 the Reformers and the Old Body could each raise more than treble that amount.

There being no Episcopalian church nearer to Great Horton than Bradford or Thornton, a movement was started for the erection of a church, and the Old Bell Chapel was built in the year 1806, and consecrated on July 1st, 1809, as a chapel of ease to the Parish Church of Bradford. It was a plain structure, without any attempt at architectural effect. The original cost was £1200, which was raised by subscription, Mr. John Rand the elder being one of the principal contributors. The communion plate was presented to the chapel by Mrs. Lister, of Manningham. A record of the original erection and subsequent addition is preserved in the following inscriptions:—

This chapel of ease, subject to the Parish Church of Bradford, was built by subscription in the year of our Lord 1806. This clock put up in 1808.
JOSEPH BEANLAND, JOHN BLAMIRES, Churchwardens.

This vestry built and chapel repaired by the town A.D. 1823.
Rev. J. C. BODDINGTON, Incumbent.
JOSEPH GOMERSALL, JOHN BLAMIRES, Churchwardens.

The site was taken from the waste land of Horton. The perpetual curacy, first valued at £99 per annum, was augmented in 1810 with £200 of Queen Anne's Bounty, and in 1813, 1818, and 1821 with sums amounting to £1800 in Parliamentary grants. The Vicar of Bradford is the patron. The first baptism was dated July 2, 1809, and was that of William, son of James and Rebecca Bennett. Since that date the number of baptisms has been 2785, and the burials 2817, the first burial being that of John Fox, woolcomber, aged sixty-three, who died July 25th, 1809.

The first incumbent appointed to the Old Bell Chapel was the Rev. Samuel Redhead. Mr. Redhead was not resident in Great Horton during his incumbency, but lived at Fawcett Hill, Horton Road, in the house afterwards occupied by Dr. Brown, where he kept a school described as a classical academy. Mr. Redhead laboured very earnestly in Horton till the year 1822, when the living of Haworth was presented to him, but the people of that district would not have him as their vicar, not from any personal dislike to him, but because he had been presented by the Vicar of Bradford. The strange scenes which were enacted in Haworth Church during his initiation have been oft referred to. After three weeks' possession of the living he resigned, and was afterwards appointed to the living of Calverley, having shortly before married Miss Rand, sister of Messrs. John and William Rand. He died in August, 1845.

During the incumbency of Mr. Redhead there was commenced the movement for the erection of the National School, which was built by public subscription in the year 1808. The Sunday school up to this period had been conducted in two cottages in Bartle Fold. This building also stood upon the waste, and in front were placed a pair of stocks, which were a terror to evil-doers.

The next incumbent after Mr. Redhead was the Rev. J. C. Boddington, who was curate of the Parish Church of Bradford at the time of his appointment, but came from Leamington. Mr. Boddington was well fitted for the position to which he was appointed, not only as an able minister of the gospel, but also as having considerable skill in medicine.

In his labours at Great Horton he was the means of doing great good both spiritually and bodily. He was an able pulpit speaker, a good classical scholar, and had considerable acquaintance with natural philosophy.

Although the stipend was small, the respected incumbent wanted not for means, assistance being tendered him by others. He was the only man in Great Horton who was vouchsafed the title of "Mr." Mr. Boddington was obliged to resign the living at Horton owing to ill-health, and went to reside at Cheltenham, where he died in 1851. His assistant, Dave Hartley, by frequently accompanying the rev. gentleman on his visits to the sick, also acquired a knowledge of physic, and kept up the "practice."

The Rev. John Harrison was appointed incumbent on the resignation of Mr. Boddington, and laboured in Horton till the year 1860. During his incumbency a movement was started for the erection of new schools, the Old Bell School being too small for the number of children who wished to attend. A committee was appointed for the purpose of collecting subscriptions for the erection of the schools, which were commenced in the summer of 1859, the memorial stone being laid on Saturday, December 3rd, 1859, by Mr. F. S. Powell. The schools were opened in November, 1860, when the occasion formed a "red-letter day" in Horton; no fewer than 1200 persons sat down at the tea party in connection with the event. The site occupied by the schools was conveyed to Mr. Henry Mason on behalf of the trustees by Mrs. Charnock, of Halifax, Mr. Thomas Horsfall, of Burley Hall, and others. It previously formed part of closes of land called the Middle Field, Clover Field, and Green Field, and contained about 4851 square yards. It was subsequently conveyed by Mr. Henry Mason to the Archdeacon of Craven for the sum of £363 16s. 6d.

The premises were opened as a day-school in 1861, Mr. Dovey being the first master, and Miss Armitage the first mistress. The present master is Mr. Robt. Waite, under whom the schools have flourished for many years. The Old Bell Chapel has been converted into an infant school.

The Rev. J. Harrison married a sister of Sir Wm. Wright, of Hull, formerly of Bradford, and exchanged livings with the Rev. G. M. Webb, vicar of Aughton, in the East Riding, in April, 1860.

During Mr. Webb's incumbency the new church of St. John the Evangelist was erected, and also the present vicarage, a site for the latter being begged by Mr. Webb, who also solicited all the money required for its erection. As a safe foundation for a steeple could not be found, in consequence of the ground being undermined, the Old Bell Chapel site was abandoned, and the new church erected on the brow of the hill overlooking the Thornton Valley, upon a plot of ground given by Mr. F. S. Powell. The foundation stone of the new edifice was laid on Easter Tuesday, 1871, by the late Mr. John Rand, and the consecration took place on March 9th, 1874.

The cost of the new church was £7000, exclusive of the tower, the erection of which was deferred for a time. Towards this large amount handsome contributions were given as follow :—William Rand, £1350 (in addition to oak pulpit, reading-desk, font, and communion plate) ; Francis S. Powell, £1100 (and site) ; Henry Mason, £500 ; J. J. Broadbent, £500 ; George Turner, £500 ; &c. The church is of large proportions, in Early Gothic, and was designed by Messrs. Healey, of Bradford. The tower and spire were added during last year, at a cost of £1800, towards which donations of £500 each were given by Messrs. George Turner, J. J. Broadbent, and F. S. Powell. Mr. Webb's labours in connection with Horton Church and Schools will not soon be forgotten. After a residence in Horton of fifteen years, he exchanged livings with the Rev. W. T. Storrs, vicar of Heckmondwike, in April, 1875. Mr. Storrs was a physician as well as clergyman, and worked hard during his short stay in Horton. The present vicar is the Rev. James Gallie, M.A., formerly of St. Luke's, Bradford.

We are debarred from indulging in the many reminiscences which are interwoven with the history of the Old Bell Chapel. Although possessing no savour of antiquity, still that history covers the lifetime of the oldest inhabitants of

Great Horton with a few exceptions, and many there are who have something to tell of its former incumbents or worshippers. We must be content with stating that Joseph Beanland, of Beckside, was the first churchwarden at Bell Chapel. Mr. James Walmsley was clerk of the chapel for twenty-six years, during the incumbencies of the Rev. Mr. Redhead and the Rev. Mr. Boddington. Joseph Lofthouse, who died in 1837, had been sexton since its erection in 1806. Nathaniel Dracup, a former bass singer at Bell Chapel, may be named as representing the choir. Among the earnest workers connected with the old Bell Sunday School were Henry Mason, Edward Cockerham, George Beanland, Richard Haley, whose labours have left impressions which will never be forgotten.

Of the early schoolmasters at the Old School, we have record of one named Sutton, who was succeeded by Tom Hirst, generally called "Hunting Tom," the secretary of the Bradford Coursing Club, and for many years steward to the Rev. Godfrey Wright. Then there was Ben Hartley, and next George Laycock. The latter had a great name in Horton. He was the son of Lazarus Laycock, chapelkeeper of the Moravian Chapel in Paternoster Fold, and had previously received his training at the Fulneck establishment.

The Paternoster Fold Moravian Chapel was established in August, 1742, the first year that the pioneers of the United Brethren came into Yorkshire, and it continued to be occupied by the Moravians till after the erection of the present chapel in Little Horton Lane, the foundation stone of which was laid on May 15th, 1838, and it was opened December 28th the same year.

The Old Chapel must have been built long before it was occupied by the Moravians. At the time it was first occupied by them there was not a building to break the view all the way to Bradford. In front of the chapel and the adjoining houses there used to be four large ash trees, and when the weather was fine the Moravians often held their meetings outside under the shade of the trees. Lazarus Laycock was chapel-keeper at Horton above twenty years; he died April 24th, 1837. The Horton Chapel was soon after deserted, and the chapel made into a cottage dwelling, which was occupied by George Laycock and his two sisters.

The introduction of Primitive Methodism to Great Horton may be ascribed to the Rev. John Coulson, of Leeds, who in May, 1821, visited Great Horton as a Primitive Methodist missionary. During the summer months meetings were held in the open air, but very soon a barn-house at Upper Green was hired for religious services, and a society was formed consisting of eleven members. This barn-house not being very comfortable, the little church rejoiced exceedingly when they subsequently had secured the upper room of a cottage in Southfield Lane.

In 1824, when their numbers had increased to forty members, it was decided to purchase the plot of land at Town End, on which the chapel now stands, with burial ground in front. The foundation-stone was laid on Saturday, the 22nd January, 1825, the collection made at the stone-laying amounting to £3 4s. 4½d. This was a very feeble commencement; but the society consisted of very poor members, and what they were short in money they made up by labour, for all the excavating work was done without cost to the society.

The total cost of the new chapel was £803 11s. 2d., the income £117 18s. 6½d., leaving a debt of £685 12s. 7½d. The persons who became responsible for the debt and who were made trustees, were John Waugh, Thomas Haigh, George Broadbent, Thomas Cockroft, James Hanson, Timothy Bartle, Edward Rawnsley, Daniel Holroyd, John Peel, Benjamin Beanland, Joseph Northrop, William Greaves, and Thomas Bartle.

The following extracts from the deed of conveyance, which was made the 21st day of May, 1825, will show with what care the trusts were guarded against loss:—

That if at any time it shall happen that the toleration allowing Protestant Dissenters to assemble together for worship shall be taken away, then the said chapel shall be sold.

That the proceeds of the said sale shall be placed out at interest, and the amount thereof paid annually to the poor belonging to said society living within two miles thereof.

That if at any time after such sale the Protestant Dissenters, called Primitive Methodists, shall be again tolerated by the laws of this realm, then the principal of such investment shall be called in, and the amount expended in erecting another building for the purposes of original chapel, &c.

These early Primitive Methodists, or "Ranters," as they were called, owing to their extraordinary zeal, would frequently walk to Leeds and back on a Sunday to hear a travelling preacher or to be present at a camp meeting. At that day they were distinguished, the women by their plainness of dress and large Leghorn bonnets, and the men by their knee-breeches and stand-collar, fish-bellied coats. Indeed, it was considered a sad conformity to the world and very heterodox when men belonging to the body of Primitive Methodists began to wear what were called "long-sleeved breeches." When it was decided to build, trade was flourishing in Great Horton, but before the village had been canvassed for subscriptions the Weavers' Union struck for an advance of wages, a great number of people were thrown out of employment, and never had the chance of further work in that branch of business. Many had to change their occupation or emigrate, which circumstance fell hard upon the chapel funds. In 1840 a new trust was formed, and subsequently, by means of a bazaar, subscriptions, and collections, the debt was reduced to £600.

In 1851 a plot of land behind the chapel at Town End was purchased at a cost of £92 5s. 11d., but it was not till 1861 that a new school was built upon it at a cost of £553, which was cleared from debt in 1863. Further enlargements took place in 1865, and again in 1868, at a cost of £1100. In March, 1864, the surviving trustees of the deed of 1840 sought to be relieved, and the trusts of the chapel and school were conveyed to Joseph Wilson, Geo. Frankland, Joseph Crabtree, Daniel Pollard, Cephas J. Wilson, Skirrow Beanland, Thos. Petty, Joseph Rhodes. Joseph Pickles, Charles Whitaker, all members of society, with David Bartle continuing trustee.

The new trustees then decided to enlarge the chapel and "pew" the bottom, which was done in 1865 at a cost of

£1080. Subsequently £350 was spent upon a new organ. In 1868 a branch school was formed at Jer Lane, and on the 25th June, 1871, the wood school chapel, at Horton Bank, which had been erected at a cost of £617, was opened. On February 4, 1883, another branch school chapel was opened at Dirkhill, near Horton Park Station, the total cost of which was £1300.

Wesley Place Chapel was erected in 1851, being the outcome of the Methodist disruption which took place in 1850. The foundation-stone was laid on Shrove Tuesday, and the chapel was opened for worship on the morning of Whit-Sunday of that year. So vigorous was the movement of Wesleyan reform in Great Horton at that time that the chapel had to be enlarged in 1852, and was made to seat 850 persons. The total cost of the original premises and enlargement was £2523.

During the ten years from 1851 to 1861 the congregation formed part of the Great Horton District of Wesleyan Reformers, the ecclesiastical constitution of which was essentially Congregational Independency. This system was, however, too far in advance of Wesleyanism to be at once easily adopted by many of those who had been trained under the latter system, and the result was that, whilst a large portion gradually became familiarised with the working of Independency, and desired to see it consistently carried out and distinctly avowed, others clung to old traditions with a tenacity which hindered the entirely harmonious co-operation which was desirable. Almost instinctively adopting Congregational principles of church order, and feeling that the movement had passed out of the Wesleyan reform stage, the Great Horton congregation proposed that the circuit should adopt the name "Congregational Methodists." The proposal did not meet the approval of the other congregations, and in 1861 the Great Horton congregation found itself alone, some of the others having become affiliated with already established sections of Methodists, and the rest retaining their original designation. Naturally the isolation thus brought about drew the Great Horton church towards the Congregationalists, with whom they are now allied.

The Congregational schools in connection with the above chapel were built in 1868. The memorial-stone was laid by Mr. Edward Baines, of Leeds, on June 2nd, 1868, and the total cost of the building, including the cost of the site and furnishing, amounted to £7254 17s. 11½d. A subscription list was opened to defray the cost, and was very liberally responded to; and what was thought at the time to be a final effort to clear off the debt on the building was made by the opening of a Fine Arts and Industrial Exhibition, under distinguished patronage, on Wednesday, August 17th, 1870, by the late Lord Frederick Cavendish. This exhibition remained open until November 30th, 1870, during which time it was visited by 71,495 persons, including season-ticket holders, and realised a sum of £1888.

What is called the "Iron Church" was erected in the autumn of 1871, and the opening services were held on the 9th day of November of that year. The church adopts Congregational principles, and seceded from Wesley Place Chapel before the decision in the "Great Horton Chapel Case," a suit at law which created considerable feeling in the neighbourhood at one time.

The "Jumpers" of Horton, as they were called on account of their fantastic manner of conducting their religious services, located themselves in a large room in Bartle Fold in the spring of 1837, and were led by a Mr. Benjamin Deighton, from Little Horton. They, however, made little progress, and eventually gave up the premises.

CHAPTER XX.

Social features of Great Horton—Working Men's Radical Association—the Democratic Institute—Liberal Club—Mechanics' Institute—Horton Old Band—Great Horton Industrial Society—the Ashton Dole—Horton Octogenarians—Conclusion.

The miscellaneous jottings with which we must conclude this series of "rambles round the townships" mostly refer to Great Horton, where, in a far higher degree than is the case in the adjoining hamlet, the characteristics and institutions of a village community are found. Indeed, it would be more proper to speak of Little Horton as a district than as the name given to a community. Latterly, by the great increase of population, that district has almost completely lost its individuality, and has become absorbed in the town of Bradford.

In the spring of 1837 thirty or forty young men regularly assembled at a building at Low Green, where they were taught without charge the rudiments of education by Mr. Jude Yates. Notwithstanding their defective knowledge the majority were possessed of political notions, and not a few were enamoured of the philosophical speculations of Paine. The result of this gathering was the formation of the Working Men's Radical Association. The society had a vigorous existence, being visited at times by Feargus O'Connor, Henry Vincent, John Cleaver, and other pronounced Radicals, such as Peter Bussey, Squire Farrar, John Jackson, Chris.Wilkinson,&c. The Chartist agitation already alluded to upset the arrangements of the association, but the effect of the training thus received was not lost. In the year 1842, after a revision of the rules of the Mechanics' Institute, a number of members became disaffected in consequence of the prohibition of the discussion of political subjects in the Institute, and a new institution called the "Democratic Institute" was formed in a house at Upper Green, which combined the discussion of political and religious questions in addition to the subjects usually comprised within the compass of the Mechanics' Institute. This society had a prosperous existence for many years, and continued till 1869, when its effects were sold or distributed amongst the members. There is no doubt that the above associations exerted a great influence in educating the inhabitants in those advanced Liberal principles for which the Great Horton Ward is distinguished.

The present Great Horton Liberal Club was established in February, 1871. For three years a cottage in High Street was used as a place of meeting. Subsequently a limited liability company was formed for the erection of a club house, which was opened on March 20, 1876. The building is lofty and commodious, and was erected at a cost of £2000, exclusive of the site. A Conservative Club has also been recently established in High Street.

In the latter end of March, 1839, four persons, viz., Messrs. John Wood, Chas. Topham, George Sunderland, and Ephraim Watmough, remained after the close of the night school then conducted by Mr. Wood in the Church school, usually called the Bell school, to consider the propriety of forming a Mechanics' Institute in Great Horton, and an engagement was entered into by those present to bear the cost of convening a public meeting for that purpose. A placard was issued on April 23rd, 1839, in the Church Schoolroom, and a meeting was held, Mr. John Wood, schoolmaster, in the chair, when it was resolved—" That an institution be immediately formed to be called the Horton Mechanics' Institute, or Society for the Acquisition of Useful Knowledge." Twenty-four members were enrolled at the meeting, and the society continued in existence for about thirty years, when the library and effects were sold to liquidate its debts. Among the early workers in the movement were Mr. Peter Fox and the late George Laycock.

Long ago Great Horton was famous for its band of instrumentalists, a revival of which has been set afoot within recent years. The name of the earlier society was the Horton Old Band, its meeting place being Pickles Hill Top. As it may be interesting to learn the composition of this famous band, we append the names of the players in the year 1820, and the instruments they used, viz. :—Leader, Edward Topham, who played the clarionet ; 2, Isaac Rawnsley,

Rambles Round Horton.

clarionet ; 3, Richard Swaine, do. ; 4, John Hartley, do. ; 5, William Swaine, serpent ; 6, Jos. Blamires, do. ; 7, Eli Dracup, do.; 8, Levi Holgate, trumpet; 9, Jonathan Wardman, trombone ; 10, John Holdsworth, do. ; 11, George Hardcastle, do. ; 12, James Carter, bugle ; 13, Richard Haley, do. ; 14, Chas. Wardman, French horn ; 15, William Parker, flute ; 16, Abraham Jowett, bugle ; 17, Matthew Wood, bassoon ; 18, Edward Flather, triangle ; 19, Henry Hindle, drummer. All the above are dead, and the Horton Old Band has long since become defunct.

The Horton Old Choral Society was also an institution of some note and influence in its day, of which Mr. Ed. Bartle was the leader. At Beldon Hill and the uplands of Horton the custom of "Christmas singing" is kept up as in the olden time, a band of vocalists and instrumentalists turning out in all weathers to herald Christmas morning.

Great Horton boasts a musical composer of no mean order in the person of Mr. Wm. Hollingworth, whose father and grandfather were also musicians, the latter being choirmaster at Horton Lane Chapel in old John Skelton's days. Mr. Hollingworth has composed many instrumental works, glees, part songs, chants, anthems, and fantasias for brass bands, one of his glees, "Here's life and health to England's Queen," having gone through six editions.

We might have some difficulty in offering statistical confirmation of the fact, but there are grounds for the assertion that a greater amount of thriftiness and husbanded resources exist at Horton than in any other township of the borough in proportion to population. The people, being of a saving turn, naturally adopted the co-operative principle of trading during its early introduction into these parts. The initiatory step was taken at a meeting held at Hew Clews Bottom in the year 1859, the following fourteen working-men being present, namely :—Aaron Shepherd, Rei Riley, George Lofthouse, Alfred Shepherd, Samuel Watmough, John Preston, Harry Topham, John Priestley, John Shepherd, Ellice Atack, Matthew Shepherd, Wm. Shackleton, Wm. Fox, with George Laycock, the latter being secretary. A quantity of flour, groceries, &c., was bought wholesale, and retailed to the

P

fourteen members in the rooms of the Democratic Institute in High Street; Samuel Watmough, one of the number, being appointed to act as salesman.

That was the beginning of the present Great Horton Industrial Society, Limited, which grew to such an extent that the club-room was soon too small, and a shop just below the Institute was taken, and opened, first only at night, afterwards all day. Even this building was soon found altogether inadequate for the business of the society, and a movement was started which resulted in the erection of the present handsome stores in the year 1861, the site of which (including some old cottages) was purchased from Samuel Suddards, of Tong, for £1100. The society has six branches in addition to the central stores, and about 1500 members. Its capital amounts to £17,332, and since the year 1863, when the society was enrolled, its turnover has amounted to over half a million of money, out of which it has divided in profits amongst the members over £40,000.

What is known as the "Ashton Dole" is a charity, the proceeds of which are derived from property left under the will of John Ashton in 1712, to be distributed half-yearly among poor people of Horton above sixty years of age who are not in receipt of parish relief. The property originally comprised three cottages, a barn, and several closes of land in Horton, let to Jas Gomersall for £30 per annum; a blacksmith's shop, let to Jabez Balmforth and afterwards to John Garthwaite for £7 a year; a farm called Solitary, with about nine acres of land, let to George Briggs and Daniel Dracup at £16 a year. In 1813 the trust was vested in Joseph Barrans as surviving trustee. In 1826 Mr. Barrans invested the charity estate in Joseph Cousen, Thos. Booth, Thos. Ackroyd, and John Bilton as joint trustees. In 1881, however, the trust property was sold, and the proceeds invested in consols, which now realise for the benefit of the poor about £80 per annum. For a period of about ten years, the dole was distributed by Mr. John Wade. The present trustees are Messrs. James Cousen, Henry Bentley, James Dixon, jun., and Henry Cockerham. John Ashton, the founder of the dole, would in modern phraseology be termed a " miser,"

Rambles Round Horton. 227

but he made amends for his peculiarities by benefactions at his death. From an inventory of his household goods and chattels it appears that he had accumulated a large quantity of old silver coin, which sold for 5s. 1d. per ounce, and realised the sum of £147 3s.

Mr. John James gives in his "History of Bradford" a list of twenty-two persons all over ninety years of age who died in Horton between the years 1844 and 1863. They were as follow:—Daniel Nelson, Cross Lane; Elizh. Stead, Clayton Lane; John Milner, Cousen's Mill; John Haley, Paradise; Hannah Lofthouse, Horton Road; John Riley, Paternoster Lane; Jon. Briggs, Low Green; Mary Whitaker, Cordingley Fold; Elizabeth Emsley, Mill Lane; Jas. Lister, Cobden Street; Hannah Jowett, Old Road; Jonathan Tommis, Southfield Lane; Martha Greaves, Little Horton; Michael Craighton, Grafton Street, 95 (had children under twelve years of age when he died); Ann Hargreaves, Clayton Lane; Hannah Hanson, Dog Lane; Nancy Thewlis, Town End; Hannah Emsley, Harrington Street; Hannah Hartley, Villiers Street; John Gallagher, Duncan Street; John Wood, Workhouse; and Hannah Dewhirst, Beckside Road. To this list may be added the names of other Hortonians who have attained over ninety years of age, among them being three members of the Swaine family. James Swaine, of Bank Bottom, who died in 1820, followed the plough in his ninety-fifth year. It is said that a Mrs. Shepherd died at Hew Clews in her 102nd year. Joseph Wardman lived to 91 years; Thomas Priestley, Upper Green, 90; Rebecca Topham, 93; James Boocock, Great Horton, 97; John Wilkinson, 92; Joseph Greaves, Great Horton, 95. James Clough, of Little Horton, died in 1871, at 90 years of age; and Jonathan Bairstow, of Lidget Green, in 1885, aged 91. John Topham, of Cliffe Lane, died at over 90 years of age during the same year. He was the son of Moses Topham, and was one of nine children, of whom two died young, the ages of those surviving being respectively 90, 88, 86, 84, 80, 75, and 74 years.

The annals of the graveyards at the old Bell Chapel and the Wesleyan Chapel at Horton contain reference to many

Hortonians of the present century who reached four-score years and over. From them the following list has been compiled, viz.:—Mary Blagborough, 80; Dan Haley, 80; Sarah Haley, 81; John Schofield, 83; Squire Lofthouse (first sexton at Bell Chapel), 82; Sarah Blagborough, 86; Mary Greenwood, 84; Jane Hillam, 84; Mary Haley, 84; John Wright, 81; William Holdsworth, 85; Jonathan Holdsworth, 83; Hannah Bennett, Bracken Hill, 88; David Armitage, 83. On a tombstone marking the resting-place of Sarah and Joseph Wardman there is an inscription entitling the aged couple to the Dunmow flitch—

> This aged pair interrèd here,
> In wedlock sixty-seven year,
> Who ne'er knew either brawl or strife,
> A happy husband, loving wife.

Sarah died at 85; Joseph, her husband, reached 91 years; Margaret Hallewell, 86; Joseph Holdsworth, 81; Ann Holdsworth, 87; Jeremy Haley, 81; Grace Haley, 81; Martha Fox, 81; Ben Shackleton, 82; John Littlewood, 81; Sarah Littlewood, 83; Joseph Bottomley, 80; Sarah Dracup, 80; Roger Milnes, 87; Squire Knowles, 86; Sally Knowles, 86; John Hanson, 84; Mark Barraclough, 86; Mary Blackburn, 84; John Hudson, 82; Mary Hummel, 85; John Smith, 84; Susan Harland, 82; John Kellet, 82; Isaac Wade, 80; Mary Bennett, 84; Nancy Wardman, 80; John Shackleton, 80; Stephen Hartley, 83; David Topham, 88; Aaron Topham, 86; Samuel Peel, 83; David Shepherd, 82; Ann Carter, 86; Abram Bentley, 81; Ann Bentley, 81; Sally Roper, 84; Henry Dewhirst, 80; Jonathan Jowett, 85; John Bakes, 80; Sarah Binns, 83; Mary Edmondson, 83; Prudence Hartley, 84; Jonas Fox, 83; Stephen Farrand, 84; Timothy Jennings, 84; Eli Suddards, 86; Elizabeth Suddards, 80; Hannah Suddards, 87; Mary Cliff, 86; Jonas Priestley, 88; Mary, wife of Joseph Swaine, 83; Jonas Jowett, of Beldon Hill, 81; Jonas Jowett, 82; Peter Butterfield, 80; Joshua Ormondroyd, 85; David Crossley, 88; John Ormondroyd, 81; Joseph Wood, 83; Betty Emsley, 82; Sarah Dracup, 81; Betty Barraclough, 80; Mary Shackleton, 80; Alice Smith, 87;

Rambles Round Horton.

Joshua Milnes, 80 ; Joseph Wood, 82 ; Sarah Sutcliffe, 88 ; Timothy Jennings, 85 ; Ann Jowett, in her 90th year; Eliza Holdsworth, 83, Thomas Hudson, 87 ; Mary Greaves, 83 ; Hannah Armitage, of Beldon Hill, in her 84th year. Mary Wade, Blacksmith Fold, aged 82 ; John Holroyd, a Waterloo veteran, aged 82 ; Joshua Jowett, Stephenson Fold, aged 86 ; Mary Verity, Knight's Fold, 89 ; Susey Boyes, Bartle Fold, 87. The above list, although monotonous to the unappreciative reader, bears ample testimony to the healthiness of Horton, taken in conjunction with the relation which frugal and temperate living has upon the vital ststistics of a community.

The branch of the Great Northern line of railway from Bradford to Thornton was opened for traffic to Great Horton on October 14, 1878.

The following record of the population, taken at each decade, shows the rate of progress of the Horton township during the present century as follows :—Census of 1801, 3459; 1811, 4423 ; 1821, 7192 ; 1831, 10,782 ; 1841, 17,615 ; 1851, 28,143 ; 1861, 30,187 ; 1871, 40,722 ; 1881, 46,030.

APPENDIX.

20 Jan., 1642.

WILL of JOHN LISTER, of Ovenden, Yeoman.

Gives to DANIEL LISTER, his son, and his heirs, all lands in Northowram which he had purchased of Jeremy Holdesworth, and one messuage and lands, &c., in Shelf, in occupation of James Wallis. Messuage, tenement, &c., and all lands belonging in Ovenden, which he had purchased of Gilbert Deane, Caleb Kempe, and Moses Jenkins. Also, all that messuage and lands, &c., in Horton, in Bradford dale, in tenure of Andrew Shyers. Remainder to JOSEPH LISTER, his (testator's) son, and his heirs and assigns.

Gives to said son, JOSEPH LISTER, four messuages, tenements, and three cottages, and all the lands, &c., belonging, in Ovenden, which he had bought of John Weddall, merchant, and Mary, his wife. Also, a messuage and tenement in Clayton, in Bradford dale, in tenure of John Lun. Remainder to aforesaid DANIEL LISTER.

Gives to said DANIEL and JOSEPH LISTER, his sons, six acres of land and buildings thereon, in North Bierley, which he and a certain Matthew Houldsworth purchased of a certain John Nettleton and Richard Nettleton, in moieties, with remainders to either brother.

JOHN LISTER, the testator's son, and heir apparent, not 21 years of age.

Gives two messuages and lands, in Wibsey and North Bierley, to SUSAN, his wife. Reversion thereof to DANIEL and JOSEPH LISTER, his sons.

Leaves Legacies to his Sisters ELIZABETH, GRACE, and MARTHA, and to his Brother, JOSEPH LISTER.

To his FATHER and MOTHER a pair of gloves a piece.

SUSAN, his wife, executrix and residuary legatee.

Witnesses—JAMES FOXCROFT.
E. HANSON.

Proved 1st October, 1644, by Susan, the widow, to whom was committed the guardianship of Daniel and Joseph Lister, her "*impubes filios.*"

Mr. FRANCIS SHARP POWELL was elected Member of Parliament for Wigan at the General Election in November, 1885.

GLOSSARY.

WORDS AND PHRASES IN USE AT GREAT HORTON.

Abaght—about.
Aboon—above.
Addle—to work for wages.
Afore—before.
Agate (" Ger agate ")—to do something.
Ageean—again.
Ahr ta bahn--are you going.
Aht—out.
Akin—related to.
All shirt-neck--cutting a great figure out of nothing.
Ashelt—likely or probable.
Ass-neuk—under the fire grate.
Awf—half.
Awkert (Awkward) — queer and comical.
Awl—all.
Awlus—always.
Awner—owner.
Axt—asked.
Az—as

Bacca—tobacco.
Backart—backward.
Badger—a grocer.
Baght—without.
Balderdash--talking without sense.
Bang—to beat, to throw down.
Barn—a child.
Batin' time—time for refreshment.
Bawk—to disappoint.
Beck'n—to call with the fingers.
Becoss—because.
Beest—first milk after calving.
Behunt—signifying behind.
Bein'—being.
Belesses—bellows.
Belling—making a loud noise.
Bench—a seat.
Benjey—a straw hat.
Bezzler—a drunken fellow.
Blackish—inclining to black.
Blain—a boil.

Blame it—an exclamation of disappointment.
Blatter—of which pancakes are made.
Bleb—a blister.
Blendit—mixed.
Blegs--blackberries.
Blurred - blotted.
Bocken—to loath.
Boggard—a subject for scare.
Bolt—to run away.
Bonny—beautiful.
Bonkful—filled up.
Booze—to drink.
Booath—both.
Bowd—bold.
Brag—to boast.
Bray—to hammer.
Bray'd—to be thrashed.
Brat—a pinafore ; a child.
Brass—money.
Brazzen—bold, shameless.
Breikfast—the first meal.
Breeter—brighter.
Breyk—to break.
Brig—a bridge.
Brigs—used to put upon the fire in cooking.
Britches—trousers.
Broiched—introducing a subject.
Brokken—broken.
Bruarts--the brim of a hat.
Brussen—over-full.
Buckstick—a smart young fellow.
Bugth—great size.
Bump—a knock
Bup--addressed to a child to drink.
Burly—thick, clumsy.
Butty--joint partnership ; a mate ; word used by boys.
Buzzard—a moth or butterfly.
By t' mess—an exclamation of surprise or disgust.

Glossary

Cackle—to talk loud and foolishly.
Cadging—begging.
Canker'd—rusty.
Cant—vigorous, healthy.
Can't feshun—shamefaced.
Capp't—astonished.
Carl—to thrash ; a clown.
Catterwauling—to imitate a cat.
Cawf—a calf.
Cawf-heead—a disparaging remark.
Chap—a sweetheart.
Chary—reluctant, cautious.
Childer—children.
Chimley—chimney.
Chock-full—filled to the top.
Chomping—chewing.
Chonce—chance.
Chumps — wood for Gunpowder Plot fire.
Clahd—cloud.
Claggy—thick, sticky.
Clammy—greasy.
Clatter—noise.
Clegged—dry in the mouth.
Cletch—a brood of chickens.
Clink—to shake up.
Cloise—warm, sultry ; a close or field.
Clotted—sticking together.
Clutter—all in a heap.
Cocker—fair play.
Collops—slices of bacon.
Copp't— caught.
Cowd—cold.
Cowk—a cinder
Craan—crown.
Craps— rendered fat.
Crash—to break with noise.
Cratch—an arm chair.
Cronk—to sit low down.
Crony- a boon companion.
Crumple—to disarrange.
Cubbert - cupboard.
Cuddn't—could not.
Cuzzen—cousin.

Daahn—down.
Dab- a blow.
Daddle—to reel.
Dahn down.
Daft—witless.
Darn to mend a hole in a stocking.
Dauntle—to fondle.
Deeing—dying.
Deeath—death.

Ding—to strike.
Dingle—to make a noise.
Dish-claat — cloth for washing dishes.
Dither—to tremble.
Doady—a stupid person.
Dock—to cut off.
Dofft—undressed.
Dowter—daughter.
Donn'd—dressed up.
Donk—a pot marble.
Doy—term of endearment.
Doytches—ditches.
Dree—dry, tedious.
Drizzle—to rain softly.
Dub—a hole ; a door.
Dubbler—a large dish.
Dungon—knocked.
Dursn't—dare not.

Ealt—ailing.
Eaving—the eaves of a house.
Eawner—owner.
Eawt—out.
Eawther—either.
Eawer—an hour.
Een—eyes.
Elliker—vinegar.
Etten—eaten.
Eyt—eat.

Fadge—a bundle.
Fagged—tired.
Fawt— fault.
Fell-aht—to finish a warp ; also to disagree.
Fellah—fellow ; a husband.
Fend—to stir about.
Fettle—to clean up.
Fib—an untruth.
Flash—fine, showy.
Flay-craw—an unsightly object.
Flayed—frightened.
Flecked—unevenly spread.
Flegs—a causeway.
Flick—a side of bacon.
Flittin'- to remove.
Flunter—in great haste.
Flusk—to fly at.
Foisty—stinking.
Fowd—fold.
Fowk- folk.
Fra'—from.
Fratch—to quarrel with.
Freeten—to frighten

Glossary.

Fussock—a term of reproach; also a donkey.
Fusty—to smell bad.

Gad abaht—to gossip.
Gape—to yawn.
Gape-seed—to stare about.
Gate—way.
Gaters (Goin' gaters)—accompanying part of the way.
Gawby—a dunce.
Gawmless—stupid, senseless.
Gavelock—an iron crowbar.
Gerse—grass.
Gern—to look savage.
Giggle—to laugh sillily.
Ginnel—a narrow passage.
Gipp—to vomit.
Girds—sick fits.
Gleys—to squint.
Gleyd—an evil-tempered person.
Glent—a sly look.
Glopp't—suddenly frightened.
Gobble—to swallow without chewing
Gooid—good.
Gooid for nowt—a worthless fellow.
Gooms—gums.
Gradely—handsomely.
Gripping—clasped or clinching.
Gronny—grandmother.

Hahsumiver—howsoever.
Hahse-praad—proud of home.
Happen—perhaps.
Han' claat—towel.
Haver-bread—oatbread.
Hawve—half.
Hawpenny—halfpenny.
Heft—handle of a knife.
Heigh-flown—high notions.
Heusings—edge of slates on house.
Hippins—napkins for infants.
Hook or Crook—by one means or another.
Howd—to hold.
Hug—to carry.
Hugger-mugger—secret ways.
Hursen—herself.

Inklin'—a slight knowledge.
In a pickle—in trouble.
I'm dahn on't—no faith in it.
Ittha—hear thou.
Ivver—ever.

Jackanapes—a term of derision.
Jannock—fair play.
Jawms—the supports of a door or mantel-piece.
Jerry-berrin'—a previous experience.
Jock—food.
Jossled—crushed, knocked abcut.
Jowled—to be run against.
Juggled—swindled.

Kah—cow.
Kahcummer—cucumber.
Kallin'—gossiping.
Keel—to cool.
Kersnin'—christening.
Kersmas—Christmas.
Kester—abbreviation for Christopher.
Kesting—casting off.
Kink—to lose the breath with coughing.
Kink-cough—whooping cough.
Kist—a chest.
Kit—a vessel to carry water.
Kittle—ticklish; liable to be upset.
Kittlin'—a kitten.
Knodden—kneaded.
Koil—coal.
Kuss—a kiss.

Lackey—a servant.
Laith—a barn.
Laking—playing.
Lap—to wrap up; to drink.
Leather-heead—a term of reproach.
Leet—light.
Leet-on—to get a sweetheart.
Lick—to beat.
Lig—to lie.
Limp—to halt.
Lippen—to expect.
Living tally—unmarried.
Loft—a chamber.
Loich—straight.
Loizins—losses.
Lug—to pull by the hair.
Lumber—household rubbish.

Maalack—a disturbance.
Maddled—stupefied.
Map cloth—floor cloth.
Maunder—to murmur.
Mawky—proud.

Glossary

Mell—to meddle with.
Mess-abaght—active to no purpose
Midge—an insect; a little person.
Middlin'—tolerably well.
Monny—many.
Mooin—moon.
Mough—a mow of hay.
Mullock—to get into a mess.
Mun—must.
Munch—to chew.
Mysen—myself.

Na ahn ta—thou will not.
Nab—to steal.
Nah—now.
Nap-hand—a clever workman.
Nasty—queer-tempered.
Nawn—known.
Near—mean.
Neet—night.
Nettled—irritated.
Newk—a corner.
Ninny—a simpleton.
Nobbut—only.
Nominy—a long, prating statement.
Nowt—nothing.
Nudge—to jog with the elbow.

Odds an' en's—odd, trifling things.
Offans—often.
Offen—often.
Oined—pulled down; "put on."
Oist—over it.
On tick—on credit.
Oppen thi gob—open your mouth.
Ossiting—coughing.
Owd—old.

Pash abaht—to go about hurriedly.
Peffing—applied to a short cough.
Peggies—an infant's first teeth.
Peggy—to stir clothes in washing.
Pey—a pea.
Peyls abaht—to go about in a rough manner.
Pickle—to put away.
Piggin—a lading can.
Poky—being forward.
Pooak—poke.
Popped—annoyed; pawned.
Prig—a pan or posnet.
Pumping—obtaining information by close questioning.

Quirk—to shirk duty.

Quizzing—to obtain information by questioning.
Quicksticks—in a hurry.

Raffle-coppin—a vagabond.
Rarely—excellently.
Reckon—to suppose.
Reek—smoke.
Reet—Right.
Reezy—rancid.
Reyt—right.
Rift—to belch wind.
Rig—ridge of a house.
Rive—to tear.
Rodney—to idle time away.
Roughshod—without consideration for another.
Ruttle—a noise in the throat.

Sark—to suck.
Saar—sour.
Sackless—innocent.
Scale—to poke a fire.
Scawp—head.
Scrawm—to climb.
Scrunty—little.
Secks—sacks.
Secktacle—a hoist.
Seed—seen.
Sell'd—sold.
Seln—myself.
Shaat—to shout.
Shackle—the wrist.
Shilly-shally—empty; purposeless.
Shoin—shoes.
Sift—to get information slyly.
Sken—to look aslant; to squint.
Slap—a blow.
Slape-shod—shoes taking water.
Slash—to cut.
Slapp't—whipped.
Slavver—the spittle.
Slake—to quench the thirst.
Slaumin'—sleepy or drowsy.
Sloppy—wet, dirty.
Slur—to slide.
Slush—thawed snow.
Slutter—to fall down.
Smack—a sharp blow.
Smooring—smothering.
Snappy—short; bad tempered.
Sneck—a door fastener.
Snig—to pilfer.
Snook—to smell.
Snod—smooth.

Glossary.

Snuffle—making a noise through the nose.
Sodden—to soke with wet.
Soltch—a heavy fall.
Sops—children's food.
Split—to tell a secret.
Spooin—spoon.
Stalled—wearied.
Starken—to stiffen.
Stawp—to stand still.
Steyl—a handle; the act of stealing.
Stint—so much and no more.
Stown—stolen.
Stooil—a seat.
Stroak—two pecks.
Stuff—to cram.
Suds—a lather.
Summat—something.
Swad—shell of pea or bean.
Swaith—a single row of mown grass.
Swarm—to climb.
Swarthy—tawny.
Swatch—a sample-piece of cloth.
Sweeat—sweat.
Sweal—to melt.
Swelting—overcome with heat.
Swig—a hearty drink.
Swill—to wash lightly.
Swop—to exchange.
Syle—to put through a sieve.

Taan—taken.
Tak—take.
Tawk—conversation.
Tenger—a deceiving person.

Tengs—fire tongs.
Tent—to attend; to nurse.
Teych—to instruct.
Thoil—to give ungrudgingly.
Thowt—thought.
Thump—a heavy blow.
Tidy-betty—ashpan.
Tippling—secret drinking.
Tit—a horse or pony.
Titter—giggling laughter.
Topple—to fall over.
Tramp—a vagrant.
Trice—speedily.
Twig—to catch the meaning.

Upreyt—upright.

Varry—very.

Wack—to strike sharply.
Wahr—worse.
Wakey—short of sense.
Wallop—to beat.
Wamble—to walk unsteady.
Ware—to spend.
Wart—an excrescence.
Warter—week-day.
Wax—to grow.
Wick—alive.
Wisk—a bundle of rushes.
Wizzened—shrunk.
Wokken—to wake up.

Yahm—home.
Yus, ahnt ta—yes, thou will

INDEX

A

Abbot, John, the blacksmith 182
Ackroyd, Cowling, Notice of......183, 184
Ackroyd, Francis, worsted piece maker ; his numerous family ...138, 139
Akeroyd, James, Primrose Hill......... 177
All Saints' Church, Horton Green, description of; architect, contractor, and cost 135, 136
Anderson, Rev. Dr., of Troy, U.S.A., successor of Dr. J. R. Campbell, Horton Lane Chapel............... 71
Annesley Chapel.......................... 79
Area of Township, in acres 14
Ashley, John, spinner, and presentation to 35
Ashfield, or the "Happy Valley"... 209
Ashton Dole............................. 226
Atkinson, Jonas, clerk................. 178
Atkinson, Rebecca, married to Richd. Gorton 178

B

Bacon, William, and his widow 56
Balme, John, one of the original trustees of Horton Lane Chapel ... 56
Balme, Misses, bequests to Airedale and Horton Colleges 56
Balme, Abraham, assistant overseer 17, 141, 142
Balme, Joshua Rhodes, his labours at Lidget Green 192
Bamburgh Castle, its historic importance, one of the residences of Dr. John Sharp................ 127—129
Baptist College, founded in 1805 ; institution removed to Rawdon in 1859 80
Bairstow, Abraham, a celebrity, and founder of Paddock Dyehouse ... 164
Barracloughs of Horton............180—203
Barraclough, Tommy, ... 181
Barraclough, Mary, married to Rev. James Charnock 181
Barrans, Jos., farmer, horse dealer, and piece maker 142
Beacon Hill, height of, ... 3
Beanland, Joseph, corn miller and colliery proprietor 174
Beldon Hill 5
Beldon Hill derived its name from Benny Beldon, formerly called Upper and Lower Haycliffe ; old denizens on Beldon and Pickles Hills ; public Gardens on Beldon Hill...................................... 160
Beldon Hill, road dispute and trials 19, 20
Bell Chapel ....16, 214—218
Bentley, Nathan 201
Birks Farm, owners and occupiers of 198
Blagborough family 182, 228
Black Horse Inn, Pal Hammond, the hostess ; her "native Doric" and fine old oak bedstead 152, 3
Blamires family, once numerous and still well represented ; descendants and their occupations ; Timothy, son of William, accounted the strongest man in Horton ...... 167—169
Blamires, John, first steward on Bridges' Estate........................ 141
Boddington, Rev. J. C................. 215
Booth, Charles, Barrister, takes the name of Swaine, and acquires the property of Swaines and Booths ; married Hannah Gilpin Sharp, and also added name of Sharp 107, 108
Booths, early residents on Horton Green ; " Skinny Booth," his penurious disposition........................ 137
Booth, Thomas, piece maker, Horton Green, ... 139
Boundaries of township.............. 1, 2
Bower Family ; Jeremy and Thomas, mercers, during the reign of Queen Elizabeth 49, 50
Bowling Lane, Manchester Road, in the early part of the century 73, 74
Bradford incorporated in 1849 ; and Horton divided into two wards...... 22
Bradford Union, including Horton, formed in 1837........................ 18
Bradford Union Workhouse........... 18
Bradford Horn 187, 188
Bradford Waterworks originally supplied from Haycliffe Hill to near Judy Barrett's shop in Westgate 158
Proprietors and Number of Shares; opposition by some of the inhabitants 159
Bracken Hall and Holly Bank......... 172
Bridges, Rev. W., Rector of Castleford 117
Bridges, Francis Sharp, inheritor of the Leeds and Horton family estates 118
Bridges, Thomas, a noted antiquary and intimate friend of Thoresby... 118

Index.

	PAGE
Brick Castle in Hunt Yard	186
Broad-dole	112
Broadbent, J. J., purchases Harris Court Mill, notice of	182, 183
Brooksbank, an old family; Gilbert, a favourite Christian name; mentioned in the Subsidy Roll of 1608; and another Gilbert paid the Hearth Tax in 1666; and a third Gilbert paid a large land tax in 1704; residences of the family and their property	177—180
Brooksbank, Mary, the elder	181
Brooksbank, Joseph, gent.	181
Brooksbanks, the last of	181
Brooksbank Property, to whom descended	180
Brooksbank House	182
Brownroyd, Wibsey-like names	154
Brunton, John, leather breeches maker	66
Buckley protest	38, 39
Huckle, John	185
Burglary at Horton Old Hall	138
Butterworth & Brookes' disastrous failure	31

C

"Calico Coach," run to Manchester	30
Calico Manufacturers attending Manchester market	30
Calimancoes, how made and singed	25
Campbell, Rev. Dr., and his ministry	71
Carriers of Cotton Goods to Manchester	29
Carter, Tom, Workhouse Master	17
Centenary Chapel	79
Charnock Family	181
Charnocks, allied to, acquired property of the Brooksbanks	180
Charnock, Rev. James, married to Mary Barraclough	181
Chapel Green, site of the first Presbyterian meeting house	155
Chapel House, the home of the Thorntons	155
Chapel Lane Chapel, in 1719	52, 53
Chapel Lane, old residents	49, 50
Chartist Movement	27, 28
Chimney Accident at Cannan's Mill	35
Church School, erected in 1808	213
Church Sunday School, erection of	216
Churchwardens, names of earliest	16
Clayton, James, mathematician, meteorologist, and writer	143
Clayton, John, introduced mule spinning by hand; his sons woolstaplers	143
Clayton Lane, once contained a Jerusalem Church, and many followers of John Wroe	79
Clothiers and Stuff Makers	24

	PAGE
Clough, William	184
Clough, John	184
Close Top Farm, owners, tenants, and alterations in	157
Coal staiths and waggon roads of the Low Moor Company	150, 151
Coach Road between Bradford and Halifax	
Coal got in Horton in 1350	159
Cockerham, Edward	185, 186
Cockpit Hill, Beldon and Pickles Hills, resorts for cockfighting	162
Congregational Schools	222
Constables appointed by the Court Leet	16
Cordingleys, fellmongers, gave the name of Skin House to Jacob Hudson's farm	78
Cork-leg business, first makers	66
Cousens, see Horton Villa	148
Cousen, William, manufacturer, purchased the manor in 1858; acquired the Blamires property by marriage; his son James, lord of the manor; the family remarkable for stature	148, 173—189
Cousen, John and Charles, eminent line engravers; titles of some of their chief works	146—148
Cowling Mill	182
Cricket and Athletic Club, Park Avenue	148, 149

D

Dean, Rev. John, Unitarian minister, and treasurer of the Bradford Library	53
Democratic Institute	223
Denton, Richard	184
Denton, John	178
Dixon, Jeremy, bequest to Unitarian Chapel	55
Division of Township	15
"Doles," "gates," and "butts"	156
Domesday Book description of Horton	6
Domestic habits of cottagers	25
Dracup, Saml., and his improvements in the jacquard and card-cutting machines	37
Dracup, Nathaniel, first Methodist in Horton	211, 212
Drop Farm, the site of Horton Bank Reservoir	163

E

Early Methodists in Horton	213, 214
Early Schoolmasters at Horton	218
Ebenezer Chapel and its founders; minister; chapel re-built in 1861; removed to Mannville in 1879	57

Index. 241

F

"Fair Becca," Popular legend of: account of her untimely fate; remorse and confession of her murderer 170, 171
Fawcett, Dr., born at Lidget Green; his Commentary on the Bible 191
Fawcett, Stephen, the poet of Legrams 204
Fawcett, Richard, early engaged in the wool trade; owner of the Holme Mill, and built another in Union Street; epithet of "King Richard"; his sons, Canon Fawcett and Richard, a woolstapler...62, 63
Fawcett, Canon, where born 187
Field Head Estate 207
Field Head Dyeworks 207
Field Head Mills 208
Field House 208
Fine Arts Exhibition at Congregational Schools opened by Lord F. Cavendish, Aug. 17, 1870 222
Fitzgerald, Colonel Thos. Geo., his descendants 89
Four Ashes tree blown down 210
Four Ashes Inn 177
Fox Family, property owners 163
Fox, E. K. 185
Freeholders' List, from the subsidy roll of 1608 .... 10, 11

G

Gallie, Rev. James, M.A. 217
Gas, where first used in Gt. Horton 15, 16
Glossary of Words and Phrases 233—238
Glyde, Rev. Jonathan 71
"Good Old Times": Fare and Clothing " 26
Goodmansend, first interment in Quaker burial ground 152
Gorton, Richard 180
Gospel Pilgrims' Chapel 150
Great Northern Railway, opened to Horton 229
Great Horton Liberal Club 224
    "   "   Conservative Club ... 224
    "   "   Mechanics' Institute... 224
Great Horton House 182
Great Horton Industrial Society 226
"Greens," no longer open spaces ... 4
Greenwoods, of Brownroyd Fold ... 154
Growth of Trade: primitive modes of working .... 23—25
Guytrash Stories, and form of the boggard.................. 172

H

Haley Family 185
Haley, Sally 185

Q

Hailstone, Samuel, attorney, his family 58, 59
Hailstone, Edward, F.S.A., ... 100, 109
Haigh, David, the reputed inventor of cork legs 66
Hall Yard 188
Hall, James 188
Hall, John 188
Harrison, Rev. John 216
Harris Court Mill 182
Hare and Hounds Inn, Landlords of 162
Hawmonds or Hammonds, an old Horton family, landowners, and mentioned in the poll-tax of 1379; present family 154
Haycliffe Lane, the residence of a branch of the Swaines.................. 157, 158
Haycliffe Hill 156
Hearth Money in 1666, and number of hearths.................. 12
Heinekin, Nicholas Thos., Unitarian minister 54
Hemingway, Henry, attorney 89
Heywood, Oliver, visits Horton Hall 101
Hew Clews, name of and associations; droll stories of the natives 170
Highway Board: officers and their salaries; re-election in 1849; superseded 1851 .... 20, 21
Highway Surveyors' Meetings: where held 21
Hill Top Presbyterian Chapel.......... 45
Hill, Edward, ejected by the Act of Uniformity 91
Hinchliffe, Joseph, a Moravian, an excellent schoolmaster, author of several educational works 12, 13
Hirst Tom, schoolmaster 203, 210
Hodsden, Mrs. 89, 138
Hodgson, Thomas, of Birks.......... 198
Hodgson, Thomas, of Scholemoor... 181
Hodgson, Thomas, of Bolling.......... 93
Holme Top Mill, builders, tenants, and owner.................. 140
Holme Top House, past owners...... 113
Holdsworth, George, his descendants 101
Hollingreave Lands, alias Spittle Roods 112
Hollingwood Lane, said to have obtained its name from the holly hedges; the name of long standing 103
Hollingworth, William, musical composer 225
Horton Amateur Thespians,.......... 26
Horton, named from the manor; branches of the family 6
Horton nomenclature.................. 10
Horton Magna, or Great Horton, sparsely tenanted in the beginning of the present century.................. 107
Horton, primitive character of the neighbourhood.................. 96
Hortonians, thrifty and "saving:" ardent politicians.................. 23

Index.

	PAGE
Horton Old Hall, built for the younger branch of the Sharps	97
Horton Hall ; the home of the elder branch; description of the building; early resort of Nonconformists for worship ; here Rev. Thomas Sharp officiated some time, afterwards at Morley, and Leeds	99—109
Horton Hall, occupants of	107—109
Horton Hall, purchased by F. S. Powell, in 1871	109
Horton Listers, long residence in the neighbourhood ; their descent and pedigree	83—90
Horton Grange	201
Horton Villa	146
Horton House Academy	82, 83
Horton Lane Chapel and its founders ; Trust Deed and conditions of Membership ; successive Enlargements ; Ministers and Churches sprung from	69—71
Horton Public Park ; extent, description, and cost	149, 150
Horton Bank, New and Old Roads described	164
Horton Green and its Associations	136, 137
Horton Green—Old Residents of	141
Horton Old Band	224
Horton Old Choral Society	225
Hortons of Howroyde	6, 7,
House Building extraordinary	151
Howley Hall—Materials used for the erection of Chapel Lane Chapel	53
Hudson, Jacob, and his Wife ; their industry and frugal habits ; acquisitions and singular will	75—78
Hulme, Nathaniel and Joseph, born at Holme Top, two distinguished sons of Mr. S. Hulme, of Kipping, Thornton	146
Hunt Yard, Legend of, property purchased by Fox	186, 187
Hunt Yard Wesleyan Chapel ; first Trustees ; Opening of	212

I

Illingworth, Robert, attorney	163
Illingworth, Dr.	185
Iron Church, Congregational	222

J

Jackson, John, the "old Chartist"	203, 204
Jennings, John	14, 17, 189
Jennings, Jonas	18
Jennings, John, the miller	199
Jer Lane Old School, conducted many years by John Benn	161
Superseded by Board School	162
John of Gaunt	187

	PAGE
John Northrop	187
Jowetts, formerly considerable owners of land and tenements in Horton	162
"Jumpers" of Horton	222

K

Kaye, Benjamin, Cotton Manufacturer ; a large dealer ; removed to Allerton Hall	140, 141
King's Arms Inn, sold to Mrs. Trout, came to the Rudd family ; sold to the Bradford Corporation	180
Knight, John, " one of the kings of Horton" : with his brother erected a cotton mill, but failed in 1826 ; mill re-built by Harris & Co., and adapted to worsted	30
Knight's Bankruptcy	180
Knight's Mill	182

L

Lacy, Henry de, Earl of Lincoln	2
Lacy, Robert de, grants the Manor to Hugh de Stapleton	6
Lacy and Horton families, and their tenantry	7—9
Lacies and their servitors in 1342	8, 9
Land and Property Owners in 1704, 1802, and 1839	12—14
Land Owners, four principal	4
Land tenure and service under the Lacies	8, 9
Lapse of the cotton trade, and growth of the worsted	31
Laycock, Lazarus	218
Legrams Lane, an old pack horse road	2, 3
Leventhorpe William	95
Lidget Green, early seat of Nonconformity	190
Lister, Robert, a privileged dyer in 1382 ; succeeded by Richard, who was constable of Halifax, and paid the highest rent to the lords of the manor ; the Ovenden and Northowram Estates continuing in the family till 1756	84, 85
Lister, Thomas, lands and tenure ; descendants ; Shibden Hall branch of the family; marriage alliances,&c.	85
Lister, John, inherited the Horton and Ovenden Estates	86
Lister, John, Will of (Appendix)	
Lister, Samuel, J.P., of Horton, his bequests	86, 87, 88
Lister, Samuel, of Manningham, an attorney	88, 89
Lister, John, M.A.	86
Listers, zealous Parliamentarians ; their sufferings during the Civil War	91, 92

Index. 243

Lister, Joseph, account of the siege of Bradford 91, 92
Lister, Thomas, of Manningham, a major under General Fairfax......... 117
Lister, Abraham, of Bolling, an attorney 113
Lister Pedigree 88
Lister's Arms, a favourite call house in the coaching days 79
Lister Hills, origin of..................... 205
Lister Hills Chapel........................ 209
Low Close Farm............................ 189
Low Green 188
Low Green Working Men's Radical Association 223
Lower Hall Brooks........................ 181
Lumby Family, of Scholemoor ...16, 197
Lumby, Sammy............................16, 197

M

Mansion House, Southfield Lane 181—185
Manor Court records 7, 8
Manor Court steward and judge ... 17
Manor, recent and present owners ; descent from the Lacies to the Horton Family ; sale in 1858 to Wm. Cousen, and old mill to S. Dracup ; mill long tenanted by Joseph Beanland 7, 173, 174
Manor House 188
Manor of Leventhorpe 96
Mann Brothers, stuff merchants ; Thomas also carried on the corkleg business......................66, 67
Marshall's Mill, built in 1818, burnt down in 1822.............................. 33
Maynard's valuation of the tythes in 1638 11
Maude, Dr. William 202
Meeting-houses registered after the passing of the Toleration Act...... 51
Midgley Family ....196—197
Mills erected between 1817 and 1850 ; their owners and tenants ....32—37
Milk stick and its use.................... 26
Ministers at Chapel Lane Chapel from its erection ....50—55
Mires—Myers 162, 168, 170
Myers, Thomas, assistant-overseer...18, 20, 35, 162
Miry Pond, site 161
Mitchell Bros., large worsted spinners 33
Mitchell, Francis and John, ... 33
Moravian Chapel, Paternoster Fold ; do., Little Horton Lane............... 218
Mortimers of Scholemoor 195, 196
Mossman Family 43, 44
Mount Carmel Chapel 150
Mount Pleasant School, trustees of..192, 193
Moulsons ; family long engaged in the stone and building trade........139, 140

N

Names derived from trades 84
Nathaniel Dracup, first Methodist in Horton 211
National School, Lidget Green 193
Nettleton Fold : old residents 161

O

Oates, William Henry 207
Octagon Chapel, first Wesleyan place of worship in Bradford ; land purchase and original trustees ; purchased in 1810 by Richard Fawcett 63, 64, 65
Old Bell Chapel, erection of ; first incumbents ....214—216
Old Homestead at Bank Bottom, built about 1600 165
"Old House at Home" ; ascribed to Isaac Sharp ; passed into the Lister family ; different occupiers 144
Old Road hostelries 164, 165
Old Skinhouse, a seventeenth century homestead, owned by Jacob Hudson, purchased by Thomas Dewhirst 78
Old Todley, site of ; Wesleyan School at Old Todley ....182—211
Old inhabitants of Horton ...227, 228, 229

P

Parker 20, 32, 75, 162
Parkinson, Stephen, built houses at Summerseat Place 180
Parkinson, John, bookseller, builder of Mount Carmel Chapel ; afterwards became a Primitive Methodist local preacher 150
Pickles Hill : derivation of name ... 166
Pilling, Joseph, the miller.............. 199
Plug Riots, said to have been due to Chartism ; great excitement in Horton 28, 29
Poor Relief in the early part of present century 17
Poll Tax of 1379 ....9, 10
Population of Horton 229
Powell, Rev. Benjamin, father of Mr. F. S. Powell............................... 117
Powell, Francis Sharp, educated at Wigan and Sedburgh Grammar Schools, and graduated at Cambridge ; called to the Bar ; sat four times in Parliament ; presented with portrait of himself in 1884 ; erected All Saints' Church, Parsonage, and Schools; his Yorkshire residence, Horton Old Hall ; description of the hall ; relics, family portraits, articles of *vertu*,

Index.

armour, carved oak, and other antiques; elected member of Parliament for Wigan (see Appendix); pedigree of...118, 119—121
Preston Place School, how named; Preston Place 208
Presbyterian Chapel, erected at Little Horton soon after the Revolution of 1688 .... 50, 51
Presbyterians of Chapel Lane became Unitarians during the Rev. John Dean's ministry 53
Presbyterian Ministers .... 51—53
Primitive Methodism in Horton; erection of chapel 219, 220
Primitive Manufacturing, wool carded and spun at home; modes of life and furnishing and fare; cotton industry and long hours of labour 24, 25
Price, Morton (Charles Horton Rhyss), sold manorial property in 1858 7

Q

Quaker Lane, so called from its leading to the early burying place of the Friends; list of interments ... 152

R

Radical Reform Club.................. 204
Ramsbothams, origin and descendants of, their connection with the Rands and Swaines 43, 44
Ramsbotham, H. R., founded the firm of H. R. Ramsbotham and Co. 44, 203
Ramsbotham, John, surgeon, adopted Hahnemann's views, his family ... 44
Ramsbotham, Henry, Swaine, and N. Murgatroyd, in 1798 erected the first worsted mill in the Holme 38
Ramsdens honourably connected with the Bradford Trade; sprung from Upper Green 172, 173
Rand Family, early pioneers of worsted trade.................... 40, 41
Randall Well Close bequest......... 66
Redhead, Rev. Samuel 215
Red Lion Inn, owners and occupiers 142
Reevy Beacon Hill 161
Rent, ancient forms of, and service; "Red Rose," "Boynes," and "Hens"; "Gafol," a tribute...... 114
Richardson, William 148
Riley, Joseph and Edmund, schoolmasters; the latter an author of poems and tales 141
Robin Hood and Little John (old hostelry in Hunt yard) 186
Rushworth, heir of.................. 187

S

Sams Mill, ancient corn mill 199
Sawrey, Faith, the last lineal descendant of the elder branch of the Sharps 107
Scarr Lane 186
Scholemoor, origin of name............ 193
Scholemoor Estate, ancient owners of; bought by Bradford Corporation 197
Scholemoor Cemetery.................... 198
Seebohm, Benjamin..................... 202
Sharps of Horton, their long connection with the township; possessions, how acquired 94, 95
Sharp, James, his identity; exact relationship not certain; descent claimed from a Christopher Sharp 96
Sharp Family, branches of the same; divided into two; residence of the elder, Horton Hall; the younger, Horton Old Hall; espoused opposite sides in religion and politics 96, 97
Sharp, Thomas, his inheritance; his two sons; the younger of the main branches of the family......... 98
Sharp, John, the noted Parliamentarian under Fairfax, and present at Marston Moor; two of his sons, the Rev. Thomas Sharp, vicar of Adel, and Abraham, the mathematician 98, 99
Sharp, Rev. Thomas, Vicar of Adel, deprived by the Act of Uniformity, afterwards an ardent Nonconformist minister at Morley and Leeds .... 98—101
Sharp, Dr. John, studied at Leyden; his outfit and journey to Holland... 102
Sharp, Abraham, educated at Bradford Grammar School; his devotion to scientific pursuits; friendship with Flamsted, and employment at Greenwich Observatory; curious medley of entries in memorandum book; his studious life at Horton 105—7
Sharp, Thomas, yeoman and clothier in 1607; added greatly to his paternal estate..................... 111
Sharp, John, an ardent Royalist, received a blow from a battle axe during Civil Wars; his sons partisans on the king's side ...115—117
Sharp, John, D.D., Archbishop of York; born in Ivegate; educated at Bradford Grammar School and graduated at Cambridge; obtained the Archdeaconry of Berkshire, and three other preferments the same year; Dean of Canterbury, and created Archbishop of York in his forty-seventh year; his diary and life; a prolific writer, and collector of coins 122, 123, 124, 125, 126, 127

Index. 245

Sharp, Thomas, younger son of the Archbishop, Archdeacon of Northumberland; Sharp, John, Prebendary of Durham, Archdeacon of Northumberland, Vicar of Hartburn, and curate of Bamburgh...... 127
Sharp, Granville, the most distinguished son of the Archdeacon: his life and philanthropic labours; the earliest abolitionist of slavery; his trials for setting slaves free; secured Sierra Leone as a settlement for the liberated slaves; earnest labourer in behalf of religious and literary institutions, and a voluminous writer.............................. 129, 130
Sharp, James, of Horton; his descendants 131
Sharp, John, of Tong, father of Wm., of Bradford family, and distinguished relatives—the Heys ... 131
Sharp, Wm., an eminent surgeon at St. Bartholomew's Hospital 129
Sharp, Wm., M.A., Marcham Rectory, Boston........................... 132
Sharp, Wm., an eminent Bradford surgeon, house surgeon of St. Bartholomew's Hospital, settled in Bradford, in 1792; monument formerly in the Parish Church, now in the corridor of the Infirmary ... 132
Sharp John, M.A., Vicar of Horbury 132
Sharp, Richard, of Gildersome, the father of three distinguished sons 132, 133
Sharp, Wm., M.D., F.R.S., F.G.S., succeeded his uncle in 1833; his lectures on Natural Philosophy; one of the founders and president of the Bradford Philosophical Society; surgeon to the Infirmary; removed to Rugby; his careful investigation of Hahnemann's theory; marriages and family 133, 134
Sharp, Madam 107, 108
Sharps' marriage alliance with Stapleton, Bridges, and Powell 117
Sherebrig Beck Close................ 181
Shibden Hall; a fine example of timber-built residences 86
Smith, Samuel, of Bradford, Mayor, notice of........................207, 208
Smith, Lawrence....................... 203
"Smith, Dick," at one time the largest worsted spinner in Bradford...............................142, 143
Smithy Hill, or Old Todley............ 182
Soke Corn Mill, in Horton, in 1311; tenants and rent 173
Southfield Lane; Saughfield or Southgate; name illustrates the custom of the open-field tenure; the system explained..........156, 157
Southern Half-acres..................... 112

Springfield 198
Stamp, Rev. W. W. 213
Stewards of the Bridges Estates 138
Stony lands 180
St. Andrew's Church................... 209
St. John's Church, Manchester Road.
The new Church of St. John the Evangelist, in Horton Lane, built in its stead............................. 72
St. James's Church, erected by John Wood, junr.; first incumbent the Rev. G. S. Bull, an earnest advocate of the Ten Hours Bill; his successors 73
St. John the Evangelist, Great Horton, erection of................... 217
Sterne, Richard, Archbishop of York 92
Sterne, Laurence, author of "Tristram Shandy," educated at Hipperholme Grammar School......................... 92
Sterne, Simon; numerous family; their descendants 92, 93
Stephensons of Horton Green......... 138
Steadman, W., D.D., personal appearance and labours............... 80, 81
Streams and their Courses 1, 2
Storrs, Rev. W. T. 217
Swaines, a very ancient family; numerous branches; marriage alliances; pedigree .... 44, 45—8
Swaine, Joseph 180
Swaine, Samuel 201
Swaine, Dr. W. E., physician extraordinary to the Duchess of Kent... 47
Swaines of Gomersal 46, 47
Swaine, James, said to have ploughed when ninety-five years of age 165
Swaines, noted for longevity 47, 48
Swaine & Ramsbotham's Mill in the Holme, the first of the kind in Bradford; great fire, and exertions of the Bradford Volunteers... 42
Suddards, Eli 86, 189
Summerseat Place 180

T

Tan House 203
Taylor, Rev. Thos., Minister of Horton Lane Chapel............. 70, 71
Tempest Field 181
Tenants of Horton Old Hall ... 118, 119
Tetley Charles ("Pump Tetley")... 35, 36
Thomas, Abraham ("Dr. Tom"), notice of 185
Thorntons of Scholemoor............. 194
Thorntons of Little Horton........... 155
Thornton Lane, the Thorne, part of Lady Hewley's Charity 155
Thief Score Lane 200
Toby Lane 186
Tod (or Toad) Well Farm; an old homestead 151

Index.

	PAGE
Topham	162, 224, 225, 227, 228
Turner, John and Robert	202
Turner, George	202
Tythes in 1638, and list of contributors	11

W

Wade, John, a good type of the Horton character; Churchwarden, Poor Law Guardian, and Town Councillor 20, 21, 169, 170, 226
Walker, James, physician, inheritor of Bank Bottom Farm; tenants 165, 166
"Waste Lands," "Enclosures," and "Common Fields," 113
Watmough 224, 225, 226
Webb, Rev. G. M. 217
Weddall, Mr., Account of 123, 124
Well Close House, built on the site of the Old Workhouse 17
Wesleyanism in Horton 212
Wesleyan School, first erected; trustees of 182
Wesleyan Sunday School 213

Wesley Place Chapel, erection of; becomes Congregational 221
West End Building Society 206
West Lodge 210
Westbrook House 62
Westbrook Place 209
Whitaker, Wm., principal partner in the Old Brewery 39
Wickham, Rev. Lamplugh 60
Wood Family; possessions derived from the Lacies of Cromwellbotham; transfers of land to the Sharps 112, 113
Wood, John, senr., Southbrook Lodge, manufacturer of horn, ivory, and tortoise-shell combs, &c. 62
Wood, John ("Spectacle Wood"), first postmaster of Horton 184
Workhouse, Old, pulled down about 1822 17

Y

Yates, Jude 223

www.ingramcontent.com/pod-product-compliance
Lightning Source LLC
Chambersburg PA
CBHW021359230426
43666CB00006B/585